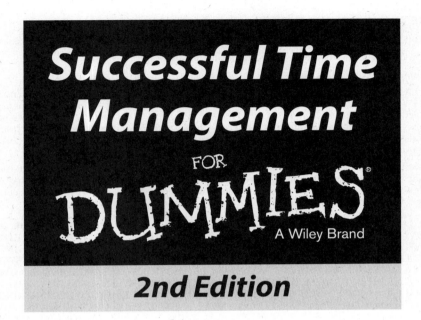

Successful Time Management

FOR DUMMIES®
A Wiley Brand

2nd Edition

by Dirk Zeller

FOR
DUMMIES®
A Wiley Brand

Successful Time Management **For Dummies®, 2nd edition**

Published by John Wiley & Sons, Inc., 111 River Street, Hoboken , NJ 07030-5774 www.wiley.com

Copyright © 2015 by John Wiley & Sons, Inc., Hoboken, New Jersey

Published simultaneously in Canada

For general information on our other products and services, please contact our Customer Care Department within the U.S. at 877-762-2974, outside the U.S. at 317-572-3993, or fax 317-572-4002.

For technical support, please visit www.wiley.com/techsupport.

Wiley publishes in a variety of print and electronic formats and by print-on-demand. Some material included with standard print versions of this book may not be included in e-books or in print-on-demand. If this book refers to media such as a CD or DVD that is not included in the version you purchased, you may download this material at http://booksupport.wiley.com. For more information about Wiley products, visit www.wiley.com.

Library of Congress Control Number: 2014954667

ISBN: 97-811-1898266-2

ISBN 97-811-1898267-9 (ePub); ISBN 97-811-1898268-6 (PDF)

Manufactured in the United States of America

10 9 8 7 6 5 4 3 2 1

Contents at a Glance

Table of Contents

Introduction

• •

Time is the only resource that people can't borrow, buy, or barter. And time refuses to follow one of the main tenets of the law of supply and demand: the idea that when the demand goes up to a high level, the supply will increase to meet the demand. People may use different amounts of time to accomplish results, but everyone is endowed with the same amount of time each day: 86,400 seconds.

Your ability to manage that time is really one of the top two causes of success or failure in your life. Investing greater amounts of time into a need, goal, objective, or even weakness can tip the balance of success in your favor. At numerous crossroads in life, I had to be willing to apply more time than my competitors to achieve a competitive advantage over them in the marketplace. I certainly didn't take for granted that my mental power was far superior to that of my competitors. Rather, my willingness to invest more time in certain tasks or use my time more effectively equalized the playing field.

Of course, if you invest too much time at work, you can be a success at the office but a failure at home. A true champion always has his or her pulse on home life and invests the right amount to keep vital relationships in life growing and thriving. The good news is that this book has both arenas covered. Congratulations on investing in yourself, your success, and your life!

About This Book

Successful Time Management For Dummies is about using your time more effectively to create greater results at the office and at home. Note that in the spirit of saving you time, this is a reference book. In other words, you don't have to read it from cover to cover. Just look up what you need and put those ideas in action.

Personally, I think you should read every word of this book. I wrote it, after all! However, if you're the bare-bones-info type, you can skip the sidebars that appear throughout the book. Those gray boxes contain interesting, often anecdotal information that's related to the topic but not essential to understanding it.

This book

- ✔ Helps you with your organizational habits, discipline, systemization, goals, values, management style, persuasion, and even travel.

- ✔ Offers real techniques, strategies, and tools that I've personally used, taught, coached, and spoke about. I've seen them bring forth a bounty of results in my life as well as in the lives of countless others.

- ✔ Helps you mentally wrap your brain around the problems of time management.

- ✔ Explains how to establish a solid system that you can replicate over time.

- ✔ Introduces you to prioritization systems, time-categorization systems, time-blocking strategies, and appointment-setting strategies.

- ✔ Helps you grab back control and distill time management down to its essence.

- ✔ Sets you up for success and then helps you establish and align your goals with your time.

- ✔ Delves into prioritization strategies and tools.

- ✔ Takes you deep into the most important characteristics of a great time manager.

- ✔ Tells you how to time-block your way to greater success.

- ✔ Contains the tips for you to take your business and career to the highest level, no matter your job title.

Icons Used in This Book

To help you navigate this book a bit better, you can rely on the icons in the book's margins. The icons act as little signposts pointing out the important info.

This bull's-eye icon points out little-advertised nuggets of knowledge that are certain to give you an edge in increasing your time-management skills.

This icon denotes critical information that you really need to take away with you. Remember these points, if nothing else. They address the issues that you come across repeatedly with time management.

Consider this the flashing red light on the road to making a sale. When you see the Warning icon, you know to steer clear of whatever practice, behavior, or response I indicate.

These icons tell you that I've cracked open the archives of my life experiences or my successful clients' life experiences to help illustrate a point.

Foolish Assumptions

When I wrote the book, I assumed a few things about you, dear reader:

- ✔ You want to use your time better. You expect to gain more time with your loved ones, you want to ramp up your success at work, or you're looking for a little of both.

- ✔ You know that effective time management isn't a one-stop fix; it's a comprehensive effort that requires looking at all time-draining culprits. You're willing to invest the effort needed to develop your time-management skills (or create them if they don't currently exist!).

- ✔ You're willing to be patient with yourself throughout the difficult process of self-betterment, knowing that in the end, all your efforts will pay off.

Beyond the Book

There is much more information available from your author, and from the *Dummies* brand, for your learning pleasure. Check out these resources to learn more about the art of successful time management:

Find the Dummies Cheat Sheet for this book at www.dummies.com/ cheatsheet/successfultimemanagement. The cheat sheet gives you a quick reference to help you manage your time and stay on track.

Extra online content can be found at http://www.dummies.com/extras/ successfultimemanagement. Here, you can find short articles on ways to trim down wasted time. From how to plan a trip to getting your yard work done, you'll find these articles helpful.

Where to Go From Here

In this book, I use the classic *For Dummies* fashion: You have easy access to the precise information you need when you need it. You can start at Page 1 and read through, or you can hop around, targeting the areas you need the most help with first. Keep this book close by to help you wring the most you can out of life in the scant 24 hours you have each day.

Part I is a good place to start because it helps you deal with the mental barriers to time management that can seem to form an unscalable wall. After that, you may want to pick topics that cause you the most challenge or frustration. For instance, you can check out Chapter 16 for ways to beat procrastination or see Chapter 18 so you can get a handle on upcoming meetings. On the other hand, if you feel you have your time strategy pretty much under control but are looking for a tune-up, you may go right to Part V first. There, I address how to take time management to the highest level through customized plans for your job or job title.

The truth is that no matter where you take your first plunge, the water's fine. You can find plenty of valuable information that you can use to increase your performance without increasing your hours at work.

Part I
Beginning the Revolution: Simple Steps to Start With

getting started

with

Successful Time Management

In this part . . .

✔ Learn how to remove key barriers from your life to encourage greater productivity. Assess where you stand in terms of time management.

✔ Create an organizational planning and implementation process, and discover the importance of setting up a system.

✔ Discover how the habits of tidiness and orderliness can save you hundreds of lost hours annually [md] imagine life without always looking for lost stuff!

✔ Understand that time is money; learn how you can calculate the value of your time.

Chapter 1

The Essence of Good Time Management: Organizing Yourself

Time management boils down to a mindset of focusing on your priorities, goals, and objectives for a specific time period — a week, a day, or even an hour. It's the awareness that you are the one who lays claim to your success with the allotment of time you have for today.

Time management is a set of skills that are learned over time. The skills taught in this book — for example, of time blocking, single handling, controlling interruptions, and others — don't provide you with overnight success, nor can you implement or perfect them quickly. They require patience to fail, adjust, proceed, and then repeat the process many times. But by sticking with it, you can accomplish what needs to be done without too much stress and panic, and maybe have a little extra time left over.

This book is about taking control of the time you have in each day. Effective time management requires a little introspection, some good habits and organizational skills, and a handful of logistical and tactical tools. So take some time and get ready to learn how to manage it successfully.

Planning in Advance

The planning process for a project, your workday, or even a vacation is more vexing than the execution. Many people invest countless hours planning that perfect vacation to Hawaii. They research the different island options, review recreation activities, lodging, air travel, dining options, the list is endless. But few people plan their day or week with such zeal.

You have to fall in love with advance planning. You are likely faced each day with tasks you would rather not do, but frequently they seem to be high priorities. For example, most salespeople don't wake up each morning saying, "How exciting today; I get to call people I don't know and ask for their business!" Most moms don't get up and say in an excited tone, "I get to remind my seventh-grade son ten times to make sure he packs his homework before he goes to school!"

This is where advance planning brings big dividends to your life. Before your day begins — maybe the night before — plan to do the toughest but most important things first. Usually tough tasks become more challenging to complete throughout the day as more projects, deadlines, and emergency items crop up. So a good rule is to clear out the tough tasks first.

The sheer act of planning is the key to unlock your creativity, problem solving, mental strength, and clarity. It also increases your mental and physical energy because you see the pathway to a productive day.

The better you use planning strategies and techniques, the more you can avoid procrastinating away what you don't want to do. At its base level, planning is simply creating a list. You increase your productivity by more than 25 percent by simply writing down what you need to accomplish. The advantages of creating a list are as follows.

Achieving peace of mind

Create your life as you wind down for the day so that you're ready to take on tomorrow. You likely are able to rest and relax more, knowing that your following day is planned. You sleep better when you don't have unresolved issues weighing heavy on your mind. You won't get that middle-of-the-night wake-up call of "Did I get that done?" You can achieve a deeper slumber by knowing you have your time and tasks under control.

Activating your subconscious mind

You also trigger your subconscious mind while you sleep. Because you have created your list, your subconscious works on that list while you rest. Your subconscious mind turns the challenges and problems over and over like a rotisserie, and eventually it comes up with strategies and solutions. Have you ever gone to bed with a problem or challenge only to wake up with a couple of new ideas on how to solve them? Your subconscious mind created those ideas while you slept. Always give your subconscious something to do at night by . . . handing it a list.

The 1,000 percent return

There is always a large payoff for planning. Many studies have indicated that for every minute of planning you save ten minutes in execution. That is a 1,000 percent return on your time with proper planning. Those numbers don't really illustrate a return of 1,000 percent; a monetary example can put the proper scope on it.

If you have $10,000 and you got a 1,000 percent return in one year, at the end of the year you would have $100,000. If you receive a 1,000 percent return the next year, you would have $1,000,000. The initial investment went from $10,000 to $1,000,000 in less than two years. That's the type of return you can receive each day from planning properly.

Frequently the response I hear is, "I am too busy to plan." I have even tried to use that excuse myself. The truth is that even if you planned out everything in excruciating detail by forcing yourself to do it, you most likely would not invest more than a few minutes a day in the whole planning process. Strange as it may sound, sometimes you may need to slow down in order to speed up. Planning is the only pathway to greater productivity and quality of life.

The wasted time and mistakes you make are most likely related to a lack of planning. The most epic failures have commonality in lack of planning. My single most disastrous business failure came from lack of planning. I rushed into a decision without giving it the thought, planning, research, and care it deserved. It cost me a year of my life and hundreds of thousands of dollars in income. It was an expensive lesson on planning in time and treasure.

Assemble all that is needed

After you have planned out your day, a project, or even dinner, you then need to gather your materials to start and complete the project. I frequently cook with my kids, both Annabelle and Wesley. They get so excited that when we decide which recipe to make together they are instantly ready to crack the eggs and start mixing. I have to slow them down to read the recipe, gather all the ingredients, the measuring cups, pans to bake in, bowls, hand mixer, and so on. I want all of the tools on the counter in an organized fashion for a couple of reasons.

The kids and I might find a trip to the store is necessary for a missing ingredient before we start. That certainly will add time to the project. We could find something else to cook where we have all the ingredients, saving us a trip. We save time by not wandering around the kitchen from pantry to refrigerator to food preparation area. It saves time in cleanup because the mess is concentrated in one area rather than all over the kitchen. By assembling all that is needed, you save considerable time.

Before you start on anything, ask yourself these key questions:

- ✔ What data or information would make completing this quicker?
- ✔ Is there some information I don't have that would save me time for this project?
- ✔ Do I really have everything I need?

The cycle of planning, to gathering, to implementation is the cycle of success and efficiency. If you have to backtrack to gather resources after you've begun implementation, or go back to planning because your execution is stalled, and the waste of your time in the backtracking is a significant loss.

Handle everything — just once

In today's technology world, you deal with less paper because of electronic documents; even with electronic documents you tend to handle and review them multiple times before acting on them. This review is as if you had paper stacked on your desk; it's just now in your computer and email inbox. The shuffling and reshuffling just happens inside your computer, so it seems far more efficient. The truth is you can just store more stuff easily so your productivity can really plummet.

If you're like me, at times you tend to hoard stuff. Because you can store so much in electronic files you tend to keep rather than purge. You can be more efficient with your time if you throw away documents, files, and paper that you don't need. Anything that is not relevant to your life, family, business, or goals, throw it out. Ask yourself, "Is there a negative consequence to throwing this out now?" If the answer is no, throw it out now.

If you need this information in the future, is there another place you could easily access it? The truth in our society is, information is becoming a commodity. Information is readily available, so keeping it because you might need it in the future only overloads you with files, documents, and stuff.

Grabbing the Three Keys to Personal Organization

Your personal organization is one of the largest influences of your success and happiness in your life. Your personal organization skills and systems help you feel more fulfilled, productive, and achieve a mental state of well-being overall. There are three keys that you want to apply frequently to improve your personal organization. Take a look at the next three sections to key in on these skills.

Stepping back to evaluate

Evaluating your key work areas can reveal a lot about the person working there. By stepping back from your desk or work area, you can ask the questions, "What type of person works at this desk? Are they organized or unorganized? Does it appear they have an effective system in getting work done? What changes should they make in their organization? Would I trust this person with an important task based on this work environment? What are the reasons I would or wouldn't?"

You need to have an honest evaluation with yourself, as if you hired a third party or neutral authority to review your workspace. What do you see, and what would they see? Then repeat that process for your home office. Does it have the look from an outsider's as a productive environment? What does your briefcase, computer files, car, purse, closet, house, yard, garage look like? Who is the person who would live this manner? Would you entrust this person with an important task to be completed?

Developing neatness habits

For some of us, including myself, this one is really tough. I admit of all the concepts, systems, and strategies this one is my Achilles' heel. I am better at this by following some of my own counsel, but I am clearly a work in progress. There is no question we can save time and increase productivity by organizing or even cleaning up our workspace. We all need a sense of order and organization to feel calm, relaxed, and in control of our surroundings. Your actual work environment can create a feeling of pleasure and satisfaction or stress and frustration. By instituting order and neatness, you can increase your productivity.

When you create this ordered environment, your self-esteem increases. You're more self-confident in a successful outcome. That self-confidence emotion creates a willingness to be creative, innovate, try new things, and take risks. You feel more in control with more power.

All this neatness removes the roadblocks of frustration and generates more energy. The higher energy level taps into your resources and determination to accomplish the task at hand faster and more efficiently. Establishing neatness habits has far-reaching benefits, reducing your time while increasing your wellbeing and the results you achieve.

Refuse to excuse

"Refuse to excuse" should be a life mantra and not applied only to time management. Too many people let themselves off the hook with excuses of why tasks and chores didn't get done or why these folks didn't accomplish their mission. People who are messy frequently make excuses to justify or cover up a mess. "That's just the way I am," or "I know where everything is," or "I work better this way."

When you review the time spent, messy people are deluding themselves into thinking they know where everything is located. Frequently a large part of their day is spent trying to find or remember where they put things, instead of being productive at the office or home.

Refuse to excuse a messy desk or work environment for this week. If you have to clear your desk to be able to start on a project, just do it. Take the one task or tool you need to work on, and clear the rest off your desk. If you have to put everything else in drawers, cabinets, closets, waste baskets, or even on the floor, do it. Test this on yourself. Unclutter your space. No excuses for a few days, and see how productive you become.

Chapter 2

Setting Yourself Up for Success

*T*ime is the great equalizer — everyone has the same amount in a day. No matter who you are, where you live, and what you do, you clock the same 24-hour cycle as the next person. One person may be wealthier than another, but that doesn't earn him a minute more than the poorest people on the planet.

If that simple fact seems a bit discouraging, think of it this way: You may not have the power to get yourself more time, but you *do* have the power to make the most of it. You can take your 365 days a year, 7 days a week, and 1,440 minutes in a day and invest them in such a way that you reap a return that fulfills your life and attracts the success you dream of.

That's what this book is about: taking control of how you spend your time to make sure you're using it how you really want to. You really are in control of your time, even though you don't always feel like it — even if you have a job that demands overtime; even if you have kids who keep you in the carpool loop; even if you have dreams and goals that involve developing new skills or furthering your education.

All in all, discovering how to manage your time well is part mental restructuring and part creating a system. Effective time management requires a little introspection, some good habits and organizational skills, and more than a few logistical and tactical tools. But all are achievable, so if you have the time — and I assure you that you do — get ready for a journey that's certain to, if not buy you more time, show you how to make the absolute most of the 24 hours in your day.

Getting to Know Yourself

Although everyone gets the same number of hours to work with each day, what people don't have in equal amounts are other valuable assets: skill, intelligence, money, ambition, energy, passion, attitude, even looks. All these unique reserves play into your best use of time. So the better you understand yourself — your strengths, weaknesses, goals, values, and motivations — the easier it is to manage your time effectively. In this section, you look at your strengths and goals, think about how much your time is worth, and observe personal energy and behavior patterns that affect your focus throughout the day.

Assessing your strengths and weaknesses

As a young man, I thought I was good — okay, I admit it; I thought I was *great* — at a much larger group of skills, tasks, and jobs than I do today. In fact, the older I get, the more I realize the list of what I'm *not* good at dwarfs the list of things I *am* good at. Being consciously competent at those few, however, gets me a lot further than being unconsciously incompetent, as I once was. Despite my poor academic record in high school, as a young adult, I was a quick study at what I needed to do to be as successful in life as I wanted to be. At some point, I saw the light and realized I needed to face up to what I had to do to get where I wanted to go.

First, I took stock of my assets: I tallied up my strengths, skills, and even my weaknesses. And I identified things I needed to work on and things I needed to leverage. That's when I realized that although some people were smarter, were more educated, had more money, and knew more influential people than I did, I had the same amount of time as anyone else. And if I wanted to get ahead, it was up to me to harness my time and invest it in such a way to get a greater return. My willingness to invest more time to gain the edge helped equalize the playing field for me and help me achieve the success I enjoy today.

Chances are that by this point in your life, you've discovered some skills that you come to naturally or perhaps have worked hard to acquire. Maybe you're a master negotiator. Or a whiz with numbers. You may be a good writer. Or you may have a silver tongue. Whatever your strengths, developing the handful that brings you the most return on your efforts, propelling you forward to attain your goals, is a more productive course of action than trying to be the best at everything. For most people, these strengths typically number no more than a half-dozen.

In addition to pinpointing your strengths, you need to identify the areas where your skills are lackluster. Then figure out which tasks are essential for meeting the goals you want to accomplish, and build those skills. Invest time in honing and maintaining your strengths, and improve the weaknesses that you need to overcome to reach your goals. *Remember:* To be successful, you need to be selective.

Naming goals to give you direction

You know how it is: When you're working toward something, keeping your focus is much easier. A woman may want to lose weight, for example, but perhaps she struggles to stick to a diet or exercise plan. But if her son's wedding is looming three months away on her calendar, she may be more inspired to stay on track, cutting back on second helpings and getting in workouts.

Your goals can serve as inspiration in adopting good time-management skills. After all, managing your time isn't really a benefit in and of itself, but managing your time so you can spend more of it doing what's important to you *is* — whether you're saving for a retirement of travel and adventure or buying the house in the perfect neighborhood.

Using your aspirations to fire up your time-management success means you have to identify your goals and keep them in the front of your mind. Pinning down what's most important to you may require some soul searching. Write down your goals — all of them — and follow these guidelines:

- ✔ **Cast a wide net.** Go for the big goals, such as joining the Peace Corps, as well as the not-so-big ones, such as getting an energy-efficient car next year.

- ✔ **Think big.** Don't rein in your dreams because they seem unrealistic.

- ✔ **Be as descriptive as possible.** Instead of "build my dream house," flesh it out: Where is this house? How big? What features does it have? What does it look like? When do you want to move in?

- ✔ **Don't limit goals to a single category.** Think about goals for your career, your personal life, your social situation, your financial status, and any other facet of life that's important to you.

The process of goal-seeking can be a fun and energizing experience, and it's one you can explore at length in Chapter 3. You also see how your current time use can affect the forecast for your future.

Assigning a monetary worth to your time

Most people think about the value of their time as it relates to on-the-job activity. The fast-food worker knows he earns a minimum wage per hour. The freelance artist advertises a per-hour rate. The massage therapist charges for her services in half-hour and hour increments. But to be truly aware of the value of your time, you need to carry this concept into your personal life as well. The value of time in your personal life is at least as valuable as your work life time. In some cases, personal time is priceless.

One of the most important points to remember as you work through this book is that it's okay not to get everything done. What's critical is making sure that the *important* things are getting done. By assigning value to your time and using the skills you acquire from this book, you can clearly identify what's important and make conscious, wise choices. For example, if you need to save another $200 per month because you want to start an account for your children's college education, you may determine that putting in an extra shift at work may not be worth the loss of time with your family, even at time-and-a-half pay. Or if you really detest yard work, then paying someone else $50 to cut your grass may be a fair trade for the extra two hours of time watching the game.

Identifying your rhythm to get in the zone

Athletes talk about being *in the zone,* a place where positive results seem to stick like a magnet. Well, I'm here to tell you that the zone isn't some magical place where wishes come true. Anybody can get there, without a lucky token or fairy dust. What it takes is focus, singular focus.

Throwing away money

I once saw a woman in a parking lot throw pennies on the ground. When I asked her what she was doing, she told me she'd just read about a multimillionaire who had calculated his worth, and based on the value of an hour of his time, he determined that it wasn't worth the few seconds it'd take for him to pick up a dollar bill from the sidewalk. She, however, had decided that although it was worth her time to pick up a dollar, she could afford to part with a few pennies.

I think she missed the point, but there's a lesson in this experience: You're always on the clock. Time is money, and yours has a value. Giving away your precious time without a sense of its value is like throwing money on the sidewalk. By knowing what your time is worth, you can prioritize those tasks that yield the greatest return, delegating or eliminating those tasks that provide little to no return on your time investment.

As an ex-professional athlete in racquetball in the 1980s, I can say I've been in the zone a number of times. And I've experienced that same distillation of focus and electric energy on work projects as well — times when my volume and quality of work was bordering on unbelievable. If you can get your focus under control, you can visit the zone every day and make great things happen.

If you know your rhythms — when you're most on, what times of day you're best equipped to undertake certain tasks — you can perform your most important activities when you're in the zone. Everyone works to a unique pace, and recognizing that rhythm is one of the most valuable personal discoveries you can make. Some of the aspects you need to explore include the following:

✔ How many hours can you work at a high level each day?

✔ What's your most productive time of the day?

✔ How many weeks can you work at high intensity without a break?

✔ How long of a break do you need so you can come back focused and intense?

Breakout! Sharpening your focus with time off

About ten years ago, as I was evaluating my sales results, I puzzled over a drop in my numbers at the tenth week when I'd been working without a break. It didn't take me long to realize that my lower results reflected my drop in focus. And it's a pattern I could see in previous months. I realized the best course of action, rather than gutting it out, was to get out. I needed a vacation.

I also found that I didn't need a full week's vacation to return to work revitalized and refreshed. I simply needed a mini-break, about five days over the course of a long weekend to step away from the work routine and see the world through another lens, whether holing up with my family or making an escape to the beach. In the last few years, I've recognized again that span of time spent at work has been reduced from ten weeks to a nine-week schedule. It could be attributed to age, increased responsibility, pre-teen and teen children, or a couple of ongoing health issues. I have learned that getting out is still the best course of action.

To this day, I lay out my whole year in advance, now based on the nine-week rhythm. This ensures I use my time for maximum benefit. I'm either working at a high level, or I am out recharging myself for five days to come back strong.

Following a System

Effective time management requires more than good intent and self-knowledge. To keep your time under careful control, you need a framework. In your arsenal of time-management ammunition, you want to stock organizational skills, technology that helps keep you on track, and planning tools that help you keep the reins on your time, hour by hour, day by day, week by week, and so forth.

Establishing a solid system you can replicate is a key to succeeding in managing your time. Systems, standards, strategies, and rules protect your time and allow you to use it to your best advantage. These skills are applicable whether you're the company CEO, a salesperson, a midlevel manager, an executive, or an administrative assistant. No matter your work or your work environment, time management is of universal value.

Scheduling your time and creating a routine

Sticking to a time-scheduling system can't guarantee the return of your long-lost vacation days, but by regularly tracking your meetings, appointments, and obligations, you reduce your odds of double-booking and scheduling appointments too close. And by planning ahead, you make sure to make time for all the important things first.

For years, I've followed the time-blocking system, which I detail in Chapter 5. The system ensures that you put your priorities first (starting with routines and then moving to individual tasks/activities) before scheduling in commitments and activities of lesser importance.

Such time-management techniques are just as applicable to the other spheres of your life. There's a reason why I advise you to plug in your personal commitments first when filling in your time-blocking schedule: Your personal time is worthy of protection, and you can further enhance that time by applying time-management principles.

Organizing your surroundings

A good system of time management requires order and organization. Creating order in your world saves time wasted searching for stuff, from important phone numbers to your shoes. But even more, physical order creates mental order and helps you perform more efficiently.

The schedule will set you free

Too many people feel that all this structure is too restrictive. They think the freedom they seek with their schedules and their lives is contained in a more flexible environment. They're afraid establishing a routine will keep them wrapped in the chains of time.

However, most people waste too much time figuring out each individual day on the fly. They react to the day rather than respond. Reacting is a reflex action that turns over your agenda to others, and that can't possibly lead to freedom. Responding is a disciplined act of planning that determines where and how you'll invest your time.

For example, suppose you have a set place in your schedule to respond to phone calls and problems. You've established the routine of dealing with these issues in predetermined time slots. You can hold off on your response until later — when you're calmer, more focused, and in a problem-solving mentality — instead of reacting because you're dealing with the issue now.

Planning how to spend your time, which at first glance seems opposed to freedom, is the only pathway to the true mastery of time. With the right routine come simplicity, productivity, and freedom. The "what am I going to work on today?" or "what's my schedule today?" never happens. And when you get the important work out of the way, you free yourself to do what you really enjoy.

If you're a free spirit and what I'm suggesting just fried your circuits, start with a small amount of routine. Ask yourself, "Can I establish a daily routine to try it out? What can I do without having it send me into withdrawal?" Then implement a new routine every week. You'll add more than 50 new pieces of structure to your schedule in a normal work year and see a significant improvement in your freedom.

Yes, your workspace should be clean and orderly, with papers and folders arranged in some sort of sequence that makes items easy and quick to find. Your desk should be cleared off, providing space to work. Your important tools — phone, computer, calculator — ought to be within reach. And your day planner, of course, should be at your fingertips. Your briefcase, your meeting planner, even your closet has an impact on your time-management success.

Overcoming Time-Management Obstacles

Anyone can conquer time management, but it's not always easy. If your experience is anything like mine, sometimes your days feel like a video game, where you're in constant threat of being gobbled up on your course to the finish line. But instead of cartoon threats, your obstacles are your own short-comings (poor communication skills, procrastination, and the inability to make wise and quick decisions), time-wasting co-workers and bosses, phone and people interruptions, and unproductive meetings.

Communicating effectively

Communicating effectively is one of the best ways to maximize your time. One of the biggest time-wasters on company time is, no surprise, talking with co-workers. But what may be a surprise is that the abuse *isn't* a function of weekend catch-up discussions that take place at the water cooler or the gossip circle at the copy machine. Rather, it's the banter at the weekly staff status reports, the drawn-out updates of projects that never seem to conclude, the sales presentations that get off track. It's all the meetings that could be as brief as ten minutes but somehow take an hour or more.

At your disposal, however, is an amazing weapon for taming these misbehaving encounters: your words. With a few deft remarks, you have the power to bring these meetings to a productive close.

In Chapter 14, I provide specific insight on which types of situations are most appropriate for each of the primary communication methods — face-to-face, verbal only, and written — and I present plenty of ideas for communicating your message and posing questions strategically, succinctly, and successfully so your communication ends in results, action, and decisions — whether you're leading a meeting or simply attending it.

Circumventing interruptions

Interruptions creep into your workday in all sorts of insidious manners. Besides the pesky co-worker stepping into your office with "Got a sec?" interruptions come in the form of unproductive meetings, phone calls, hall conversations that drift into your office and distract you, even the "you've got mail" icon that creeps onto the lower corner of your computer monitor. You now have more of these interruptions than ever before. You get sidetracked by instant messaging and social media such as Facebook and Twitter. The list of five-minute-here-and-there interruptions is endless.

Additionally, most poor time managers interrupt themselves by trying to do too much at once. Study after study supports that multitasking isn't the most effective work style. The constant stops and starts disrupt a project, requiring startup time each time you turn back to the task. I truly believe being a good time manager at work depends on how you create, craft, and implement your interruption system and strategy. Each day, interruptions cost hours of lost productivity for businesses.

Getting procrastination under control

Sometimes, it's tempting to use interruptions as an excuse to postpone a project or a task. How nice to have someone else to blame for not getting started! And before you know it, you've found so many good reasons not to do something that you've backed yourself into a really tight 11th-hour corner, and the pressure's on.

Say you're writing a 400-page book and you have ten months to complete the project. You have almost a year to put this thing together. Looking forward, your task requires you to complete 40 pages per month — little more than a page a day. That's too easy! You can afford to put it off for a while. Wait for a couple of months, and then you'll need to produce 50 pages a month. Still doable. But at some point, *doable* starts to morph into *impossible*. But when? When you're down to four months and pressured to crank out 100 pages per month? Or do you wait until the last minute and find yourself struggling to complete nearly 15 pages per day?

Procrastination has a lot of causes, but most of the reasons to procrastinate leave you headed for trouble.

Making decisions: Just do it

One of the easiest things to put off is making a decision. Even sidestepping the smallest decisions can lead to giant time-consumption. Think about it: You scroll through your email and save one to ponder and respond to later. You revisit a few times and still can't bring yourself to a commitment. So you get more email from the sender. To stave off making a decision, you ask a couple of questions, which requires more time and attention. By the time the issue is resolved and put to bed, you may have invested five times more attention than if you'd handled it at once.

Many factors create the confusion and uncertainty that prevent you from making sound but quick decisions. Often, part of the struggle is having too many options. Most people have a tough enough time choosing between pumpkin and apple pie at the Thanksgiving table. But every day, you're forced to make decisions from choices as abundant as a home-style cafeteria line. Having options is usually a good thing, but too much choice is overwhelming, even paralyzing.

Being able to handle email, paperwork, and tasks leverages your time. Being able to decide on a course of action, whether you handle an issue or delegate it to someone else, creates a surplus of time.

Garnering Support While Establishing Your Boundaries

Sometimes your family, friends, and co-workers are your biggest challenge to managing your time successfully. Whose phone calls interrupt your train of thought when you're on a roll? Who expects you home for dinner, despite a pressing proposal deadline? For whose meetings do you have to take a break from your critical research?

Yet despite all the challenges they throw your way, these same folks can also serve as your allies as you pursue the quest of better time use. Getting them on board and perceiving them as comrades in shared goals is a great way to offset the interruptions that they also inevitably bring to the table.

Balancing work and time with family and friends

All work and no play, as they say, means something is askew with your life balance. Recognize that although your job and career are critical components of who you are, they're also a means to support aspects of your life that, I suspect, are more important to you: your personal life, which includes your family, your friends, your community, and your leisure and social activities.

If you find yourself constantly putting in long hours at work for months on end, something's off-kilter: Either you're not managing your time effectively, or something's wrong with your job. No one — not even Wall Street lawyers — should be putting in 70-hour weeks on a regular basis. A 70-hour work week leaves little time for sleep, recreation, family, or relationships.

Still, getting the support of family members is critical for success. There's no doubt that my family comes before my job, but that doesn't mean I can drop work whenever I want. So my wife, Joan, and even my two children, 13-year-old Wesley and 9-year-old Annabelle, are my supporters, and we all work together to manage our time so we have more of it together. There have been occasions based on workload and deadline when the only option to meet the deadlines is to be out of balance. Interestingly you're reading words that were written in an out-of-balance time.

The first step to creating time-management success in out-of-balance times is to recognize the potential in advance; stress is reduced if you plan for out-of-balance times. The next step is to approach your family. For example, I discuss openly with Joan, Wesley, and Annabelle the need to spend more time at the office, traveling, writing . . . whatever is causing my time to be out of balance.

It's important to determine and discuss the timeframe. In time management, short out-of-balance time periods likely won't hurt your health or relationships. And at the end of the out-of-balance time period, offer a reward that's shared by all: a reward that your family or friends can experience together. Discuss the reward and come to a consensus so everyone benefits, not just yourself or your business.

Streamlining interactions with co-workers and customers

Most people find themselves in a work environment in which they regularly interact with others, whether co-workers, business associations, or customers. The workday is rife with opportunities for interruption, distraction, and time-wasting. In addition to the phone calls and cubicle pop-ins, you have business appointments, associates who keep you waiting, or meetings that are unfocused and poorly run.

Maintaining control of your time at work requires you to develop some ways to manage meetings, appointments, and other work interactions so they're as efficient and productive as possible. Whether you initiate the interaction or you're merely a participant, you can have some control over the meeting.

Because of my background, I tend to have a soft spot for sales. If you're in sales or a customer service capacity, in such positions, taking control of your time is a little more challenging. To make the sale, you want to take as much time as your prospect wants. And when addressing a service issue, your most important objective is to make the customer happy. But you can be successful in sales and serve your clients well and still keep control of your time. In fact, in Chapter 20, I show you how to speed up the decision-making process during sales so you get a positive answer sooner.

Keeping Motivation High

According to Earl Nightingale, the dean of the personal development industry, "Success is the progressive realization of a worthy goal or worthy ideal." His definition doesn't confine achievement to a fixed point but instead presents success as a journey. Like most goals, mastering your time-management skills isn't something that happens overnight.

Throughout the process of working to improve the way you manage your time, you'll occasionally encounter points where you start feeling disappointed, wondering whether your efforts are paying off. Whenever you hit those lows — and you will — remember to give yourself credit for every step you make in the right direction. One great way to stay motivated is to link incentive to inducement: In other words, reward yourself. For example, if you complete certain actions that tie to your goals, give yourself Friday afternoon off. Or savor an evening on the couch with a good movie or dinner at a favorite restaurant. Do whatever serves as an enticing reward.

Take motivation to the next level by involving others in the reward. Let your spouse know that an evening out awaits if you fulfill your week's goals before deadline. Tell the kids that if you spend the next couple of evenings at the office, you can all head for the amusement park on Saturday. I guarantee this strategy is a sure-fire way to supercharge your motivation.

As you work through this difficult but worthy bout of self-improvement, keep your mind on the positive side and remember two simple truths:

- You're human.
- Work always expands to fill the time you allow for it.

No matter how productive I am, whether I have just a couple things to accomplish or a sky-high pile on my desk, and whether I leave work on time or stay late, there's always something that doesn't get done. So I don't get hung up on those things I don't accomplish — I just keep my eyes on the goal, prioritize accordingly, delegate what I can, and protect my boundaries carefully so I take on only as much as I know I can handle while still remaining satisfied with all parts of my life. When you start to get frustrated about the never-ending flow of work that comes your way, remind yourself that you're blessed with more opportunities than time — and that's not a bad place to be.

Chapter 3

Linking Time Management to Life Goals

*T*oday, more than at any time in history, you have limitless opportunities, especially if you're living in the United States. However, having so many choices can lead to confusion, distraction, and wasted time. Achievement in anything in life takes focus, diligence, and patience. So the question arises: Can getting a handle on your most precious lifelong dreams and desires help you get more done on a day-to-day basis? Absolutely! Say, for example, you and your spouse have always dreamed of taking six months to travel the world while you're still young enough to hoist a backpack. Such a focus may motivate you to put in extra hours or accelerate your sales quotas at work to build up the necessary funds and time for that adventure.

Even long-range goals can shape the way you use your time in the here and now. Suppose your goal is to retire to a modest cabin in the Smoky Mountains and spend the rest of your life writing the Great American Novel. Even if that goal is 30 years away, your priority *now* is more likely to be on investing your income and perhaps taking some writing courses rather than on building a 4,200-square-foot home and learning to ski — or it should be, anyway, because the preparations you need to make first and foremost are the ones that'll enable you to build that cabin and have the money and time to write.

Everyone has dreams and goals for the future. But in order to accomplish more in less time, to create a sense of urgency and command efficiency, having a clear sense of goals and purpose is critical. In this chapter, I guide you in the process of committing your goals to paper; categorizing, balancing, and breaking them down into manageable chunks; and allowing that powerful action to spur your productivity.

Understanding Why You Need to Put Your Goals on Paper

Some studies calculate that only about 3 percent of goal-setters document their aspirations. And I can assure you that these folks are the ones who have the most money, influence, power, prestige, freedom, and time to work toward their dreams. Why? Because, as numerous studies suggest, people who clearly define and write down their goals are more likely to accomplish them — and in a shorter time frame and more direct fashion. People who don't clarify and write out their goals invest more time and accomplish less.

When you take the time to write down your goals, you clarify them and sharpen your vision for attaining them, which allows you to do the following:

- **Take control of your life.** By identifying what's most important to you and putting it on paper, you tell your brain that this isn't a dream to be ignored as a hope-to, wish-to, or would-like-to. It's really something for which you're willing to invest time, effort, energy, and emotion.

- **Map out the most direct route to achievement.** When you put your goals in writing, you're setting your sights on the destination before you begin. Your life goals become the framework for how you prioritize and manage your time. You begin the process of planning and strategizing about the steps you can take to achieve that goal. Your brain starts to look for the best, most direct route and the route with the lowest time investment.

- **Limit detours.** Ever hear the saying "If you don't know where you're going, any road will take you there"? Problem is, if you head off on just *any* road, you're likely to end up in a place you don't want to be. By documenting your goals, you can more easily gauge whether an effort is likely to bring you closer to or further away from them. With your goals in front of you, you make fewer wrong turns and invest less time in trial-and-error dead ends. If you know that "be an outstanding father" is at the top of your written list, then overtime, extra assignments, travel, and other actions that take you away from your kids won't distract you as easily; you know you're more likely to achieve this goal by spending time with your kids, going to their games, taking walks, throwing a ball, playing dress-up, going to the park, or writing a note.

✔ **Stay motivated.** Written goals fuel motivation, inducing you to perform at a higher level and at a faster rate in order to achieve.

Establishing Your Fabulous 50

As you put together your list of goals, you need to consider the five core aspects of wants that I cover in this section. My mentor Jim Rohn taught them to me when I was in my 20s. These five questions dramatically reduced the amount of time I needed to achieve many of the goals that are now crossed off my goal sheets, and these same questions can help you expand your thinking so you can have more, be more, and achieve more.

As soon as you finish reading this section, read no further until you get your goals on paper. Your task after reading this section is to come up with at least 50 goals that you want to accomplish within the next ten years. As you brainstorm your list of goals, keep a few points in mind to make your goal-setting effective:

✔ **Make sure your goals line up with your *wants*.** Don't evaluate goals based on what you think you need, deserve, or can realistically achieve; attack it by what you want. Your success is determined by how you invest your time each day.

✔ **Think big.** "Go big or go home" is a philosophy I encourage my clients and workshop participants to embrace. Many shy away from setting big goals for a range of reasons, from fear of disappointment to concern that they may not have the drive to pursue them.

If you approach your dreams conservatively — going after what you think is reasonable or realistic — your odds of getting beyond that are slim to none. But if you let your imagination go and pursue the big dream, the odds of reaching that level of joy and fulfillment are in your favor. Big goals and big dreams cause you to stretch, strain, and go for what you really want in life. They connect with the best use of your time and energy.

✔ **Pick a time somewhere in the future and work backward from there.** For any goal that stretches further than ten years, break it down into smaller goals with shorter time frames to increase your focus, intensity, and commitment. See the later section "Assigning a time frame to each goal" for details.

✔ **Make your goals measurable.** When you establish a measurable, quantifiable goal, you know you can't fudge on whether you achieved it or not.

You either hit the target or you don't. You also know where you stand at any given time. Goal measurement naturally falls into two categories:

- **Number-based goals:** Measuring your progress toward a goal is pretty easy when the goal is number-based. You know when you've acquired a million dollars or lost 30 pounds, for example. The bank statement or scale is pretty simple to read. As you craft financial and other goals that are associated with numbers, be specific. Do you want to earn a certain annual salary? To put away a certain amount of money each year? To run a certain number of miles by September?

- **Non-number-based goals:** To measure a non-number-based goal, focus on how you'll know when you've accomplished it. For example, will some organization's seal of approval establish you as a world-renowned archeologist? Will being elected president of the chamber of commerce constitute being a business leader in the community? Will having your children expressing greater thanks for your efforts as a parent equate to being a better dad or mom?

As you identify and record 50 goals you'd like to achieve in the next 10 years, contemplate the following five core questions to guide your goal setting.

Using what works for you

Individualism is key when crafting your goals, and it applies to both *what* you record and *how* you record it. You can put your goals in Evernote, enter them in an electronic spreadsheet, post them on a visual whiteboard, or even use them as wallpaper for your phone . . . whatever is easiest for you and triggers the constant reminder. Or maybe you find that your thoughts flow best when you write them down by hand. The important thing to remember is that whatever method best enables your mind to flow freely and inspires you to craft your goals is the one you should use. Don't let others sway you in how to craft and define your goals or what your goals should be.

Consider this little-known fact about yours truly: I have written ten books, and all have been written by putting pen to paper. This archaic approach may seem ridiculous in today's high-tech publishing environment; dictating my thoughts into Dragon or some software would certainly be easier and less time-consuming than writing everything by hand. But not for me. For whatever reason, the direct connection among my hand, pen, eyes, and brain enables me to create a better book. Inspiration comes to me frequently while writing thoughts down, so I stick to my routine and get someone with more time to type my writing into an electronic file.

What do you want to have?

The question of what you want to have focuses on material acquisitions. What possessions do you yearn for? A swimming pool? A sailboat? Do you fantasize about owning a sports car? Do you dream of a formal rose garden landscaped into your backyard? Someone to cook and clean for you? Your own private jet? Winter vacations in the Caribbean? If your home environment is a priority, imagine the place you want to live. An expansive ranch overlooking the Pacific Ocean? A Fifth Avenue penthouse? An off-the-grid abode that runs on solar and wind power? A villa in Tuscany?

Although possessions are important to consider, they're typically a means to an end: They enable you to create the lifestyle that you want to have.

One of the best goals I set and achieved was to own two houses, one as my primary residence and one to which I could retreat. Achieving that goal also motivated me to better invest time during work hours so I could enjoy spending long weekends at my second home. Our second home also created an opportunity to become involved with a church that connected us with two birth mothers we would not have otherwise known. I'm a father because of divine intervention — because of the original goal was simply to have a vacation home.

What do you want to see?

When you ask yourself what you want to see, think experiential acquisition. Travel is likely to be a key focus. I'm certain you can easily come up with at least ten places you want to see. Have some world wonders fascinated you? The Pyramids of Egypt? The Great Wall of China? I travel internationally a few times a year on business, and it only fuels my desire to see more parts of the world and expand my awareness of how other people live.

Your desire for new sights may lean toward unfamiliar geography — the desert lands of the Southwest if you're a New England native or the Rocky Mountains in winter if you hail from a lowland home. Perhaps your *see* goals are more personal. You may have always wanted to visit the country your ancestors came from or even visit the small town in the Midwest where your great-grandparents met and raised a family.

What do you want to do?

Most likely, many of your goals are connected with the question of what you want to do at some point in your life. Whereas the possessions you want to acquire help create your lifestyle, the action-oriented question you consider here focuses more on bigger events and feats outside the daily realm. Because this category is vast, I have my clients consider three main aspects of this question:

- **Activities:** You may want to include some once-in-a-lifetime experiences, such as snorkeling with sea turtles or hiking Mt. Kilimanjaro. What about a goal of regular exercise four times a week? Or maybe you want to see a particular artist in concert.

- **Skills:** For example, have you always wanted to speak Spanish or Mandarin Chinese? Do you wish you could play the piano or electric guitar? Have you put off a new experience — snow-skiing, surfing, fly fishing — because you thought it was too late to learn? Whether these skills can enhance your career or financial state or are simply actions that bring personal pleasure, cast a wide net and list the ones that intrigue you most.

- **Career:** How do you want to seek fulfillment through your career? Be honest with yourself and sort out how you'd like to measure that success. Do you yearn to be recognized as the top authority in your field? To win an international award? To write an influential book?

What do you want to give?

Andrew Carnegie, the great steel entrepreneur, met his goal to amass a fortune in the first half of his life. His goal for the second half was to give it all away. Many of the public libraries in the United States, Canada, and the United Kingdom exist today because of his philanthropy.

An important way to balance all the *want, see,* and *do* items on your Fabulous 50 list is to include *give* goals as well. What are you willing or interested in giving back? How do you want to share your good fortune with others? Which causes are near and dear to you?

Your *give* list may include specific monetary goals — "give 10 percent of my income to charity" — but you may find more fulfillment by tying in your giving goals to your other interests. For example, if your career aspirations involve writing a bestseller, supporting a charity that champions literacy, or volunteering to teach adults to read may be goals that touch a chord with you. If you dream of traveling to exotic destinations, you may participate in a humanitarian mission, bringing medicine and other important supplies to people in a developing country. If you care deeply about environmental initiatives, maybe you want to look into ecotourism or green volunteering opportunities.

Who do you want to become?

To a degree, what you want to have, see, do, and give determine the person you want to become. But you should still envision and write down how you see yourself developing *while* you achieve these goals. The real value of goals isn't what you achieve — it's in the accumulation of knowledge, skills, discipline, and experience you gain through learning, changing, improving, and investing yourself as you work toward your goals. Often, those newly discovered or carefully developed traits are the only lasting acquisition that stands the test of time.

Don't get me wrong — I'm not suggesting that you become someone other than who you are; rather, I'm encouraging you to earnestly and honestly evaluate the characteristics and disciplines best suited for your ambitions. To identify the areas you should focus on, take a look at all the goals you've written down so far (if you haven't yet read the preceding sections, complete them before moving on here). Then ask yourself the following questions when considering your goals as a whole:

- ✔ **What personal characteristics do you need to change or improve?** Do you need assertiveness training to deal more effectively with your boss or co-workers? Do you need to work on interpersonal skills? Does your anger get in the way of your success because you get frustrated so easily?

- ✔ **What disciplines do you need to work harder at practicing consistently?** Are you able to delay gratification and do what you need to when it needs to be done? Are you able to save regular amounts from your current paycheck, or are you waiting to make more money before you start the savings process? What if that extra money never shows up?

If you're struggling to identify areas where you need to work on personal development, take at look at people who have achieved what you want; then evaluate your characteristics and disciplines as compared to theirs.

Appreciating personal growth

Consider this true-life story: I made my first million by the time I was in my early 30s, but I can wholeheartedly say the value I gained from attaining that goal wasn't the money (which, unfortunately, I lost a pretty good chunk of through some poor investments I made). Of deeper and lasting value are the personal characteristics and skills that I gained through the process of strategizing, acting, and investing my time on my way toward the goal. Because I'd changed as a person as a result of the process, the steps toward reaching that goal again weren't nearly so challenging, and the char-

acteristics I developed through the process enabled me to meet other goals as well.

I grew with each new goal I worked toward. To reach my goals in real estate sales, I had to increase my focus and discipline. When I decided to go into coaching and speaking, I had to develop better behavioral analysis and leadership to get others to follow my coaching and teaching. And to reach my goal of writing books that would help readers achieve success, I had to gather new skills in organization, critical thinking, and patience due to all these editors in the publishing business.

Labeling and Balancing Your Fabulous 50

After you draft a list of the 50 goals you want to achieve in the next 10 years, your next task is to assign a category and time frame to each of them. Creating categories for your goals and establishing time frames to achieve them sharpens your focus and increases your intensity, which can reduce the time required to achieve your goals. It also allows you to quickly and easily see whether your time investment to the various areas of your life as well as the size and difficulty of your goals are appropriately balanced.

The objective isn't to spread an equal number and depth of goals among the six categories; the aim is to identify whether one or two of the categories is light compared to the others and to determine whether you need to pay more attention to those areas of your life to develop them. In the end, the purpose is to create a well-rounded system of goals that addresses your whole person and that you'll have the motivation to actually work toward.

Assigning a time frame to each goal

I firmly believe you can have anything you want; you just can't have it all at once and all right now. Just because you establish a goal to lose 20 pounds doesn't mean you'll wake up tomorrow with 20 pounds missing from your body. Realizing your goal involves a process that requires specific activity and time.

The vast majority of people who set financial goals to acquire wealth or financial independence achieve those over time. In many cases, if the amount is comparatively large, it requires 20, 30, potentially even 40 years to achieve. It requires consistent application toward the goal.

I recently did a full review of my financial goals and the progress I have made toward them. It was gratifying in that review to know that in my present savings and investment return pace, I will cross the goal completion line in less than seven years, well within my plan. It's a wonderful feeling, knowing that financial freedom is within my reach.

There are no unrealistic goals, but there may be unrealistic time frames. The world is full of people who have accomplished great things with the application of extensive time. Edison, for example, was said to have failed in excess of 10,000 times in his search for the right filament for the incandescent light bulb. Imagine the time frame necessary to fail 10,000 times!

Remember that your Fabulous 50 list names goals that you want to accomplish within the next 10 years. That said, you may want to see some of them come to fruition much earlier. Some may be immediate — just a year away. Others may require you to first achieve some intermediate goals. For instance, say your goal is to double your income within three years. You know you're unlikely to receive anywhere *close* to a 100-percent raise at your current job, so you start exploring other options: a new job that pays more and has a fast-track career path, a second job, freelance or contract projects that you can do on your off-hours, or a real-estate investment that brings in rental income.

Before you head to the next section, go back through your list of 50 goals (which you create earlier in "Establishing Your Fabulous 50") and write a 1, 3, 5, or 10 next to each goal to indicate whether you want to achieve that goal within 1, 3, 5, or 10 years.

When you start thinking about the time you need to attain your goals, make sure you're being reasonable. Whether or not the time frame for your goals is reasonable depends entirely on your situation. To help you stay on track, follow these steps:

✔ **Consider the time frame you'd *ideally* like to accomplish this goal.**

Would you be happy if you accomplished it one year or even three years later than your ideal, or are you intent on accomplishing it by a certain time?

- ✓ **Assess the complexity of the goal.**
- ✓ **Determine what new knowledge or other resources you may need to accomplish the goal.**

  See the "Pinpointing Your Resource Needs" section, later in this chapter, for guidance.
- ✓ **Consider what time frame someone else needed to accomplish a similar goal.**

After you label each goal with a time frame, tally up the number of goals you have for each time slot and record those totals in Figure 3-1. Then assess the spread of your goals across those time frames to see whether they're well balanced.

Especially when finances are involved, keep in mind that you should enjoy the *process* of working toward your goals. Although planning for the future is important, you're guaranteed only the present. You don't want to rob yourself of all enjoyment now — better to live a balanced life while you implement your plan and adjust it as needed when circumstances throw you for a loop.

Categorizing your goals

After you assign a time frame to each of your 50 goals, your next step is to assign a category to each one. Typically, your goals fall into one of six categories:

C = Career

F = Family

H = Health

M = Money/financial

P = Personal

S = Spiritual

Figure 3-1:
Balance your goals across time frames with this chart.

Timeframe	Number of Goals in This Timeframe
1 year	
3 years	
5 years	
10 years	

When determining which category each goal falls under, you'll find that some goals fall naturally in one specific category. A goal to get be promoted to supervisor at work, for example, is an easy C. Other goals, however, aren't so easy to peg. Going back to school to earn an MBA may be a C for career, but it also may be a P for personal. Place the goal in whichever category you most closely associate with it or feel free to place some goals in multiple categories.

Now go back through your list of 50 goals and write the appropriate category letter next to each one. After you label each goal with a category, count the total number of goals you have for each category and record those numbers in Figure 3-2. Then assess the spread of your goals across those categories to see whether they're well balanced. Are you light on health goals? Should you pay more attention to your spiritual life?

Category	*Number of Goals in This Category*
Career (C)	
Family (F)	
Health (H)	
Money/financial (M)	
Personal (P)	
Spiritual (S)	

Figure 3-2: Balance your goals across categories with this chart.

Targeting 12 Goals to Start With

At this point, you should have a list of 50 goals you want to accomplish over the next 10 years, all labeled according to the time frame you want to achieve them in and the aspect of your life that they fall under (see the preceding section). A large list ensures you have new goals to move to when you accomplish your first goals. However, concentrating on all your goals at once leads to frustration, distraction, and ultimately, failure.

The next step is to break down your list of 50 into some manageable chunks, which helps you focus your energy where you need it most. You won't allow others to interrupt you as frequently, and you'll work with a greater sense of urgency because you have things to do, places to go, people to meet, things to see, time frames in which to accomplish them, and goals to cross off.

Narrowing down your list

To whittle your long list of goals down to a manageable size, choose the three most important goals within each time frame: three that you want to achieve within one year, three before the three-year point, three within five years, and the last trio within ten years.

As you accomplish goals on your top-12 list, revisit your Fabulous 50 and recalibrate your top 12, adding new goals and crossing off the ones you've completed. Keep reviewing your goals on at least a monthly basis. You want to see the progress you're making. With your increasing confidence, you're likely to feel more comfortable with more daring, bolder, and challenging goals. And by resetting your goals, you continue to stoke that momentum.

Noting why your top-12 goals are important to you

Too frequently, people fixate on how they'll accomplish or achieve something. However, the real magic to achieving goals is contained in the *why*. If the *why* is large enough, the *how* becomes easy.

It's been nearly 25 years since I first read Napoleon Hill's landmark book, *Think and Grow Rich!* He guided me to delve deep within myself to explore the *whys* of my aspirations and motivations — and so much more. I'm now known worldwide for my success in real estate sales and my ability to sell 150-plus homes a year on a four-day work week. That was no accident — it was a goal of mine from the start, and I'm certain I've succeeded because I had a clear understanding of the *why* behind it.

Here's my story: My dad worked a four-day week when I was growing up. He was always around on Friday when I came home from school. But the biggest benefit came in the summer, when we left Portland every Thursday afternoon to spend three days at a second home on a lake near the Oregon coast. Some of my fondest childhood memories are of swimming, sailing, waterskiing, walking the beach, and playing at our lake house. I wanted to replicate that life exactly. As I built my real estate sales business, that desire drove my success. It led me to build a vacation home in Bend, Oregon, where Joan and I spent three days a week for more than five years. We enjoyed the lifestyle so much that we eventually moved there and made it our home.

Although my *why* happened to come from a positive childhood experience, keep in mind that reasons can just as easily come from a negative place — either way, they're motivating factors to keep you pressing on. Thousands of success stories have germinated from the seeds of abject poverty or personal tragedy. My father's *why,* for example, was born out of his love for my mother, who was diagnosed with multiple sclerosis when I was 3 years old. By the time I was in the second grade, she never took another step. My father's goal was to earn enough income as a dentist to provide my mother with the most extraordinary life possible: to travel in a wheelchair to Mexico, Asia, Hawaii (annually), and many other locations — always with three sons in tow. But mostly, he wanted to be able to care for her in her in the home where she raised her children and to give her the best quality of life imaginable for someone in her condition.

As a coach, I can only ask questions and guide you to your unique *whys,* regardless of whether they come from happy memories, adversity, or the love and commitment to another. After you determine which 12 goals you'll start on, evaluate why each one is important to you and write it down. Why did you choose these 12 goals over the others? What will these goals accomplish for you? What are you going to feel like when you accomplish them and cross them off your list?

Reading your goals list aloud is a great way to assist your subconscious processes. This action reinforces the message in your brain. Regular repetition and review, coupled with your solid grasp of the *whys,* keeps your goals front-of-mind — even when they're at the back of your mind!

Pinpointing Your Resource Needs

Achieving your goals requires resources, be they money, contacts, knowledge, skills, time, and so on — or all the above. Some fortunate folks may have an abundant supply of all resources, but most are short on at least a couple. I may have the income to allow me to train to become a world-class figure skater, but because I lack the skill, I'm unlikely to have enough time to become good enough to achieve the goal of qualifying for the 2018 Winter Olympics in Pyeongchang, South Korea.

Even if you approach your goals with an imbalance of resources, by carefully leveraging those that you have at your disposal, you can overcome many shortfalls. If you're lacking in one or more resources, you may have to invest more of the resources you have. Take my Olympics example: I'm short on time and skill, so I may need to invest more money to devote myself to full-time training, or I may have to borrow time and aim for the 2022 Olympics, instead.

As you read through the following sections, evaluate the resource requirements for achievement for each of the top 12 goals that you identify earlier in this chapter. When you complete this step of the goal-setting process, you'll have an effective set of goals that you can integrate into your time schedule, which I discuss in depth in Chapter 5.

Accruing funds: A capital idea

Most goals, if they aren't *about* money, seem to require money — building your dream home, taking a cruise, sending your kids to an Ivy League school, opening your own coffee shop. Even a goal such as landing a job at a high-powered corporation, which seems to be about earning money, may require you to get some additional education or purchase suitable interview attire.

If you find that your goal requires capital, do your best to quantify the amount. Then determine whether you have enough money to achieve your goal or whether you need more. Ask the following questions:

- ✔ Do you have time to earn the amount needed to fund your endeavor?
- ✔ Can you borrow the money?
- ✔ Can you leverage another of your resources to balance the shortfall?

Expanding your knowledge

Knowledge can dramatically increase the prospects of attaining your goal in the time table you've established. Trial and error is a costly means to reach your destination — especially when it comes to time investment. So if you assess your success-list goals and determine that you need more information to succeed, ask the following:

- ✔ What, exactly, is the knowledge you need to realize your goal?
- ✔ What's the best way to attain that knowledge? Formal study? Online research? Talking with experts?
- ✔ How long will gaining this knowledge take, and does it fit in with your goal's time frame?

Honing your skill set

For the fulfillment of many goals, additional skills are required. Don't confuse knowledge with skill. *Knowledge* entails the gathering and processing of information in a way that you can use to gain a deeper understanding of a subject. *Skill* involves putting that understanding into effective action. You can study the heart and understand how it works — even know how bypass surgery works to prevent heart failure — but you don't want to perform such a procedure without having the skill of an experienced surgeon.

Examine your success list again to evaluate where additional skills may be necessary:

✔ What skills are required for each goal?

✔ Are these skills that you already claim, or do you need to acquire them?

✔ Are these skills that you can learn within the time frame? If not, then how can you make up for that skill shortage? Can you find someone who has the skills and ask for his or her help?

Tapping into human resources

Most people have accomplished what they have because someone else helped them along the way, so don't overlook the *people* component as you tally up your resources. The right contacts can be valuable in helping you attain your goals. Consider that dream of working for the high-powered corporation, for instance. Knowing someone who works for the company — or who has inside connections — is one of the best ways to get your foot in the door. But people resources can help in achieving other types of goals as well, from buying that cabin in the woods (Uncle Sydney always believed that real estate is the best investment) to learning to play the saxophone (the waiter at the local coffee shop is only too happy to earn some extra money giving lessons). Here are some questions to ask yourself as you evaluate your human resources:

✔ Do you know anyone who achieved a goal similar to yours, someone who may be willing to advise you?

✔ If you need additional schooling but are short on funds, do you know people who may be able to help you acquire the knowledge you need, or can you utilize their talents?

✔ Do you know someone who has the knowledge, skill, connections, or money that you need to reach your goal?

✔ Can you tap into your people resources and use the skills of someone else to compensate for skills you can't attain yourself?

✔ Do you know someone who knows someone else who may be able to help you?

Think of ways that the people you plan to approach can benefit if you attain your goal. Can you compensate them monetarily for their help? Can you offer something in trade that has value for them? Even just asking for help and saying thank you in advance is enough for some people. (Though many times, people are more willing to help when there's something in it for them.)

If you can't find anyone to help, you're forced to take the personal education route. The good thing, though, is that lots of books, classes, and seminars are available to help you, so take advantage of them.

Chapter 4

Putting a Value on Your Time

Depending on your values, different kinds of numbers may be important to you: To some, it's cholesterol count and blood pressure figures; to others, it's the number of years they've been married. To many, the sum total in the retirement account is the number-one number, and some people zero in on the amount left on their mortgage.

But I contend that your per-hour worth should be among the top-of-mind numbers that are important to you — no matter what your values or priorities are — even if you don't earn your living on a per-hour rate. Knowing the value of your time enables you to make wise decisions about where and how you spend it so you can make the most of this limited resource according to your circumstances, goals, and interests.

Obviously, the higher you raise your per-hour worth while upholding your priorities, the more you can propel your efforts toward meeting your goals, because you have more resources at your disposal — you have either more money or more time, whichever you need most.

In this chapter, I guide you toward optimizing your value so you can reap the rewards and attain what's most important to you. I start by showing you why your hourly value is crucial to effective time management. From there, I help you calculate the overall value of your time based on your employment income. (If you have an hourly job, you can skip that section.) Then I help you decide how to leverage your time and money, both in your career efforts and in your personal choices, so you can boost your hourly value and get the most out of your time investment.

Getting a Good Grip on the Time-Equals-Money Concept

Your per-hour value translates to your quality of life, both now and in the future. Not only does your income influence how you spend your nonworking hours, but it also determines how much leisure time you have to spend.

As you can imagine, your hourly value reaches beyond the basics: It impacts your health, too. For instance, studies show that lower-income earners have more health problems, including heart disease and diabetes, which are often attributed to poor diets and a lack of medical care. Also, low-income earners have less free time to invest in exercise because they have to invest more time to provide for the basic needs of their family. Additionally, the challenge of trying to make ends meet can cause great stress, leading to not just physical illness but also to depression and other mental health problems.

And though it's important to live in the present, it's also important to keep an eye toward the future. How well you prepare does have an impact on your quality of life right now. Making enough money to be able to save for retirement and other major life expenses — including a child's education — results in a sense of comfort and safety about your future.

Your personal time has value, too. And by having a grip on the value of your work hours, you gain a better grasp on what your downtime is worth. After all, most people work so they can make the most of their personal time, whether they're devoting it to family, hobbies, volunteer work, travel, or education.

I was recently on a coaching call with an amazing client who sells real estate in Fredericksburg, Virginia. She has more than doubled her income in the last few years. Her challenge is balancing her thriving business with her true priorities in life — her boys and husband. Because she has raised her hourly rate in business, some of the *home tasks,* such as laundry, meal shopping and preparation, and house cleaning need to be reevaluated as to their value.

Before you get ahead of me here, certainly someone needs to do those functions for any family. The point I made to her is that it didn't have to be her. Because of these tasks, she was staying up late or getting up early to complete them. These *normal* activities caused her to work longer hours, miss opportunities in business, and feel detached from the family fun because she needed to get the laundry done or the house cleaned. After discussing and evaluating I said, "You could hire someone to clean the house, do the laundry, and prep a few meals a week for you for about one to two sales per year.

Would that be worth it to you?" She just needed understand to trade her time from a lower-value activity to a higher-value activity.

When you recognize that your free time has a monetary value, just as your work time does, you gain the perspective you need to make choices:

- ✔ Is the extra money you gain by working overtime worth giving up your holiday with your family?

- ✔ Could you go part-time and stay at home with your small children?

- ✔ Can you afford to take a leave of absence to do a volunteer stint in Haiti?

- ✔ Should you take on a freelance project that means giving up all your free time for three months to fund your dream trip to Bali?

But what is an hour of your personal time worth? Well, that's not a question you can easily answer. How do you put a price on time with your young children? Or apply a dollar value to travel experiences that bring you in touch with new worlds? Or equate the quiet therapy of a walk in the woods with the stress of a work presentation?

The harsh truth is that you don't get paid for not working. But that doesn't mean your personal time has no monetary value. Just thinking about your time as a commodity with a value helps you sort through and recognize the activities that are most important to you. (For information on valuing your personal time, see the later section "Making Value-Based Time Decisions in Your Personal Life.")

Calculating Your Hourly Income

No matter your occupation, everyone sells time for a price; it's just a lot more transparent in some situations than others. Most obvious are individuals who receive a wage or a fee based on the hours they work, including minimum-wage workers and self-employed individuals such as tutors, house cleaners, and consultants.

What you are paid per hour is based on the activities you do and the skill you bring to the marketplace. A pilot, by that nature of the skill and what pilots do, has more value than a flight attendant. There are fewer people who could pilot the plane than serve as a flight attendant.

If you are a lower-wage earner, it's because the job you currently have does not have the value to pay you more. If you stay in the present position, you might gain raises over time, but there will be a limit. A fast-food counter worker will not be paid $50 an hour . . . ever.

Your objective should be to raise your value so you can advance to a higher-value job that pays more. Too many people focus on the wrong area. A low-wage job is there to help you acquire skills, show aptitude, passion, drive, and commitment. No one is supposed to stay at that pay for his or her whole life. What we are paid for our time starts at minimum wage. Wage ladders enable you to climb up to higher compensation levels, but you have to do the climbing!

Other people advertise their prices based on a per-project basis, but in reality base that fee on an estimate of project hours the job takes. Freelance writers, for instance, may charge $1,500 to write a promotional brochure, but that amount is likely a reflection of the writer's value of his or her time at a certain figure — say, $75 per hour multiplied by 20 hours of production time.

Some businesses and professions charge customers based on an hourly rate, although workers don't directly receive that per-hour fee. Instead, their salary or compensation is based on the revenue the company can bring in based on those hours. Law firms and plumbers, for example, may charge for their services on an hourly basis and pay their employees a salary or a per-hour rate.

If you earn a salary, you may not perceive yourself as having an hourly rate. But everyone does. Here's how to calculate your hourly income. This number doesn't affect how you're paid, but it puts you in touch with what an hour of your work time brings you.

1. **Calculate the number of hours you work per week.**

    Work hours/day × days/week + overtime = hours/week

    To be completely accurate, calculate your hourly rate based on the hours you actually work. If you consistently put in more than 40 hours a week (most salaried folks aren't paid overtime for additional hours worked), add those hours to your total. Here's an example:

    8 hours/day × 5 days/week + 2 hours overtime = 42 hours/week

2. **Figure out how many hours you work per year.**

    Work hours/week × weeks/year = hours/year

    Make sure you subtract time off. For instance, if you take three weeks of vacation each year, subtract that from your total number of weeks worked. If your salary is based on a three-week vacation and an average 42-hour work week, here's how many hours you work per year:

    42 hours/week × 49 weeks/year = 2,058 hours/year

3. Divide your gross salary by the number of hours you work per year.

Salary ÷ hours/year = hourly income

For instance, $80,000 divided by 2,058 hours is $38.87.

Boosting Your Hourly Value through Your Work Efforts

Money isn't the scarcest and most valuable resource; time is. There are plenty of ways to make more money, but there's no way to add more minutes to an hour. You have a limited amount of this precious commodity, so you want to protect it and spend it as if it's your own personal trust fund.

Most people think that if they work more hours, they'll automatically make more money. That's faulty thinking: You can devote more hours to work, but if you invest the hours in the wrong actions, you gain nothing — and you lose time.

The solution may be to ask for more money for your time. Some workers have a good deal of control over their hourly income and can therefore charge more per hour for their services. The freelance writer can raise her hourly rate from $65 to $70 and bring in an additional $50 on a ten-hour project. A tax accountant can increase the fee for income tax preparation from $450 to $510. If he needs six hours to prepare the average income tax return, the accountant just gave himself an increase from $75 to $85 an hour.

However, the simple fact is that most people don't have the luxury of raising their income at will. So what's the next best step? Change how you use your time so you get the best return on investment — after all, what you do with your time leads to greater prosperity.

To increase your hourly value, you have to decide whether you'll work toward earning more money or earning more time. Then focus on performing high-value activities to achieve that goal; the process of discovering the really important actions or items you can invest your time in can help you change your hourly rate. The decision of how to increase your hourly value — whether to work toward generating more money in the same amount of time or generating the same amount of money in less time — depends on your circumstances:

- ✔ If you're in a commission or bonus compensation structure, you can increase productivity to earn additional income.

- ✔ If you're in a salary-based position, you can find ways to be more productive within the 40 hours week and reduce the additional hours you put in.

If, however, your job doesn't enable you to increase your hourly value, whether in terms of money or time, then you have bigger decisions to make. Other changes you can make to directly impact your income are to simply do the following:

- Find a similar job at a company that pays a bigger salary or offers more freedom with your work hours.

- Improve your performance and earn a raise or a promotion. Know, however, that the success of your efforts toward a raise or promotion is ultimately up to the higher-ups.

When evaluating time-for-money trades, be sure not to limit your definition of *return* to money: Ask yourself whether the exchange improves the quality of your life. Look at how your life would change outside of work if you were to double or triple your hourly rate. If what you're trading for dollars does any of the following, it's a good trade.

- Increases your ability and opportunity to earn more money

- Increases your amount of family time

- Decreases your work hours

- Enhances your physical and mental fitness

- Provides an opportunity for someone who needs it

- Removes something you don't enjoy or don't do well from your life

So that's a simple look at the overall strategy behind improving your return on investment. Chapter 5 takes you through the specifics, helping you schedule your to-do list each day so you make sure all your efforts align with your goals, which you outline in Chapter 3.

Making Value-Based Time Decisions in Your Personal Life

When you consider the way you live your personal life, divide your focus into two categories: chores/responsibilities, and leisure time. Although personal time may seem straightforward, there really is a difference between chores and leisure activities, and the way you approach your time-management decisions hinges on that difference. But however you spend your personal time, you can assign that time a value equal to your work worth — even though no one's paying you — to help you decide how to spend it.

Deciding whether to buy time: Chores and responsibilities

When you have a handle on the value of your time in hourly increments (see the earlier section "Calculating Your Hourly Income"), you have the information you need to make better time choices. The chores have to be done, whether you do them, or delegate, or even pay someone else to do them. The question with chores is whether you want to do them yourself or to exchange dollars for someone else to do them. You have to ask, "Is the cost of the time this task would take me greater than or less than the cost to hire someone to do the work?" Here, you're simply comparing numbers. Think of the laundry list of household chores and personal errands that can eat up every bit of personal time you have. If you could pay someone to do some of those tasks at a rate equal to or well below your hourly rate, wouldn't that be a good return on investment?

I have to admit I am not a big fan of yard work. It might date back to my father owning a number of real estate properties and from about the age of 10 I was the chief landscape guy for his properties. I have mowed acres of lawn, pulled tons of weeds, spread thousands of cubic yards of bark dust. I have done my fair share of yard work in my life. I was paid well for my efforts in my formative years, learned commitment, how to work hard, hitting deadlines . . . and many other valuable life lessons.

I haven't touched a mower, edger, or weed whacker in more than 20 years. The value I can create in life with my family or in business doesn't warrant the activity of yard work. I can pay a professional $100 to $150 a week for the couple of hours it takes to maintain my yard. The value of any time is well beyond the $30 to $50 an hour to have this done. All time in life is a trade. You are trading your time for something you desire, want, or need. I'm blessed that I have the option to trade away things I don't want to do in exchange for things I do want to do. The evaluation is based on your value of time and enjoyment of a particular action or activity. If you have all kinds of free time on the weekend — and you enjoy being out in the yard — paying someone else to cut your grass may be a money-time trade that has no value for you.

If you love to garden but hate cleaning the house, and cleaning the house takes you 4 hours ($200 if your time is worth $50 per hour), why *not* pay a housecleaning service $70, $80, even $100 to buy back the four hours it'd take you to do it all? And you buy yourself four blissful hours puttering over your zinnias and scarlet runner beans.

Making time-spending decisions: Leisure activities

With leisure activities, your decision simply hinges on whether you want to do them at all. Unlike chores, which you have to deal with in some way, you can get away with forgoing certain pastimes. When you're faced with decisions on whether to accept an invitation or volunteer for a committee or do any other activity, that can affect your leisure time.

Looking at rewards

A leisure activity has to bring you as much joy or value as your hourly income rate. Some things you do will be priceless, whereas others are worthless or even less than worthless because they drain you rather than fill you up. So with leisure activities, you aren't comparing numbers — you simply decide whether a given activity is worth your hourly value. Consider the value of the activity in terms of

- Your personal enjoyment
- The service you want to do for someone
- The support to those who are less fortunate than yourself
- The desire to pay it forward
- The legacy you want to leave to others

Factoring in monetary and time costs

Another factor to consider when choosing leisure activities is the cost of your free time. Often, that time isn't so free — you undertake activities that require some recreational funds. When you have to pay to enjoy certain recreational or leisure activities, take the cost of the activity and add it to the monetary time-cost you'd have to pay for the activity. In short, would you pay the cost in your hourly value (plus any costs of the activity itself) to participate in that activity?

Say your income equates to $35 an hour. If an acquaintance you're not all that crazy about invites you to her jewelry party on a weeknight, you'd be looking at, say, a two-hour cost of $70, plus any money you'd spend while there. Should you go? Probably not, if this acquaintance really isn't someone you prefer to spend your time with.

Or how about this scenario? A local nonprofit asks you to be on a committee that requires an average of ten hours per month. Total value: $350 worth of your time each month. Is the value earned from your time donation worth the cost to you? How does it factor into your overall goals? Do you enjoy being on the committee and do you feel passionate about the nonprofit's mission? Do you have other more important things you have to tend to first?

The money-to-time-value consideration extends to even the seemingly most mundane of activities — for example, dining out. Going out to a two-hour dinner with a family of four may rack up $80 or more. If you earn $80 in one hour, this may seem like a fair trade — you're paying $80 for something that would cost you $160 in time. But if your income is $20 per hour, you're essentially paying $80 for something that's worth only $40 in time. That may seem steep for a midweek convenience grab; however, if you're celebrating your child's first straight-A report card, it may feel like a fairer trade.

How about a week of vacation? Travel, hotel, and food on the road can add up fast. If you and your partner total up $3,000 in expenses for a beach resort getaway, at $80 an hour, that's 37.5 hours — not quite a week's worth of work hours . . . and not a bad deal, you may think. The fact of the matter is this: The decision of whether an activity is worth its cost is completely subjective. That idea is certainly empowering and freeing, as long as you make conscious choices about where you dole out your hours.

Staying open to experiences and using time wisely

The process of evaluating your leisure time is meant to help you use your time well, not to limit your experiences. If you're unsure about a certain activity but you had fun and found it worthwhile in the past, you should probably go. Also consider going if it's part of your current or future goals. If you enjoy the people but not an activity, you can suggest a change of venue and make the outing more worthwhile.

If you give up activities and find yourself mindlessly wasting the time you gained in front of the TV or online, you likely need more clarity in your goals. Or your goals may not be compelling enough. Chapter 3 can help you sort out your goals and pinpoint the activities you find most fulfilling.

Helping kids understand the time-versus-money balance

Business travel can eat up a lot of the personal time you count on for recreation and renewal. You may still tie up your workday at 5:30 p.m., but instead of going home to the family, you retreat to your hotel room for the night. And your weekend may be consumed with long travel days to get home.

I know the price of a job that requires business travel. It's a price that I pay, my wife pays, and my kids pay. By the end of the year, I'll have traveled to five different continents speaking to sales organizations in countries around the world. I'll be away from my family for days — and in some cases, weeks — at a time.

When my son Wesley was 5, I was getting ready to leave for a week of speaking engagements. He was crying and begging me not to go. When I see my children cry, I'm a pushover, but I knew I couldn't *not* go, so after I saw that all my reassurances weren't working to stop his tears, I went out on a limb and tried to reason with my son.

I explained to him that I already promised the people that I'd be there and it wouldn't be right for me not to show up. I assured him that if he wanted me to, I'd be willing to stop speaking and spend more time at home. But we'd all have to make some changes: We'd have to sell our home and buy a smaller one because Daddy would be making less money. We would need to cut some things out of our budget like some vacations, eating out, toys — the new bike he'd been asking for. I wound up my explanation and asked him gently, "Do you understand?" He looked at me thoughtfully for a second and then said, "Bye, Dad. See you later." And off he ran.

Part II
Establishing a Good System

When you're organized, your productivity increases, your frustration level decreases, and without clutter, your mind can focus on the tasks at hand. Here are the top five ways to get your workspace in order.

1. **Purge your office:** De-clutter, empty, shred, get rid of everything that you don't need or want. Look around. What haven't you used in a while?

2. **Revise your filing system:** The digital age has eliminated the need to store many paper files. Ask yourself what you can store digitally and what files might be duplicated. You may be able to lose some of the files and folders you've used in the past.

3. **Clean and organize your desktop:** Your first step is to take everything off your desktop and give it a good cleaning. Then put back only the items that you use on a daily basis. Use desktop organizers or containers to organize the items on your desk; use trays for papers and containers for smaller items.

4. **Organize your drawers:** Use drawer organizers for little items, such as paper clips, tacks, and so on. Put items used together in the same drawer space — for example, put stamps with envelopes. And be sure to use a separate drawer for personal items.

5. **Clear your stacks of stuff:** With your clean and organized office, you won't create piles of paper anymore! But you still have to sort through the old stacks. Go through it all, a little at a time if necessary, and put everything in the appropriate place . . . or dump it.

In this part . . .

✔ Learn how to take control of your schedule, make time for what matters most, and achieve your most precious life goals and dreams.

✔ Navigate around the pitfalls of the home office [md] from interruptions, to kids, through even the disconnected feelings so many telecommuters struggle with.

✔ Tackle your workspace by learning new organizational skills.

✔ Give your computer, database, and electronic filing system a technology makeover. Learn how to revamp your scheduling systems and appointment requests to enhance your productivity.

✔ Get familiar with cloud computing so your schedule and appointments have the portability you need in today's mobile world.

Chapter 5

Focusing Your Efforts, Prioritizing Tasks, and Blocking Your Time

. . . .

In This Chapter

▶ Identifying vital tasks and goals with the 80/20 rule

▶ Prioritizing activities

▶ Developing the habit of time-blocking

▶ Staying on the road to successful time-blocking

. . . .

*W*hat you do with your time is more important than how much time you have. Just as recognizing and understanding your life goals helps you achieve successful time-management skills, the effective use of your time goes a long, *long* way to shortening the journey to those goals. By investing your time with care and consideration, your journey toward your dreams is certain to be a smoother road. In fact, an old time-management adage says that for every minute you invest in planning, you save ten minutes in execution. Spend an hour planning your trip, and you'll free up *ten* hours — to achieve better business results, reduce stress, and add quality time at home.

The best way to achieve your goals is to prioritize them and develop an ordered plan to reach them. A universally recognized method for maximizing productivity, called the *80/20 rule,* has proven successful time and again, for more than 100 years. In this chapter, I explain the general concept and show you how to apply it — at work, at home, in your relationships, and beyond.

People who are most productive have another common trait: They treat everything in life as an appointment. These people value their time and the activities to which they commit, whether business or personal. They lend importance to their duties, commitments, and activities by writing them down and giving them a time slot, whether they're one-time occurrences or regular activities. They even make appointments with themselves.

To ensure you act on your priorities in the order that's most important to you, you need to follow a method to your scheduling — and that's what this chapter is all about. Here, I help you match your overall time investment to your goals (which you outline in Chapter 3), prioritize your tasks, and create a schedule to take you safely to your destination.

Focusing Your Energy with the 80/20 Theory of Everything

In 1906, Vilfredo Pareto noted that in his home country of Italy, a small contingency of citizens — about 20 percent — held most of the power, influence, and money — about 80 percent, he figured. That, of course, meant that the other 80 percent of the population held only 20 percent of the financial and political power in the country. Pareto found a similar distribution in other nations. In the 1940s, Joseph M. Juran applied the same 80:20 ratio to quality control issues, and since then the business world has run with idea of the "vital few and trivial many."

The basic principle that in all things, only a few are vital and many are trivial is known as the *80/20 rule* (also referred to as the *Pareto principle*), and you can apply it to almost any situation. I've heard it used in the workplace ("20 percent of my staff makes 80 percent of the revenue") and even by investors ("20 percent of my stocks generate 80 percent of my income"). You can also apply the 80/20 rule to time management, as I explain in this section.

Matching time investment to return

Generally speaking, only 20 percent of those things that you spend your time doing produces 80 percent of the results that you want to achieve. This principle applies to virtually every situation in which you have to budget your time in order to get things done — whether at work, at home, in your relationships, and so on.

The goal in using the 80/20 rule to maximize your productivity is to identify the key 20-percent activities that are most effective (producing 80 percent of the results) and make sure you prioritize those activities. Complete those vital tasks above all else and perhaps look for ways to increase the time you spend on them.

In this section, I show you how to implement the 80/20 rule.

Step 1: Sizing up your current situation

Before you can do any sort of strategizing, you need to take a good, honest look at how you use your time. For people who struggle with time management, the problem, by and large, lies in the crucial steps of assessing and planning. Start your assessment with these steps:

1. **Observe how you currently use your time.**

   Through the observation process, you can discover behaviors, habits, and skill sets that both negatively and positively affect your productivity. What do you spend most of your day doing? How far down the daily to-do list do you get each day?

2. **Assess your personal productivity trends.**

   During which segments of the day are your energy levels the highest? Which personal habits cause you to adjust your plans for the day?

3. **Take a close look at the interruptions you face on a regular basis.**

   During what segments of the day do you experience the most interruptions? What sort of interruptions do you receive most frequently, and from whom?

Later in the chapter, in "Blocking Off Your Time and Plugging in Your To-Do Items," I explain how to control and plan for your time through time-blocking your day.

Step 2: Identifying the top tasks that support your goals

Some folks tend to follow the squeeze-it-in philosophy: They cram in everything they possibly can — and then some. These people almost always end up miserable because they try to do so much that they don't take care of their basic needs and end up strung out in every possible way. The quality of what they do, as well as the amount of what they do, suffers as a result of their ever-increasing exhaustion.

To work efficiently, you need to identify your 80 percent — the results you want to achieve. Break out your list of goals (which I help you think through and record in Chapter 3). Take a good look at your top 12 goals and identify the tasks you need to do that align with those goals. If your number-one goal is to provide your kids with an Ivy League education, for example, then your priorities are less likely to center around taking twice-yearly vacations to the Caribbean and more likely to revolve around investing wisely and encouraging your offspring to do well in school (can you say "full-ride scholarship"?).

After you identify what you need to do — your vital few — spend a bit more time in self-reflection to double-check that you've correctly identified your goals and essential tasks. One of the biggest wastes of time for people is changing direction, priorities, objectives, and goals. Successful people and successful time managers take the direct route from point A to point B.

Here's what to ask yourself about these key tasks:

- How much time do you devote to those activities? Twenty percent? Less? More?
- What are you doing with the remainder of your time?
- How much return are you getting for the investment on the remainder?

Step 3: Prioritizing your daily objectives

After you identify the tasks and activities that you need to accomplish to achieve your goals, assign a value to those goals so you can decide how to order your daily task list.

Take the send-your-kids-to-an-Ivy-League school scenario that I bring up in the preceding section: Even though another of your priorities is to be home for your kids, you — as a nonworking parent who values the type of education you can provide for your 3-going-on-18-year-old more than the short-term joy of being a stay-at-home parent — may decide to return to the workforce as you see tuitions skyrocketing. You can make this decision because you have a clear idea about how you rank your priorities. This clarity may help direct you to a job with hours compatible with your kid's schedule.

To personalize how you prioritize your goals at work, follow these steps:

1. **Look at your long-term career goals.**

    Do you want to advance to a particular career level? Do you want to achieve a particular income? Or is your goal to fine-tune your skill set before figuring out where you want to go next?

2. **Review your company's priorities.**

    Having a solid understanding of the company's priorities, goals, objectives, and strategic thrusts guides your own prioritization so you can get the edge on the company's competition. To get a global perspective, review your company's mission statement, review its published corporate values and goals, and see how they pertain to your position. Ask your direct supervisor for further elaboration on these statements and on his or her priorities so you can make sure you align yours accordingly.

The vital 20 percent: Figuring out where to focus your energy at work

Used effectively, the 80/20 rule can increase your on-the-job performance. From boardroom to lunchroom, executive suite to mailroom, this time-management principle can help you accomplish the most important tasks in less time and help you advance in your career.

The 20-percent investment in the 80 percent of results remains relatively constant. In more than 15 years of working with business leaders to improve performance, I've witnessed it firsthand: What's truly important for success changes very little within a given profession. The two global objectives of any successful business are profit and customer retention. What differs among professions is how those global objectives translate to match individual objectives.

For example, here's how the 80/20 rule factors into some major job categories:

- ✔ **Ownership/executive leadership:** As an executive or owner, your most important role is to establish the vision, goals, and benchmarks for the business. What are the core values and core purpose for the business? What are the goals for the year and then next quarter? What are the most pressing problems that need to be solved? What are the strengths, weaknesses, opportunities, and threats the company or marketplace is experiencing? You then have to convey those answers consistently in clear terms for your lieutenants to follow and hold the lieutenants accountable to the standards.

- ✔ **Sales:** For sales professionals, lead generation leads to 80 percent of your return. Without new leads and new prospects to sell to, your customer and prospect base remains fixed to your current clients. So in sales, your most important tasks are prospecting and following up on leads; you should put a priority on securing and conducting sales appointments and building personal relationships.

   Don't forget your existing client base as well. They usually follow the same 80/20 rule, where 20 percent of them contribute 80 percent of the revenue. Spend your time with this group to increase sales and referrals.

- ✔ **Management:** For those in leadership positions, your vital 20 percent is the coaching and development of people. You use coaching strategies to encourage and empower your employees, and you monitor your staff's adherence to the company's strategic plans. In addition, you help your employees acquire the knowledge, skills, attitude, and actions to advance their careers.

✔ **Task- or service-based roles:** This group of people varies the most because it's the broadest. To identify your vital tasks, take a look at your company's objectives, your department's objectives, and your own objectives to get a well-rounded picture of how your role fits into the bigger picture. Then decide which of your job responsibilities increase sales or improve customer retentions.

After that, consider the value of the product or service you offer, and weigh the importance of quality versus speed or quantity — your ultimate goal is to serve your customers better so you retain and grow your relationships with them. (If you're not sure how much weight each element deserves, talk to your supervisor about where you should focus your efforts.)

- If quality takes higher priority, ask yourself how you can deliver a better product or service in the amount of time you're given.

- If delivery speed or quantity is more important, ask yourself how you can deliver that product more efficiently while maintaining quality.

✔ **Administration:** If you're in an administrative role, your goal is to enhance the company's performance, whether you're supporting front-line sales staff or assisting the corporate leadership in steering the business toward profit. If you're in sales support, how can you help free up the salespeople to do more selling? Can you fill out reports for the salespeople? Research new market opportunities and get contact information? Can you repeat that help for the sales manager in reports and better tracking of the salespeople's numbers so the manager can do more coaching and shadowing of the salespeople?

If you're working in customer service, is there a recurring customer service problem that needs to be solved? Can you identify it? Can you find at least two solutions to the problem and bring them to your boss for review? You can make yourself an indispensible asset to the company with these actions and save time for yourself and your superiors as well.

Personal essentials: Channeling efforts in your personal life

The 80/20 rule isn't strictly business related, so don't lose sight of its influence on your personal life. In fact, the 80/20 rule can have the greatest impact at home. For most, personal and family life is the realm that matters most. But with all the demands of work and the outside world, it often takes the back seat. By categorizing and ordering your personal priorities, you can customize your approach to the people and priorities in your home life and make the most of your time spent with family, hobbies, leisure, and friends.

When factoring in your personal priorities, think of a variety of areas, such as time with loved ones, a worthy cause, your faith, education, and future plans. In this section, I cover the two areas of prioritization that affect most people (for other situations, follow the general process I outline earlier in "Matching time investment to return").

Investing wisely in your personal relationships

One of the great things about the 80/20 rule is that it doesn't apply only to task-oriented items — it's also about the quality of your time and the energy you put into what you choose to do with it. If you have a significant other, for example, consider how 20 percent of all the time you spend with him or her shapes 80 percent of your relationship with that person.

Outside of work, personal relationships are number one, so always consider them first, before you even start thinking about chores. Evaluate your connection with each of the important people in your life, both family and friends. In this way, you can customize your approach to the people and priorities in your home life instead of lumping everything into the generalized category of "home" and perhaps not giving any individual or activity its due attention. When dealing with people, ask yourself these questions to help you identify the 80/20 balance:

- ✔ How can you invest your time with this person to create a better relationship?
- ✔ What's most important to this loved one, and how can you serve and support these needs?

Many other questions can help get you to the root — or the 20 percent — of actions that produce a bumper crop of love, security, appreciation, and experience that build meaningful relationships at home. For example, if you're raising children, you may ask yourself these questions as well:

- ✔ How can you invest your time to nurture this child's developing interests?
- ✔ How can you show that you value this child in a way that is meaningful to him or her?
- ✔ What do you need to do each week to teach this child an important life skill?
- ✔ What shared activities allow you to serve as a positive example?
- ✔ What can you do to create a positive family memory?

ANECDOTE

Setting up family traditions

My wife, Joan, and I adhere to two traditions that don't take much time but reap huge dividends in the closeness we feel with one another and the partnership in responsibilities that we share. The first is that Saturday each week is date night. We have a standing babysitter, and even with my travel schedule, we rarely miss our Saturday-night date. We also walk together each evening after dinner. This enables us to share, interact, and exercise all with one activity.

My children and I also have a couple of long-standing traditions to foster nurturing relationships with each other. With my son, Wesley, I have Boy's Breakfast Out at least two Friday mornings per month. We spend about 90 minutes talking and laughing, and then I take him to school. He looks forward to it, and so do I. Annabelle, even at 9 years old, loves to have tea parties, so I set aside time to sit among her stuffed animals and toys while she serves me tea in doll-sized cups. We don't spend as long (fortunately — sitting in a low stool for longer than 45 minutes is murder on my back!). But she, too, eagerly anticipates tea time with Daddy.

We have two other traditions in the Zeller family. Friday night is what we call Family Friday. We go to the local high school football game or to a movie, rent a movie, have dinner out, anything that we can do as a family. Sunday night is game night. We turn off the television and play cards or board games together . . . all electronics are off!

Your 20-percent time traditions may differ from ours, depending on the age, interests, and unique traits of your loved ones at home. The important thing is to find out what brings the biggest return, greatest connection, and best memories. Of course, I have to confess that applying the 80/20 rule in relationships is much easier to write about than to execute. Although you may understand how the 80/20 rule applies to your home relationships, putting it into practice remains a challenge. Work on this with each passing day.

Balancing crucial household tasks with at-home hobbies

Face it: Your days are filled with tasks that really don't bring much return on investment. Whether it's doing the laundry or filling out paperwork, there are loads of those necessary-but-not-monumental duties that you'll never be able to eliminate. And in your personal life, these activities may include housework, home maintenance, or walking the dog.

However, you can apply the 80/20 rule to help balance how you invest your time in chores so it aligns with your hobbies. Which activities bring you the biggest return? For example, do you spend every summer evening and weekend on your back patio, entertaining or simply admiring your backyard and flower garden? Then for you, trimming, mowing, planting, and weeding may be a wise way to invest that vital 20 percent of your time. If, however, you get more enjoyment from traveling to new places, you may allocate that time to budgeting for and planning exciting vacations.

Cooking, cleaning, shopping, laundry, yard work, bill paying, and other tasks are essential, but that doesn't mean that *you* have to do them — sometimes, the added cost of hiring help is worth the time it frees in your schedule. If you gain no joy or fulfillment whatsoever in cleaning or household mainte-nance, or feel you simply don't have the time or energy to do all this without sacrificing your most important priorities, hire out those responsibilities. Sure, there's a cost involved, but you buy back time to spend on the activi-ties that mean the most to you. So send out the laundry if it frees you up to explore new menus in the kitchen, or bring in a personal chef if you'd rather be out in the garden planting tomatoes.

If you can hire someone who makes far less money than you do to do some-thing you don't enjoy, hire out the task immediately. If you can work a few more hours and increase your pay or set yourself up for promotion sooner, then work the extra hours and hire the help. In the end, you'll be doing some-thing you enjoy rather than something you despise.

Yard maintenance will never be on my vital 20-percent time investment list. In my adolescent years, I mowed, clipped, trimmed, and hedged a lifetime's worth of yards to earn money. I don't own a lawnmower and never will. And frankly, a prizewinning lawn is not tops on my list of life satisfactions. However, I do enjoy presenting my family and friends with creative meals, so I put my time into grocery shopping and cooking. It gives me a chance to help lighten the load for Joan, and it offers another 20-percent time tradition with the kids. They love to get creative in the kitchen — especially baking cookies — so we do it together.

The 80/20 rule doesn't stop there — you can also apply it to the quality of those tasks or hobbies and the results they have on your well-being. If you're a gardener, for example, think about the 20 percent of your efforts that bring forth the 80 percent of your pleasure and satisfaction from gardening. For example, maybe you don't need to sculpt a perfectly arranged flower garden to reap the personal benefits — the very act of digging your hands into the earth may give you the greatest sense of joy. So focus on the act of planting more than on the planning and shopping.

Don't forget to include those activities that support and improve your physi-cal, mental, and emotional health. Those activities that keep you sane, happy, and fit may seem insignificant when taken one at a time. But if they start getting squeezed out of the schedule, you just may start to see that sanity, happiness, and health start slipping. Be sure to account for all those little pleasures that add texture to your life — reading, study, yoga, your weekly facial.

Getting Down to Specifics: Daily Prioritization

After you identify the vital few tasks you need to accomplish to meet your top 12 goals, break them down a bit further into daily to-do items. Then prioritize them to make sure you accomplish the most important tasks first, identifying which ones you must do on a given day. In that way, you progressively work through all the minor tasks that lead to the greater steps that, in time, lead you to achieving your goals. Here's how:

1. **Start with a master list.**

   Write down everything you need to accomplish today. Don't try ranking the items at this point. You merely want to brain dump all the to-do actions you can think of. You may end up with 20, 30, even 50 items on your list: tasks as mundane as checking email and as critical as presenting a new product marketing plan to the executive board. Or if you want to fill work on your personal to-do list, the items may range from buying cat food to filing taxes before midnight.

   Remember to account for routine duties that don't have a direct effect on your company's mission or bottom line: turning in business expense reports, typing up and distributing meeting minutes, taking sales calls from prospective printing vendors. Neglecting to schedule the humdrum to-do items creates a destructive domino dynamic that can topple your well-intentioned time-block schedule.

2. **Determine the A-list.**

   Focusing on consequences creates an urgency factor so you can better use your time. Ask yourself, "What, if not done today, will lead to a significant consequence?" Designate these as *A activities*. If you have a scheduled presentation today, then that task definitely hits the A-list. Same goes for filing your tax return if the date is April 15. Buying cat food probably doesn't make this list — unless you're totally out or have a particularly vindictive cat.

3. **Categorize the rest of the tasks.**

   Now move on to B-level tasks, activities that may have a mildly negative consequence if not completed today. C tasks have no penalty if not completed today, followed by D tasks: D is for *delegate*. These are actions that someone else can take on. Finally, E items are tasks that could be eliminated, so don't even bother writing an E next to them — just mark them out completely.

4. **Rank the tasks within each category.**

Say you've categorized your list into six A items, four B items, three C items, and two D items. Your six A tasks obviously move to the top of the list, but now you have to rank these six items in order: A-1, A-2, A-3, and so forth.

If you have trouble ordering several top priorities, start with just two: Weigh them against each other — if you could complete only one task today, which of the two is most critical? Which of the two best serves your 80/20 rule? Then take the winner of that contest and compare it to the next A item, and so on. Then do the same for the B and C items.

As for the D actions? Delegate them to someone else! Everyone likes to think he or she is indispensable, but for most people, the majority of their duties could be handled by someone else. That's where the *85/10/5 rule* — first cousin to the 80/20 rule — comes into play: You tend to invest 85 percent of your time doing tasks that anyone else could do, and 10 percent of your time is devoted to actions that some people could handle. Just 5 percent of your energy goes to work that only you can accomplish. But whether at home or at work, this doesn't mean you can kick back and leave 95 percent of your responsibilities to someone else. It simply helps you home in on the critical 5 percent, allocate your remaining time to other activities that bring you the greatest satisfaction, and recognize those tasks that are easiest to delegate.

Now you're ready to tackle your to-do list, knowing that the most important tasks will be addressed first (see the nearby sidebar, "Rocking out: Putting the A-list tasks in place," for the importance of prioritizing). Don't expect to complete as large a number of cross-offs as you may be used to. Because you're now focused on more important items — which likely take more time — you may not get as many tasks completed. In my view, however, the measure of a great day is whether you wrap up all the A-list items. If you follow this system and consistently complete the As, I can assure you success. Why? Because the B and C items quickly work their way to As — and you always get the most important things done.

Don't assume that you just move the Bs and Cs up the next day. You need to complete the whole process each day. Some of the Bs will move up, but others will stay in the B category. Some of the Cs — due to outside pressure, your boss, or changed deadlines — may leapfrog the Bs and become the highest priority As.

Rocking out: Putting the A-list tasks in place

Steven Covey and A. Roger Merrill illustrated the importance of prioritizing tasks in their book *First Things First* (Simon & Schuster) with a simple metaphor. In short, a guest lecturer was speaking to a group of students when he pulled out a 1-gallon, wide-mouthed Mason jar, set it on a table in front of him, and began filling it with about a dozen fist-sized rocks. When the jar was filled to the top and no more rocks would fit inside, he asked the class whether the jar was full, to which they unanimously replied, "Yes."

He then reached under the table and pulled out a bucket of gravel, dumping some of it into the jar and shaking the jar, causing pieces of gravel to work themselves down into the spaces between the big rocks. He asked the group once more whether the jar was full, to which one suspicious student responded, "Probably not."

Under the table he reached again, this time withdrawing a bucket of sand. He started dumping in the sand, which sank into all the spaces left between the rocks and the gravel. Once more, he asked the question "Is the jar full?" "No!" the class shouted. "Good!" he said, grabbing a pitcher of water and pouring it in until the jar was filled to the brim.

He looked up at the class and asked, "What is the point of this illustration?" One eager beaver raised his hand and said, "The point is no matter how full your schedule is, if you try really hard, you can always fit some more things into it!"

"No," the speaker replied. "The truth this illustration teaches us is if you don't put the big rocks in first, you'll never get them in at all."

Blocking Off Your Time and Plugging in Your To-Do Items

After you identify and order your priorities (see the preceding sections), you place them into time slots on your weekly calendar, broken into 15-minute segments — this process is commonly called *time-blocking*. I've discovered no better system for managing time on a daily, weekly, monthly, yearly, and lifelong basis. I've seen miracle-level transformations in the lives of my clients — successes measured in income, health, relationships, personal growth, spiritual transformation, and wisdom.

Like exercise, time-blocking can be tricky because it requires a lot of thought and adjustment, both in the initial stage where you're doing it for the first time and for a while thereafter, when you're developing the skill. Everybody knows what day two after the beginning of a new fitness program feels like: Stiff joints and sore muscles have you moving like the Tin Man after a rainstorm. At first you may feel like you'll never achieve the goals you've set, but sticking to the daily program eventually brings the results you want. Figuring out how to best manage your time depends on two things:

- ✔ **Consistent, diligent practice:** If you want to build those time-blocking muscles, not only do you have to work them regularly, but you also need to increase the weight, stress, and pressure as you progress. Understanding the key to managing your minutes, hours, days, weeks, and so on takes repetition.

  I was first exposed to time-blocking at a business seminar more than 25 years ago, and for the past 15 years, I've coached hundreds of thousands of people. In all this time, I've yet to meet anyone — including myself — who doesn't need some ongoing reinforcement, repetition, and refresher course of the time-blocking principles I share with you here.

  Don't panic when you find yourself a little stressed or sore from all your time-blocking exercises. It's simply a sign that your efforts to build up those skills are working.

- ✔ **A span of time to improve:** Achieving a level of time-blocking mastery does take time — a minimum of 18 months and as much as 24 months. Why so long? Because you're developing a complex skill. A typical day has you switching from refereeing an argument between your kids to making an important presentation to the corporate executives; from putting together your department's annual budget to paying for your groceries in the checkout line. That's a lot to orchestrate, and even Handel didn't write his *Messiah* overnight. If you accept that time-blocking skills require time to develop, you're more likely to remain motivated. Your objective is to make measureable progress in reasonable time.

Implementing time-blocking to help organize your schedule takes a bit of time, but you reap huge dividends on that initial investment. This section walks you through a general outline of the process I follow.

Step 1: Dividing your day

To start, you need a daily calendar or Google Doc calendar divided into 15-minute increments. Why such small bites of time? Because even 15 minutes can represent a good chunk of productive activity. Losing just two or three of these small blocks each day can diminish your ability to meet your goals, from finishing that project at work to writing your bestselling (you hope) memoir. In the appendix, I provide a blank schedule for you to photocopy and use as many times as you'd like.

ANECDOTE

> # Time-blocking: Making small investments in big success
>
> Time-blocking doesn't require a huge commitment to produce results. A few years ago, one of my clients, a top sales performer in her region, exploded her sales by more than 125 percent in one year! I knew that time-blocking had played an important role in her success. I asked her what percentage of the time she had managed to adhere to her time-blocking schedule. She confessed that she'd stuck to the schedule only 35 percent of the time. The undeniable truth is that a little goes a long way. As you continue to use your time-blocking skills, that percentage increases, and your productivity grows accordingly.
>
> I also have a client named Sam, a salesperson, who increased his contacts by ten per day after adopting time-blocking. These ten additional contacts led to an increase of five leads per week. He averages one appointment for every 2.5 leads and has a 50-percent close ratio on appointments. So from ten contacts per day, he gains one extra sale a week. At an average $5,000 commission per sale, he has the potential to increase his income by $250,000 a year. How's that for results?

On that blank schedule, begin by dividing your day; draw a clear line between personal time and work time. When you take this step, you're creating work-life balance from the start. Don't take it for granted that Saturday and Sunday are time off just because you work a Monday-through-Friday work week. Block it into your schedule, or work activities may creep into your precious downtime. The more you take action on paper, the more concrete the time-block schedule becomes.

TIP

Apprehensive about drawing a line between work and personal time because you're wary of having to tell a business associate you can't attend a business function that extends into personal time? Not to worry. You don't have to tell a client that your Tuesday-morning workout is more important than a breakfast meeting with her — simply say you're already booked at that time. That's all the explanation you owe, and my experience shows that professional colleagues who want to do business with you respect your boundaries.

Step 2: Scheduling your personal activities

Blocking out personal activities first gives weight to these activities and ensures that they won't be overtaken by obligations that have lesser importance in the long run. Personal obligations are almost always the first thing most people trade for work; because of that, I recommend that you hold fast and tight to the personal area so it doesn't get away from you. Another advantage? You help establish a reasonable end to your workday. If you're scheduled to meet at a friend's for Texas Hold 'Em on Thursday nights, you're more motivated to wrap up your project in enough time to cut the deck.

Scheduling personal activities is twofold:

1. **Schedule routine activities you participate in.**

   Do you have dinner together as a family every night? A weekly date night with your significant other? Do you want to establish family traditions? Don't just assume these activities will happen — give them the weight they deserve and block out the time for each one. Don't forget to include your extracurricular activities here: All those PTA groups, fundraising committees, nonprofit boards, and other volunteer commitments get plugged in as well.

2. **Schedule personal priorities that aren't routine.**

   Put those personal agenda items first before filling in your day with tasks and activities that don't support those priorities.

Step 3: Factoring in your work activities

Begin with the activities that are a regular part of your job and then factor in the priorities that aren't routine. Whether you're a company CEO, a department manager, a sales associate, an administrative assistant, or an entry-level trainee, you're responsible for performing key tasks and activities each day and week. They may include daily or weekly meetings. Or maybe your responsibility is scheduling meetings for others. You likely have to prepare for these appointments. Perhaps you have to write and turn in reports or sales figures on an ongoing basis. You may have to call someone for information routinely. If you report to work daily and always spend the first hour of your day returning phone calls, time-block it into your schedule.

Step 4: Accounting for weekly self-evaluation and planning time

Your goals — whether a one-year business plan or long-range retirement vision — warrant routine checkups. Consider them as rest stops on your journey: Are you still on the right road? Is a detour ahead? Have you discovered a more direct route?

Use weekly strategic planning sessions — ideally for Friday afternoon or the end of the work week — to review your progress toward those near-future business projects as well as your larger career aspirations or personal goals. This is an opportunity to review the previous week and jump-start the upcoming week. I recommend spending 15 to 30 minutes daily and then taking a 90-to-120-minute session on self-evaluation and planning at the end of the week.

This strategic planning time is probably your most valuable time investment each week. It gives you a tremendous wrap-up for the week and a good start to next week, and it reinforces your vision for your long-term success. It also enables you to go home and spend time with your family in the right frame of mind.

Years ago, I booked a weekly appointment with myself to analyze the numbers, sales ratios, and business activities in progress. I found the results of my performance as well as that of my staff improved dramatically. I'd wasted weeks and months as I agonized whether to include this activity into my schedule. My advice? Book an evaluation and planning session first and ask questions later.

Step 5: Building in flex time

Plug segments of time into your schedule every few hours to help you to minimize the fallout from unplanned interruptions or problems. About 15 or 30 minutes is enough time to work in at strategic intervals throughout your day. Knowing that you have this free block of time can help you adhere to your schedule rather than get off track.

As you begin to build your time-blocking skills, insert 30-minute flex periods into your schedule for every two hours of time-blocked activity. This may seem like a lot of flex time, but if it allows you to maintain the rest of your time-block schedule and maintain or increase your productivity, it's worth the investment. My experience is that the best time for flex time is after you've put in a couple of hours of your most important work — whether sales calls, report-preparation, or meeting a deadline.

Don't schedule flex time right before you go into an important activity time: You're more likely to get distracted and fail to get started with your critical business. Schedule it after the work — then you can use it, if necessary, to resolve any unforeseen problems.

Assessing Your Progress and Adjusting Your Plan as Needed

Becoming comfortable with time-blocking takes time, and achieving a glitch-free schedule that you can work with for a stretch may take a half-dozen revisions. Even then, routinely evaluate your time-blocking efforts and adjust them periodically to make sure you're getting the desired results. It's not a huge time investment — you can check yourself with a few minutes a day or use 15 to 30 minutes of your weekly time to review your results. Ask yourself the following:

✔ What took you off track this week?

✔ What interruptions really affected your success with your time?

✔ Is someone sabotaging your time-block?

✔ What shifts would help your efficiency?

In this section, I discuss this review in detail.

Surveying your results

One way to determine your effectiveness at time-blocking is to check results. In as little as two weeks from when you launch your time-blocking schedule, you can probably see where you need minor adjustments. The best way to keep tabs on results is to track them on an ongoing basis. I suggest both a weekly review that focuses on the past week and a periodic review of where you stand in relation to your overall goals.

The weekly review is a time for you to replay the video of the week, looking at the highs and lows. I guarantee you'll have days where you want to pull your hair out because you face so many problems and distractions. You'll also have days that are smooth as silk. What were the differences in those days besides the outcome?

As for the periodic review, review your job description, key responsibilities, and the ways in which your performance and success are measured. Then ask yourself these questions:

✔ Are you moving closer toward achieving your goals?

✔ Can you see measurable progress in reasonable time?

✔ Are you monitoring your performance well enough to see improvement?

✔ What changes do you need to adopt now to increase your speed toward reaching the goal and reduce the overall amount of time you invest?

Your success in meeting your objectives tells you whether the time-blocking is working for you.

Looking at measurable goals

If you can measure your goals in terms of numbers (dollars or sales, for example), then checking your results is a cinch. As a salesperson, for example, you may follow your sales numbers or commissions results over several months in order to get a good understanding of the effectiveness of your time-blocking efforts. Or say you're a magazine editor who's evaluated on consistently meeting weekly publication deadlines; if your goal is to publish three articles per month in national magazines, you can assume that your time-blocking efforts require some tweaking if your review reveals that you're getting only one story in print.

Evaluating qualitative goals

If your goals aren't easily measured in terms of dollars or sales, you may need to get creative in developing your own tally for results. Family and personal goals are difficult to measure, but you can likely gain a good sense of how your efforts are tracking by just paying attention to your daily life and how you feel about it, rating your day on a 1-to-10 scale. Are your kids comfortable in talking and spending time with you? Do they look forward to being with you? Are you on friendly terms with the people in your community activities? Do you and your spouse laugh together more often than you argue?

You can also turn to other measuring sticks, which are especially useful in the workplace:

✔ What went well this week? What could you have done better?

✔ Did you accomplish what you really needed to do? How many high-priority items did you carry over to the next day or week? (See the earlier section titled "Getting Down to Specifics: Daily Prioritization" for more on prioritizing.)

✔ How would you rate your week on a 1-to-10 scale, with 1 being utterly overwhelmed and dissatisfied, and 10 being completely in control of and happy with how you spend your time?

✔ How do you feel you performed at work? How does your supervisor feel you're performing?

✔ Did you meet your goals at home?

> ✔ Has what you've accomplished this week positioned you better to achieve your long-range goals?
>
> ✔ What are the key improvement areas for you next week?
>
> ✔ What adjustments to your long-range plans do you need to make?
>
> ✔ What's diverting you from your schedule?
>
> ✔ Were you unrealistic in your time estimates for tasks?
>
> ✔ What segment of the day or activity is tipping your schedule off track?

As you're reviewing your results, be careful to do so with an open, observant mind, not a judgmental one. Give yourself a couple of weeks before you resolve to change your schedule. Doing so helps you get through a long enough period of time to account for anomalies.

Tweaking your system

Looking back at your personal behaviors and skills and the interruptions you routinely face, identify two or three steps you need to take in order to increase your success. Here are a couple of tips to point you in the right direction:

> ✔ **If you're not completing the most important tasks or working toward the most important efforts each day:** Weed out some of the trivial tasks to make room for the most important ones. (I help you do that in the "Getting Down to Specifics: Daily Prioritization" section, earlier in this chapter.)
>
> ✔ **If your most productive times of day are filled with trivial tasks:** Shift the tasks and the time slots you fit them in. (Your trouble is time-blocking, which I help you with in the earlier "Blocking Off Your Time and Scheduling and Plugging In Your To-Do Items" section.)

After you figure out what you need to change, you can adjust your schedule accordingly. Unfortunately, I can't give you a one-size-fits-all set of answers to help you figure out what to change — those decisions depend on your job requirements, your personal strengths and weaknesses, your personal goals and desires, and the amount of control you actually have over those aspects you'd like to improve. I can, however, help steer you in the right direction.

Remember the old adage "Grant me the serenity to accept the things I cannot change, courage to change the things I can, and the wisdom to know the difference"? You can apply it to the way you manage your time. If you can balance the results you expect to achieve (more productivity, greater efficiency, reduction in time worked, and greater sales) with the results you need to achieve, then you'll be successful.

Following are some examples of quick evaluation questions that can help you make the most effective, results-oriented changes to your schedule:

- ✔ **What's the standard?** Do you have a sales quota that needs to be met? Are you getting your boss's priorities done? Going home, how are you feeling about your progress?

- ✔ **How accurate does the time-block schedule need to be?** In time-blocking, a little goes a long way. The real question is how well you did this week with the most important activities — the vital 20 percent of the 80/20 rule.

- ✔ **How much have you improved?** How have you improved since you started working your time-block? How large is the improvement? Would you be happy if you improved each week for a year at this level?

- ✔ **With additional revision, how much additional productivity would you gain?** Before revising a time-block schedule, look at the anticipated return on investment. Is this change going to bring significant benefit in productivity, efficiency, or personal satisfaction?

- ✔ **How good is good enough?** Where is the point where you'll achieve diminishing returns on your effort? At some point, further refining your schedule can lead to reduced results. Where do you think that'll happen?

Perfectionism is a scourge of people who are trying to achieve more with their time. The obsession with revising, redoing, and readjusting one's time-block schedule every few days — or even hours — leads to frustration. In your time-blocking, clearly define the line of success so you can achieve your goals without going overboard.

Chapter 6

Efficiently Working from a Home Office

Because of our technology and mobile society, home offices are more of the norm than ever. That trend has accelerated with more contract, consulting, and part-time work available today. According to Global Workplace Analytics, more than 6 million people use a home office at least part of their work week; I include myself in that group. For certain hours, either early in the morning or when the kids are not home, my home office is the most productive place for me to write, plan business strategies, and use my creativity to problem-solve complex issues.

The home office can lend itself to high productivity, or it can become a wasteland of inefficiency. The difference lies in the environment, design, equipment, interaction strategy, and implementation.

Knowing Yourself and Your Environment

When you know yourself, you can create a productive environment in which to work. What types of surroundings bring you joy and energy? What type of setting would entice you to spend time there? What do you need around you to help you stay focused?

Your environment influences your success. If you create a home office space in your dark, damp basement that has no windows and your office at work is light, bright, comfortable, with a view of the park from the window, your home office will be ineffective because your desire to work there will rarely be high. You will likely find other things to do around the house than go into the dungeon of your home office.

I have been fortunate a few times to design home offices before we built the house. My preference is a large space with amenities that create a rich environment — rich wood floor and high ceilings, book cases, and a fireplace for those cold early mornings create an environment I want to come to and be productive in. You might not ever build from the ground up or have a large budget for your home office, but there are easy ways to create the environment you want.

If you can't create a closed-off, separated area from the rest of the room, paint your office area or one wall a different color from the rest of the room. By doing this, you create at least a different visual. If you have the space to utilize a bedroom, select one that is out of the main traffic pattern in your home. Use color, textures, and pictures to create an inviting environment.

Always have a few mementoes or tchotchkes that help you when you are stuck. Think of the movie *Jerry Maguire* when Jerry had to have his baseball bat to think creatively. I have a hickory-shaft golf club that I grab and swing when I'm working out thoughts and problems. This is your environment, so design it for you. Go online to www.houzz.com and see pictures and images of what can be done with home office spaces. You might invest an hour or two with an interior designer to help you get it right. I spend at least 10 hours each week in my home office. Even if it's just a day or a week working in your home office, that is 20 percent of your work time.

Working from a home office has its advantages. On some days, I get to sleep a little later, have a leisurely morning, walk the dog, work a little, and then grab lunch. Most days, however, are not like this. A day like that every once in a blue moon won't kill productivity, but more than a couple of laid-back days a week will show up in a lack of earnings and advancement opportunities.

Is working from home for you?

Working from home isn't for everyone. Some need the accountability of others to show up ready and on time at 8:00 a.m. In a home office setting, you need to be disciplined and accountable to yourself.

Let's take a little quiz to see if the home office is a good match for you.

- ✔ Are you well organized?
- ✔ Do you work well alone?

✔ Are you self-motivated and directed to start each task?

✔ You are skilled and disciplined at working through your to-do lists in spite of other distractions?

✔ Is seeing people face to face a few times a week enough social interaction for you, instead of seeing people every day?

✔ Can you create an environment in your dwelling that's uplifting and free of distraction?

✔ You love your work, but do you know when to pull the plug and be with family?

✔ Are you confident you can control home distractions (walking the dog, taking personal phone calls and texts, preparing dinner, answering the "I'm hungry" refrigerator call, doing small home repairs)?

✔ Does your family understand the meaning of the Do Not Disturb sign on your door?

✔ Is working in a home office something you are determined to accomplish in spite of the problems that might arise?

If you answered "yes" to seven or more of these questions, then having a home office is a good option for you. If you answered "yes" to five to six, a home office could work out well for you; however, you have more work to do. If you answered "yes" to four or fewer questions, the risk of failure in a home office environment is very high.

Weighing the pros and cons of a home office

There are pros and cons to any decision in life. Deciding if a home office is right for you could have a huge impact on your life and will affect your income, wealth, company advancement, family life, and peace of mind. There aren't many decisions this big in life. The problem is that most people don't realize the magnitude. Most people pine for the home office to increase flexibility, efficiency, and time savings to create a level of freedom for them. Some of the advantages include:

✔ **Setting your own hours:** This freedom allows you to align your work around family as well as your natural rhythm of your work. For example, some people work better in the evening than first thing in the morning. That's when their mental motor is firing on all cylinders. A home office gives you flexibility to work well after you put the kids to bed. You can create a work schedule that works for and with you.

✔ **Controlling costs:** For the most part, the largest cost for a small business is the rented office space and the accompanying utilities. Most building owners require years of commitment in the form of a long-term lease as well as personal financial guarantees that the monthly rent will be paid. If you work from home, you avoid all those costs.

If you run a small business in today's technology world, your customer in most business niches would never know that your office is in your home. If you have a website, social media presence, customer and prospect email lists and a phone, you have a business in today's world. On the Internet, a small company can look like a large company that has been around for 100 years.

✔ **Commuting time:** The amount of time you spend in your car getting to and from work is enormous. According to the U.S. Census Bureau, the average commute time in the United States is more than 5 minutes one way. This creates stress and tension before you even walk through the door. A home office that enables you to work from home even for a few hours and miss rush hour traffic can be a significant time- and gas-saving option.

✔ **Attending more family events:** A home office doesn't guarantee your attendance at all the soccer or t-ball games. It does allow, however, for the flexibility to step away for a few hours to attend them and then go back to work.

✔ **Hitting deadlines on projects:** Let's face it, in business there are just times where you need to go above and beyond for your bosses and clients. There are times, like when you're writing a book and your editor is breathing down your neck to submit chapters, that a designated home office can make the difference between getting it done on time . . . or not.

There are certainly positives to the home office environment, but there are also the negative traps that you need to watch out for as well. You may want to wear rose colored glasses when it comes to a home office, but there are drawbacks, such as:

✔ **Lack of formal structure and support:** If you need the structure and accountability of a work environment, a home office could be a challenge for you. Some need the structure of getting up, showering, and putting on work clothes to feel like they are at work. You also can lose your office assistant, phone coverage, ease of delegation, and other services you are provided in a typical office environment.

✔ **The feeling of isolation:** Because you are not around the office environment, you might miss the comradery and interaction with others. People who work mostly from a home office can feel isolated from their co-workers more easily. Unless you are a high-introvert person, you need to design a system to engage in interaction with your team at work. Many home office workers have animals so they aren't completely alone all day long.

✔ **A home office environment requires greater self-discipline:** A person who lacks self-management and self-discipline usually fails in a home office setting. They frequently don't demand of themselves what a boss who is watchful in an office setting might require. The skill of time management and self-discipline are vital tools for a home office worker's tool kit.

✔ **The challenge of separation from work life from home life:** There are clear lines of distinction when you have to physically prepare, commute to, and arrive at your company office. The work and home line is drawn boldly. If you are the type to slip away from family time to get that last project done, the balancing act between home and work might be too difficult.

There are other drawbacks from potential changes in child care and the resulting cost, privacy, being taken seriously as a professional, and even isolation, which I deal with in great depth later in the chapter.

Defining your space needs

How much and what type of space do you need? The square feet question is important, but generally the size of the office won't make you more or less productive. When choosing a location for your home office, you want a place that affects your productivity and ability to manage your time in a positive way. When the space is less than ideal, or when you struggle to focus on work even when you've got a great location, consider trying these tips to nurture your productivity:

✔ **Choose an out-of-the-way locale.** Look for an area that's yours alone, removed from general traffic and noise, where you can shut the door and hang a Do Not Disturb sign on the knob. The more out of the way your office, the better use you'll make of your time.

Setting up your home office in Hub Central — the family center of your home — without physical boundaries is unwise. Today's typical den off the entry doesn't provide enough physical distance between you, your work, and your family. It's right in the middle of the home, so noise from both ends of the house reaches you clearly. Your family walks by numerous times, and in newer homes, the office doors are often glass, providing no visual barrier whatsoever.

I once had an office that was nearly ideal. It was above our detached garage, which created a short commute of 47 steps from our side door up the steps and into the office. Believe it or not, those scant 47 steps substantially decreased the number of interruptions.

✔ **Employ other physical barriers if your office location isn't ideal.** If your home office isn't off in a private area of the house and your doors are glass, your best defense is a shade or visual barrier. When children see you "not working" (for mine it's when I'm thinking), they may figure it is playtime. The other necessary item is a lock on the door, which announces that you're busy and don't want to be interrupted.

Selecting the Right Equipment

My father always said, "You need the right tools for the job." The right tools and equipment in the home office environment are paramount because you can't requisition more supplies from the supply room like you can at the office. Being well prepared and well stocked can save you a lot of wasted time.

If you're a lover of new gadgets it's really easy to justify buying them just because you have a home office. A regular trip to IKEA or Office Depot can turn into a constant spending spree because you can "write it off" as office equipment.

More than a desk and chair

Your most-used tools are your desk and chair. Do you need a desk, or would more of a work table be more suited to your tasks? If you need a work area larger than a desk will accommodate, a work table might prove to be a better bet. Will your desk have your computer on it, or will there be a separate computer area? Do you use a single monitor, or are dual or more monitors required? Do you need a keyboard shelf that slides out of the way?

The aesthetics of an antique desk or a designer desk are wonderful for a home office. Most people find that they fall far short in functionality and practicality. These types of desk were not designed with today's technology in mind. Don't make the mistake of choosing form over function.

The office chair is a heavily used piece of furniture. You likely spend hours a day in it. Most chair manufacturers focus on the ergonomics for comfort and productivity. Select a chair that has good back support and enables you to adjust the height. If you can find a chair you like that tilts and has arm rest adjustments, it can reduce back strain and carpal tunnel syndrome as well. Select a chair that has a covering or that has breathable fabric or leather that will transfer heat away from your body.

I recently purchased a Varidesk. This system sits right on top of a portion of my desk. It allows me to work in a standing position while at my desk for a part of the day. This gives me a variety and helps with being seated for too much of the day. Check it out at `www.varidesk.com`.

Desktops, laptops, scanners, and other tools

The computer is most home-office users' primary tool. Whether you need a desktop or laptop depends on your movement beyond your home office. Don't go budget on a computer. You want a recent model with the highest speed, and most room for storage and memory. Most laptops and desktops come with webcams, and they do vary in quality. Because you are remote from your office you might use Skype, GoToMeeting, WebEx, or JoinMe to engage visually with your work team or sales prospects.

When in doubt between a laptop and desktop, select a laptop. You can always buy a docking station, multiple monitors, and use a standard size wireless keyboard and mouse. There are tools you can buy to make the laptop feel and function like a desktop, but not the other way around.

Check on your Internet connection speed. The typical base plan of Internet speed through your cable or DSL provider may not be fast enough. Certainly a high-quality wireless router is a must to create profitability in having a working lunch in your kitchen or outside on that beautiful summer day.

I have found more fluctuations in speed in DSL services than high-speed cable services. If you use a web conferencing service, conduct or attend web-based meetings or webinars, or make web-based presentations, these small fluctuations in DSL can cause havoc for you and others.

Most people run their home office with inadequate telephone equipment. You need a high-quality phone that is connected to a headset. Your productivity and ease of use is stunted by using your home line for business, your cell phone, or a handheld phone. A high-quality headset that is wireless allow you to move about your house while still in communication. With hands-free you can take notes, do tasks, and move while talking. You can also check on dinner progress without interrupting the conversation with your boss.

Selecting the right printer, scanner, and copier creates more efficient work flow. If you buy an all-in-one unit (that is, printer/scanner/copier/fax), be sure the quality and reliability of each part is top quality. Check the initial cost of the machine, the number of copies it produces in what length of time (nothing more frustrating than standing around, waiting for your printer to spit out a dozen or more copies), and the ease of finding and cost of replacing ink cartridges. There are vast differences in prices for makes and models. Many manufacturers sell a cheaper all-in-one knowing they will make up the cash on the cartridges you buy from them.

Managing the lighting and noise

The lighting for your office can add warmth, comfort, and creativity to your office. The windows in your office need to balance the natural light and sunlight for your office. They can also bring in glare, so be sure to have adjustable shades that enable you to regulate the natural light throughout the day.

The best home office environments have natural light, ambient light, and specific task lighting. The ambient light fills the whole room with consistent, balanced lighting. The task lighting illuminates the area or project you are specially working on now.

Noise can be a problem in a home office. Generally speaking, most homes aren't built to be soundproof. From the garbage disposal in the kitchen to the neighbor kids playing basketball in the driveway next door, noise can be a great distraction. But you have noise-cancelling options.

- ✔ **Use white noise to block out other household noises.** You can establish auditory boundaries by blocking household noises with white noise. White noise is a constant low-level background sound, such as static or a whirring fan, which quickly becomes inaudible but drowns out other, more disruptive noises.

- ✔ **Drown out distracting noise with music.** The best background music for me is Baroque piano. It's simple because it's only one instrument; also, studies have shown that Baroque music stimulates the creative side of the brain. I advise against the radio because of the constantly changing style and tempo of songs, the newscasts, and disk-jockey monologues (though some people claim to work better with this sort of background noise). I also suggest instrumental music rather than songs with lyrics — words can be distracting. I listen to orchestra and symphonic music, such as classical or easy listening.

Getting the Work Done from Home

I can't emphasize enough how crafting and adhering to a set of rules for you as well as your entire family and friends increases your chance of success when you're working at home. By drawing lines between your work time and your personal time, you allow yourself to be fully present with each — and presence is a key component of productivity. To establish a solid set of boundaries for yourself, follow these suggestions:

- ✔ **Treat a day at the home as you would a day in your office.** Start your day the same time you'd begin your commute to home-away-from-home and end it at the same you'd end your workday. Take only a half-hour lunch (but be sure to take the entire half-hour for lunch because you need that break). Regular start and stop times and set lunch breaks allow everyone to recognize your schedule and abide by it.

- ✔ **Start early.** If you work at home, you may find, as most office workers have, that you're most productive before others arrive. In the home office world, that's before your household wakes up for the day.

- ✔ **Dress for success.** Because you don't have to shower, shave, and don office clothes, you lose the empowering feeling you get that makes work seem like work. If you need formal dress to perform better and are negatively affected by staying in sweats or pajamas most of the day, by all means, get up, shower, and get dressed, just as you would if you were heading to the office. If you *feel* successful, you'll be successful, regardless of where you work.

- ✔ **Set goals for yourself.** Set goals in terms of work completed and reward yourself for achieving them, just as you would at the office.

- ✔ **Don't answer personal calls during your workday.** Using a home office to increase your productivity is an act of discipline. Others sometimes adopt the attitude that you're not really working; people who wouldn't imagine interrupting you at the office call to chew the fat, simply because you're home. Parents are often guilty of this. Be polite but firm: "Mom, I'm sorry. I'd love to talk, but I'm working right now. I'll call you back at five, as soon as I'm finished, okay?"

Fighting the home interruptions

You work from home, so undoubtedly you can take time for family whenever you want. Right? Well, not so much. Working from a home office doesn't include answering questions about the lawn, deciding what you want for dinner, and watching cartoons when the kids get home from school.

- ✔ **Control interruptions from your family members.** Patiently train your family on your work schedule and etiquette. You may want to establish set times when you allow for interruptions.

- ✔ **Even if it's difficult, set and enforce boundaries.** Setting these boundaries can be challenging, especially with the preschool set. When we were blessed with children, I decided that my work time would be "interruptible" when it came to our kids, and I stand by that philosophy. (I have to say, however, that both Annabelle and Wesley have uncanny abilities for selecting the worst possible times to interrupt!) Here's the one exception I make to the come-on-in rule: Absolutely *no* interruptions when I'm on the phone. You, too, may want to set some inviolable rules. Make them few, but enforce them rigorously.

Working at home with kids

Trying to accomplish work tasks and projects in a home office setting can be more than difficult when the kids are around. If you're home, many children feel like your time is theirs. They aren't used to being told "no" from mom or dad, but they now need to understand that the office area is off limits.

- ✔ **Bartering can empower both you and your family.** For example, while trying to finish a chapter a few days ago, I offered Wesley a trade: No more interruptions for the rest of the morning in return for an hour of fishing together. He let me complete the chapter (which took me at least an hour less to finish than it would've otherwise). Then I quit a little early, and we had our fishing contest in the golf course pond in our backyard. I lost one to four, but in spite of that, I managed to get my work done — and have a winning afternoon with my son!

- ✔ **End on time.** Being available to work extended hours can diminish the quality and quantity of family time. Set boundaries. When the office door closes, let voice mail pick up work calls. Leave the office behind.

- ✔ **Allow yourself uninterrupted time each day to decompress.** A commute allows you time to shift gears. On your way home, you move from CEO, salesperson, manager, assistant, or customer service representative to daddy, mommy, husband, wife, partner, or Fido's master. When you exit the door of your home office, the shift is over, and you're on! So when you're done for the day, take ten minutes to decompress before you walk out the door. You may even play some relaxing music so you can leave the troubles of the day behind.

Feeling isolated from the business world

If you work regularly from your home office, the biggest adjustment is the personal contact and interaction that is no longer there. The regular banter, coffee talk, and social outlet is reduced dramatically. For social people this change can be a tough adjustment. The feelings of being alone can overtake you.

ANECDOTE

Some people thrive in the more solitary environment. I find that I can work more single-mindedly on tasks from my home office.

✔ **To overcome isolation feelings, schedule regular meetings and interactions with your colleagues.** Use video conferencing, Skype, GoToMeeting, or WebEx so you have professional interaction via voice and video. Create a social media engagement time each day before your lunch hour. Grab a quick 15 minutes so you can catch up with others, and post personal reflections and observations to feel connected with others.

✔ **Create a weekly lunch outside your office.** Get out and eat with friends or co-workers to stop the walls of your home office from closing in on you. Track some of the time you are saving by not driving to and from work each day for a longer lunch hour one day a week. You're worth the flexible investment.

Chapter 7

Setting Up and Maintaining a Productive Workspace

I wish you could've heard my staff and my wife when I started writing this chapter. They howled. Okay, I admit it: What I share here is easier to write about than to *do*. Nonetheless, even if you're not 100 percent successful with every one of the techniques, tools, and strategies in this chapter (I'm speaking from experience here, folks), adopting even some of them can increase your productivity and vastly improve your overall time management.

One study I saw indicated that most people waste an hour per day trying to find papers lost on their desks (at least, that's where they think the papers are lost) or files and documents misplaced in their computers. That's not so bad, you say. But an hour per day adds up to 260 work hours per year, or more than 32 wasted days per worker annually.

Multiply that by the number of executives, professionals, and sales and administrative employees in this country, and you're talking a significant loss of time. (And that doesn't include hours spent at home trying to find misplaced eyeglasses, scissors, library books, keys, needle-nose pliers, cell phones, gym shorts, earrings, pacifiers, and so on.) Think how productive you'd be if you spent all that time, well, being productive!

If your work area is a parking lot for everything from C-level "someday" tasks to hotter-than-hot, this-project-can-make-my-career assignments, you're the Titanic heading for an iceberg. Ask yourself the following:

✔ Do you know all the tasks you have to get done, complete with time lines?

✔ Do you have all the materials, documents, and tools you need right now to take each project to completion without putting out an all-points bulletin?

✔ In short, do you have everything you need to do an exceptional job in record time?

If you can answer all these questions with truthful and unequivocal yeses, you can skip this chapter. Everyone else, read on.

Streamlining Your Workspace

"Don't touch my desk! I know exactly where everything is." I've heard that line endlessly, and I've used it myself. If you're like me, however, most of the time, as you stare at the forest of papers on your desk, or the backed-up traffic of emails in your inbox, you *are* clueless. You may have known where that phone number was yesterday, a few weeks ago, a month ago — or even a few minutes ago — but more stacks have since been added to the mix.

It's not enough to know which chart, report, snippet of paper, or electronic file is on your desk or in your computer, whether it's on the left or right side of your desk, stashed in the catch-all drawer of your filing cabinet, in your email box, filed under a client record, or in a parked file. This is your career you're talking about. Get a handle on it!

Make way! Clearing off your desk

Repeat after me: My desk is not a parking lot. My email inbox is not a parking lot. My desk is not a parking lot. If you want to get your desk under control, remember: Less is more. The more pictures, notes, boxes, tools (staplers, paper-clip holders, books), and so on that occupy your desk, the greater your odds of being distracted and the more cluttered your desk feels.

You also have less room to spread out if you're consulting multiple sources of information, using a laptop or tablet in addition to your desktop computer, or studying oversized charts or graphs. What's more, a topsy-turvy desk translates into greater stress and the misleading feeling that you have all the time in the world to complete your projects.

Remove everything that isn't absolutely necessary from your desk. Be brutal. Here are some ideas to get you started:

- ✔ Move family photos to your credenza or bookcase, where you can still see them throughout the day (and remember why you're working so hard) without their distracting you.

- ✔ If you have other pictures — perhaps of you with mentors or celebrities — hang them on the wall.

- ✔ Store extra tools, supplies, and items you use weekly in desk drawers and filing areas.

- ✔ Don't allow items you rarely use or haven't looked at since slipping them into a pile to take up desk space. Put those items away in a filing cabinet, storage box, closet, or other less-accessible area.

As for your workspace, forget the Boy Scout be-prepared motto. It's a recipe for desktop disaster, especially if you're one who likes to prepare for flood, earthquake, alien invasion, and every other conceivable catastrophe. The cleaner and clearer your desk, the better you can use your time.

Assembling essential organizational tools

Having the right tools for the job is really the start of great organization. If you haven't already done so, get all piles off your desk, even if you have to put them temporarily on the floor. Then gather these tools:

- ✔ **A desk organizer:** You need some way to keep the standard office fare — staplers, paper clips, pens, calculators — handy at your fingertips.

- ✔ **Inboxes and outboxes:** You need some type of organizational flow to your work that's based on an in-and-out system. Too often, interruptions happen when someone drops off something you don't need right now or stops by to pick something up. Setting up inboxes and outboxes outside the door of your office or cubicle keeps your desk clear and reduces chitchat.

- ✔ **Organized filing system for electronic files:** Our world is more green and efficient with so many offices going paperless. To do that, create your electronic filing system before the flood of emails and electronic documents overloads you. Here are a few hints for filing electronically. Create files based on the types of people and business you work with. For example, one folder could be titled Clients; another Customers; and another Prospects. You likely also have people who serve your business — their folder could be titled Vendors. You could also create a folder for each person with whom you interact, either as main folders or as subfolders. A good customer relations management (CRM) solution goes a long way in controlling the file and document overload in the electronic world.

If you are still attached to paper, then here are a few tips for organizing it all.

✔ **A quality filing cabinet with space for growth:** You may be surprised at how much filing space you need if you're a piler-turned-filer. I prefer lateral filing cabinets: They're more costly but can save a lot of time because you can see all the files at once. (Ah! There's that yellow folder for my volunteer project — and the blue one for my customer service committee.) If you prefer, use stacking, modular filing systems, such as those in many doctors' and dentists' offices.

✔ **Colored file folders:** Ban bland manila! I suggest using the rainbow of colored folders available today. Consider a color-coded filing system, such as a stoplight approach with green for new business and other money-generating items, red for problem issues or customers, and so on. I also find that colors jog my memory when it comes time to find the files.

✔ **File folder labels:** Labeling files is paramount to organization, efficiency, and time savings, even if you use colored folders. Labels can also be color-coded to further differentiate one file from another.

For more tools and tips you can use to organize your desk, check out *Organizing For Dummies,* by Eileen Roth and Elizabeth Miles (Wiley).

Setting up a timely filing system

Whether you are paperless or paper driven, you must have a workable filing system. Before you start going through your documents, think about how you're most likely to search for the documents you need. You can choose from numerous file-labeling strategies, but here are some possible categories:

✔ Customers (alphabetically)

✔ Past clients you no longer serve

✔ Due dates and project timing

✔ Pending projects

✔ On-hold projects

✔ To-dos, miscellaneous, or a similar catch-all type of label

You can choose to file by subject, client name, importance, or a number of other ways, but if time is of the essence, setting up a tickler filing system may be ideal. *Tickler* or *reminder files* have been around for ages. They make sure you remember to deal with delayed or deferred items at the correct times. Here's how they work:

1. **Establish two complementary tickler files, one labeled *monthly* and the other labeled *daily*.**

   Your monthly tickler can be as simple as a 12-slot expandable folder with the months written on each slot. Your daily tickler can be a 31-slot accordion file folder or even 31 hanging file folders, each labeled with dates 1 through 31. They are certainly old school, but they still work today. For a more modern approach, you could set those same parameters in your computer or tablet file system. Even using an app like Evernote can increase your ability to organize.

2. **As you receive new documents, place them in the appropriate spot in your monthly file.**

   If a document you receive in December requires no action until March, place the document in the March spot of your filing system.

3. **When you enter a new month, move documents from that month's slot into the daily positions.**

   When March rolls around, pull all the documents from your March tickler and place them in the appropriate days of the month in your daily tickler system.

Note: For many businesspeople, powerful software programs called *customer relation management* (CRMs) have replaced tickler files. Turn to Chapter 8 to find out more on CRM software and organizing computer files.

If your filing skills are truly abysmal, have someone who's a natural filer help you develop your filing system. I'm far more effective when I hand papers, reports, and memos off to an assistant. Whether a document is paper or electronic, I find I can also retrieve information more efficiently when someone else has filed it (because that person can help me find it!). Of course, only you can file some items (confidential personnel reports, salaries, information you want to keep personal, and the like). But as for the rest, use your team's strengths and gifts so you can make better use of yours.

Going paperless

One way to clear your desk is to reduce the amount of paper you handle altogether by increasing your use of electronic files. In today's technology world, you can scan most documents and create a digital version; many computers then allow you to apply optical character recognition (OCR), which changes the scanned image into text that you can edit and search through. You can also have your faxed documents turned into digital documents that can be shared by all in your department and emailed to others.

Electronic versions are especially useful when you need to retrieve files. You can organize the digital or electronic files in multiple places at one time. For instance, you can keep a prospect's information in a *prospect file* as well as in a file under the prospect's name — it's like being two places at the same time. You can also search for files or have your computer do the search while you're working on something else — the only true multitasking one can do!

Tackling piles systematically

To de-clutter yourself, you need to remember this simple rule: Put the important things where you can remember where they are and where you can get to them quickly. Here's how the de-cluttering process breaks down:

1. **Figure out what you can get rid of.**

   Here are a few simple questions to ask yourself:

   - Do you really need this? *Really?*

   - Is there value in saving this item? (If the answer isn't a definitive yes, toss it.)

   - What happens if you don't keep this?

   - What's the worst that could happen if you throw this away?

   Never throw away important documents, such as tax returns and business receipts. The IRS requires you to retain tax records and all supporting material for seven years. Before you toss, think carefully about whether an item has future value and whether copies are filed elsewhere so you can access them if you need to.

2. **Condense the offending material into smaller piles by selecting items to go into a single master important pile.**

   Many piles are simply files in disguise: documents that haven't been put away where they belong. By collecting the most important items into a single pile, you get an idea of how much time you need to dissolve this pile into nothing.

At first, you may not be able to do much more than create your master important pile. After all, you still have meetings to attend, emails to respond to, and work to finish. However, the master file ensures that you tackle the important stuff first; the smaller, less-important items have to wait.

3. **Schedule an appointment with yourself in the next 48 hours to rid yourself of your master important pile.**

   You don't need to be in tip-top mental form to file. I suggest setting your filing appointment toward the end of the week, preferably in late afternoon when your energy level is low. Friday afternoons are a good time to file with comparatively few interruptions. (If you're struggling with interruptions, turn to Chapter 15 for help.) Don't worry about your other piles yet. Using the filing system you chose (see the preceding section), focus on the most important pile until it disappears.

4. **After making your master important file disappear, go back to your remaining clutter and repeat the process.**

   Start a *second* most-important master file and move all most-important items into that pile; then file them. Then make a third most-important master file. By now, you can probably see the surface of your desk, and you may even have a substantial area cleared.

Keeping Clutter from Coming Back

Not so long ago, a handshake or verbal agreement sealed the deal. No more. Today, you need paper or electronic document as a backup to confirm an agreement, assure mutual understanding, and even organize tasks. Documents have taken over people's lives.

Whether you're at home or at the office, maximizing your time means that all those documents have to quickly find their way to the proper place, even if that place is the computer, trash bin, recycle bin, or shredder. The key to controlling paper and electronic documents before they control you is to decide quickly where to put it all.

The best strategy for maintaining a clutter-free workspace is to avoid creating piles in the first place. You need to be more strategic in your work time to circumvent pile explosion. This section gives you two quick starts to circumvent the explosive growth of piles on your desk (or credenza, bookshelves, filing cabinets, extra chairs, window ledges, floor, or any other flat surface).

Letting the mess get away from me

When I was a kid, my bedroom was a mess. My parents asked me to clean it, and I did; but like Pigpen in the *Peanuts* comic strip, I seemed to carry my mess with me everywhere I went, and my bedroom started re-accumulating clutter the minute I entered. Mere hours after I'd tidied it, it was a disaster again. In fact, my bedroom once led my father to believe we'd been burglarized: Seeing my room in complete disarray, he ran to his and my mother's bedroom to see what the thieves had taken! I've since left most clutter behind, but like mushrooms after rain, it creeps back when I'm not paying attention. I now lead a (mostly) well-organized, efficient life, and so can you.

Handling documents and papers once

Those who master documents and paper have mastered single-handling. These people touch or read a document, email, or paper one time and then take action. They don't pile, table, ponder, check, reconsider, refile, or delay. They get rid of the document the first time they handle it or see it.

If you want to become a single handler, follow the five Ds: dump, delegate, detour, do it, or depot. Otherwise, you confront a less-productive list of Ds: dawdle, daydream, deliberate, and deceive — all of which lead to your demise.

Dump it

The dump-it principle is simple: Do you need it? If you don't, dump it or dispose of it. Say no to any of the following questions, and you can feel comfortable hitting the Delete button or sending it to the shredder or recycling bin:

- ✔ Do you really need to act on this or keep it?
- ✔ Is this new, relevant information you need now or in the future?
- ✔ Does this information benefit a colleague or client?
- ✔ Are there consequences for not keeping it?
- ✔ Will this increase revenue or customer service?

Sort your mail over the recycling bin or waste basket. Everything that swirls into the bin or basket is no longer your problem.

Delegate it

Do you have an inner pack rat that wants to hold onto everything, including every paper that crosses your desk? One way to shut down this impulse is to delegate papers to someone else. Even if you *know* you could complete the task with two hands tied behind your back, that doesn't mean it's the best use of your time. Delegate and give yourself more time to work on high-value tasks while building the skills and confidence of people you delegate to.

Detour it

Handling every email, electronic document, or even sheet of paper once is a fantastic goal, but sometimes it's impossible. Maybe you need more information before you can delegate or dispose of the item, or perhaps the document raises significant questions that need to be answered before you act. If you can detour and park the email, electronic document, or paper for later follow-up, you've saved time deliberating *now*.

Don't park anything permanently! Create a detour file for delayed documents and papers, but be sure you get the information you need and deal with the issue. Don't let your temporary file grow into a pile hidden in a file.

Do it

Do it is the easiest and most straightforward of all the Ds. Take action, either to get the task done quickly or because there's a high level of urgency associated with it:

- **Tend to urgent matters.** If the task moves to the top of your priorities list after you read the paper, the best course of action is to do it now. Change your priorities and work until the new priority is completed, even if it takes you the rest of the day.

- **Get the task done quickly.** Follow the five-minute rule: If the necessary task, phone call, response, or clarification is something only you can do, and it'll take fewer than five minutes, do it yourself right now. By the time you detour it, pick it up again later, reread it, and refocus, you'll have invested far more time than the five minutes required now.

Depot it

A *depot* is a place where something is deposited or stored. You can find essential tools for filing earlier in this chapter in "Streamlining Your Workspace," so you can establish an effective depot for papers you need to keep (and *only* the papers you need to keep).

Filing regularly

Because the task of filing is mundane, it's all too easy to allow other tasks, people, and priorities to creep into the time you set aside to deal with your piles and files, and in a few short weeks, the weeds can take over your garden again. Don't let that happen! Daily filing may not be necessary, but waiting a month or six weeks is too long. Make your time spent filing a priority. At the end of filing, your desk is devoid of piles, and you can begin filing once a week — for a much shorter time — and still keep on top of it. Keep up with your filing, and you won't find it so tedious. I realize that moving an electronic file by clicking your mouse is not heavy lifting. The hard part is making the decision to take action and deciding where to put it.

Schedule a weekly filing appointment with yourself and put it on your calendar. As you look ahead to assess your week and see your filing appointment, you begin mentally preparing for it. When you're prepared, you're more likely to keep your appointment with yourself, and when the time arrives, you'll be more efficient. You may find yourself throwing away more marginal items throughout the week and completing the task in less time.

When you're facing a few hours of filing, set a goal or benchmark. If you can't complete the whole project, break it down into a portion you can complete and commit to finishing that part without fail. (For more information on completing projects by chunking, see Chapter 16. Look for my Swiss-cheese or salami-slice methods.)

Taking notes that you can track

In business, most people overlook the simple skill of note-taking as a time-saving tool. Note-taking can be done both electronically, like on Evernote, or by the more traditional pen-to-paper format. I have to admit, my mind has been programmed over the years to connect with pen to paper. It allows the three-way connection between the brain, hand, and eyes to be more efficient. Most people think anyone with a pen and paper or note-taking program like Evernote can take notes: After all, everyone learned how in junior high, right? And if you're like most people, you probably take notes on whatever's handy: sticky notes, slips of paper, cocktail napkins, envelopes, or even important documents. Wrong approach! You can face significant time-loss and embarrassment when you later find out you lost the slip of paper where you took notes. This is certainly one advantage to Evernote.

Whether you're using specially designed and cut pads printed with "from the desk of," a full 8½-x-11-inch pad that's a color other than the standard white or yellow, or a smaller white or yellow notepad, you need to use something that stands out.

If you know you'll need to file the notes, make sure you are able to scan a handwritten note for electronic storage, can easily find the note in your electronic note system, or go with large paper so you can find it later. When you finish writing, add action items to your priority list for the following day and then drop the notes into the appropriate file for record-keeping. If your action items make it to the A level during the next day's priority sort, all you have to do is pull out the file folder and find your notes there as you left them, safe and sound.

Although sticky notes are great for attaching quick reminders to your computer screen so you don't forget to buy ice cream and pickles for your pregnant wife, they're one of the worst places to jot down information. Here's why:

- **They're too small for extensive notes.** You run out of room and have to transfer information to a larger note pad or, worse, to a second (and possibly third) sticky note. Then you have a sticky note stuck to a sticky note stuck to a sticky note, and if you lose one, you lose them all.

- **Sticky notes tend to sprout legs, sticking where you don't want them to: to the wrong document headed to the wrong file.** Then you're on a frantic mission to find your all-important sticky notes (and when they've hitched a ride on an unknown document going who-knows-where, your chances of finding them are slim to none).

- **Aged sticky notes lose their stick over time.** More than once, I've lost important information because my sticky note came unstuck and fluttered into oblivion.

If you're not sharing a document with others, consider taking notes directly on the document rather than on a sticky note. You can take notes in the margins around the key issues in the document or use the white space at the beginning or end for summaries or more-general points.

Limiting the Paper You Receive

Many people receive more material via snail mail and email in one day than they can read in year. No one wants to miss news or seem out of it, but few people have time to read, let alone organize, the printed gridlock paralyzing their inboxes and mailboxes.

The question isn't how to handle the information, because you can't. All you can do is decide what's important and try to limit what you receive. You may have an information-overload problem if you

✔ Have stacks of periodicals around that you intend to read but never do.

✔ Download e-books or electronic whitepapers that you hope to read or have backed-up e-newsletters in your tablet.

✔ Buy books that sound good, only to get home and find that they're already on your shelf or in your tablet.

✔ Get frustrated because you haven't read your weekly news magazine in six months.

Here's how to cut down on the document overload:

✔ **Cancel subscriptions that you don't read regularly.** Don't immediately renew subscriptions to magazines you read infrequently, whether that's online or print. Take a break for a couple of months and see whether you really need them or miss receiving them. I can assure you that the publishers are eager to have you back and may make you a sweeter deal than if you were a regular renewal.

✔ **Move to Internet-based subscriptions.** Most quality publications now offer Internet-based subscriptions. They save time because you can search issues by topic and you can read only the articles that interest you. You can also search topics by date.

✔ **Get off mailing lists.** If you're like me, unsolicited correspondence easily makes up 60 to 80 percent of your daily incoming mail. If you're on one mailing list, your name is bought, sold, and bartered to numerous others before you can say "spring catalog."

Most reputable firms belong to the Direct Marketing Association (DMA). Write the DMA (Mail Preference Services, P.O. Box 643, Carmel, NY 10512) or visit online at www.dmaconsumers.org and ask the DMA to remove your name from its lists.

✔ **Take a sabbatical from the news.** The news can be negative, biased, and sensationalized to attract an audience. Don't let that be you. If you're interested in a topic, research it in depth (remember books?). You may find that your news sabbatical turns into a permanent vacation. (If you do need a news fix, look for the online version of your newspaper of choice.)

✔ **Create a tear file of all the articles or papers you do want to read.** I've been using a tear file for almost 20 years, and it's saved me countless hours. A tear file helps you decide quickly what's worth your time and what isn't.

It's simple: Tear out articles you want to read from trade publications, magazines, newspapers, and so on and file them in your tear file. Throw the rest of the publication into the recycle bin. Carry your tear file with you all the time, so whenever you're waiting — in traffic, at the doctor's office, at the car repair shop — you use your time productively. If the same article remains unread in your tear file for more than a couple months, pitch it.

You can also create this with the electronic news, trade reports, and other information you want to get to. Create a file in your tablet that is your tear file. Then start placing the articles or even the links to the articles so you can review them when you have a few moments.

Accounting for Ergonomics and Aesthetics

Not all time-saving techniques pertaining to your workspace are directly related to organization; elements such as comfort and positive energy also affect your productivity. Two of the most important and often overlooked areas are *ergonomics* (a fancy term for fitting the job tools to the worker, rather than vice versa) and aesthetics (how you decorate your space to make the place where you spend your time enjoyable and uplifting).

An ergonomic workspace increases your productivity, reduces your work hours, and prevents workplace injuries by placing your body at optimal angles and at distances where productivity increases and fatigue decreases. (Many work-related injuries can be traced to poor posture, poor work practices, and badly designed office chairs, desks, workstations, and computer keyboards.)

Likewise, aesthetics plays an important part in time management because it encourages you to be more productive. By surrounding yourself with things that inspire you, you help yourself keep all things in perspective, particularly the balance between your work and personal life so you can make better decisions and — on those days you feel like you're drowning — remember why you're doing what you do.

As I tell my wife, Joan, when she chooses her shoes based on style rather than comfort, ergonomics plays second fiddle to aesthetics all too often. If we're going to walk around town for an afternoon, and Joan wears her fashionable (and very attractive) slides rather than her walking or athletic shoes, I know that sooner or later, she's going to pay for her choice. The same is true in your workplace — so tend to your needs before making adjustments that are helpful but not crucial.

Setting up a proper workstation

Although today's desks are more likely to be designed to accommodate PCs, laptops, and tablets, many desks are still manufactured first and foremost for writing, note-taking, phone conversations, and getting organized.

The standard desk is a couple of inches too high for comfortable computer use, so if you spend a considerable amount — say, 50 percent — of your time on the computer, a keyboard at desk height can lead to problems with your back, shoulders, and neck. You probably know someone who's had carpal tunnel syndrome — numbness, tingling, and pain — in his or her wrists because of repetitive and incorrect computer use. That's only one ailment resulting from non-ergonomic work stations.

You probably spend the bulk of your office time sitting. To avoid fatigue and injury, invest in a good, ergonomically sound chair. Features to look for include the following:

- Adjustable height and tilt
- Adjustable back rests for your lower back
- A rotating seat
- At least five wheels

Be sure you align your keyboard and monitor, too, instead of letting pieces jut left or right. I actually have two work stations in my office. One that's the standardized desk station; the other is a stand-up work station. This allows me to move and alter location based on my energy level, mood, and with whom I'm talking.

Decorating your space

Productive people create workspaces where they enjoy spending time. You spend many hours working, so make your work environment a place where you can focus and be productive for long stretches. You may have a strictly utilitarian view of your work area (it's Spartan but functional — what more do you need?). Or it may be important to you to dress up your space a bit. Whatever your preferences, keep them in mind as you begin planning your work area. Consider the following aspects of your workspace:

- **Walls:** Do you work better if your walls are a softer, more comfortable color than the harsh white of most offices? Consider painting or hanging wallpaper or swatches of fabric.

✔ **Images:** Are pictures, art, and photographs important in your surroundings?

✔ **Floor:** Should you buy a rug to add color and form or give your office a warmer feel?

✔ **Lighting:** What's the lighting like? Most people work beneath the low hum of fluorescent lighting. To give your area a warmer feel, you may try a desk lamp or even a lamp on your credenza behind you to create better ambience.

✔ **Furniture:** Do you need to upgrade your office furniture? If it's okay with your boss, can you add a couch for afternoon cat naps or creative brainstorming? Do you need a small table for meetings with your team?

Here are a few points to remember as you personalize your space:

✔ **Limit the items on your desk to the more utilitarian variety.** Remember: The top of your desk is not a decoration zone. Use the walls, floor, and credenza to bring the environmental influence in your workspace.

✔ **Pay attention to placement.** If you're someone who dreams about better times as you toil away, right behind your desk may not be the best place for a large photo of your last trip to Hawaii. Instead, you may consider putting it on your credenza so you can look at it during a moment of relaxation and envision what you're doing all the hard work for.

✔ **Be careful not to add anything that'll add to the responsibilities you have to tend to each day.** After all, the point is to increase your productivity, not give you more to do. Consider this scenario, which I advise against in your own space: I once worked with a woman who had fish swimming in a tank on her credenza. Although her mini-aquarium was beautiful and soothing and drew plenty of attention, I often wondered how much work time she spent cleaning it — and how she persuaded her co-workers to feed her fish when she went on vacation!

Chapter 8

Fine-Tuning Organization Skills with Technology

*P*icture this: I'm getting ready to go on vacation, when a critical client asks me to make a sales presentation to one of the largest sales networks in the country. For a moment, I panic — the event is scheduled immediately after my return from my vacation. If I'm to be prepared, I'll have to disappoint my family and cancel our getaway. Ah, but then I remember — I have a similar version of that presentation wrapped up on a PowerPoint program. A few tweaks and some minor revisions, and I'll have a new and customized presentation in a couple of hours. I put in some research time, modify my PowerPoint, and head out for a week of fun and sun.

I'm a prisoner of technology, and I'm delighted. I love what technology does for me and for my business, Sales Champions. The computer is the lifeblood of my organization, from communication and data storage to organizing projects to dealing with clients, suppliers, and prospects. It must be love, or I'd never tolerate the terrible, awful fits technology occasionally gives me.

In this chapter, you discover what the love affair is all about. I point out the efficiency provided by electronic scheduling, such as using Google Calendar or your phone or tablet. I help you eliminate excess baggage on your computer, organize and name the files you save so you can access them quickly, and archive files you may need to refer to in the future in a way that minimizes the time you spend searching for them. I also show you how a customer relationship management (CRM) program can help you organize your client information and increase business. Read on.

Plugging into Electronic Scheduling

Electronic tools can help keep your time and schedule under control. A quality phone or tablet, for example, acts as your electronic assistant on the road or in your office using a calendar program like Google Calendar in Google Drive. Using some type of cloud-based scheduling system is advisable so that all information is distributed to your cloud-based tablet and/or phone devices. This section outlines your options for electronic planners, whether you're looking to use calendar software on a desktop computer or to pull out your smartphone or tablet when you're on the go. I also discuss the pros and cons of different systems and considerations to keep in mind before deciding which one to use.

The calendar-sharing benefits of electronic scheduling tools

One of the biggest benefits of using electronic scheduling tools is that you and your co-workers have access to each other's schedules *without* making a phone call or pestering administrative assistants. This slashes the time you need to set up a meeting because the software also informs you where others are, what they're doing, and when they're available. Electronic scheduling saves time on the recipient's end, too — because others can see your schedule, you receive meeting invitations only at times you're available, and you don't have to consult your schedule to see whether you can attend.

Say, for example, you've been trying to reach Bob Smith for two days. Every time you call him, he's in a meeting, and every time he calls you back, you're out in the field. You cut through the time-wasting telephone tag, check into your network scheduling system, and schedule a time for both you and Bob to talk. You can see that he's in the office but free of meetings between 2 and 3 p.m.

Using the meeting invitation system that's built into most calendars (from Outlook to Google Calendar) can save time. You can ask for, confirm, or reschedule appointments with a few clicks of the mouse or tap of your finger. This enables both you and the multiple attendees of a meeting to drop the appointment into their schedules with little effort.

Scheduling systems, such as Microsoft Outlook or Google Calendar, are great for setting up meetings for the convenience of the majority. For example, suppose you need to set a meeting next week for the ten people on your budget task force: Your attendance, as well as those of three department heads, is required. By using Outlook to schedule the meeting, you can see others' schedules before you even send a meeting invitation. You can search through the week to find the best time for the most people, ensuring your numbers and the attendance of those critical to the meeting.

And when you're not available? Don't worry: No one knows that you're actually getting a haircut at 3 p.m. Thursday — they just know you're not available to meet.

The utility of portable planners

Portable planners have an incredibly wide variety of uses. When traveling via air, I frequently see executives turn their phones or tablets to *airplane mode* as soon as the flight attendant starts the pre-flight announcements. The inflight Internet allows businesspeople to connect with the office cloud, update their appointments, and send emails long before the plane is parked at the gate.

Beware: Some smartphones don't work with some brands of CRM software (see the later section "Managing Contact Info with a CRM Program"). Be sure to check whether your smartphone is compatible with your CRM before investing in either. Also check whether you can sync from remote locations or whether you need to physically be in your office to sync. In addition, some smartphones, as well as some CRM software, won't sync if you're connected remotely. This means email you send and receive, calls you make, notes from those calls, and appointments booked by your staff won't show up in your smartphone — or in the server containing your CRM — resulting in missed appointments, duplications, wasted time, and lost revenue.

Despite all their benefits, smartphones do have drawbacks: You get married to the technology; you can be too accessible; if you lose the smartphone, it's as if you lost your whole life and database. Although most of the world has embraced the smartphone revolution, at times you may want to be *less* accessible.

When deciding whether a smartphone will save or cost you time overall, consider your job and the level of concentration that you need to perform well. Do you really need to be accessible at a moment's notice? Are you the type of person who can put it off or down? Do you answer all the phone calls that come to your home? If you're unable to screen calls at home, you may have a hard time screening your smartphone.

De-cluttering Your Computer or Tablet (and Keeping It That Way)

Is your computer a junk drawer, collecting everything you don't have time to deal with? Your computer has limited space, and sooner or later, you'll be forced to clean it or find another drawer (and computers are far more expensive than drawers!). The more junk on your computer, the harder it is to find what you're looking for. And just as an overflowing drawer gets harder to open and close, an overstuffed computer also works less efficiently.

The best way to tackle an overburdened computer is to sort its inventory and then purge what you can from it, whether you back files up to a disc and delete them from your computer or simply delete them once and for all.

Naming files and organizing them with an electronic tree

Start by creating categories for your electronic files, with one folder for each of your major areas of responsibility. Typical categories include *sales, marketing, human resources, promotion,* and *current projects,* as well as categories based on your products and services. You may also include folders for key customers. Again, just as you create subfolders under these headings in your file cabinets, create electronic subfolders for smaller, more specific categories.

Build your *filing tree* — an outline of major folders and the subfolders to go beneath them — in your computer before you begin to file individual documents. Don't start filing and *then* try to organize your files. It's difficult to see all your files at once on a computer, so that strategy rarely works. Having at least a rough outline of the files and folders on your PC, tablet, and perhaps even on paper, before you begin eliminates a lot of copying, cutting, and pasting. Result: greater efficiency and significantly less frustration.

The most challenging part of organizing, whether physical or electronic, is developing a system. The key to being able to retrieve information without wasting time is to file it correctly in the first place. The following subsections present some questions to help you devise a system that works for you.

How do you usually need to access information?

Do you need to retrieve information by date? Subject matter? Company? Project name? Everyone has different priorities based on the type of business, job description within that business, and personal preferences. If you're the keeper or primary resource of spreadsheets, reports, correspondence, or contracts, you may have to be able to pull up files quickly for others or communicate or share this information. In that case, you may need to tailor your filing system to what works best for someone else. Think about how your boss or colleague asks you for a document. Does he usually remember the name of the contact he was working with, the location he traveled to, or the time of year that he was working on the project?

If your projects are very large, break them into smaller, more easily accessed files. Here are a couple of basic breakdowns for your filing system:

- ✔ **If you do the same set of projects for several different clients, you may want to file under client names.** If you're going to file by name, decide whether to file by last name, first name, or the name of the company that person represents. (Does your client Mike Wallace of ABC Company go under *m, w,* or *a?*) Whatever you decide, stick with the system for all your files so they're grouped together and easy to retrieve.

- ✔ **If you're prone to look for files by date or if your files are continually evolving with newer versions each time they're used, structure your system so that the date information is always part of the file or folder name.** If you primarily access information based on when it was created, regardless of the client or project, the date it was created is the most important item in your document or folder title. If due date is more important, make that part of the file name.

Inconsistency and even spelling or punctuation errors can send your folders and files to unintended locations, which can make them difficult if not impossible to find later. Your computer organizes files in alphabetical and numerical order, so set some guidelines for how you plan to name your files before you start. For instance, regardless of where you place a date in your document or folder name, you need to create your date the same way each time. July 29, 2014 ends up in a different location than a document titled with 7-29-2014 or even 072914. Also be consistent in whether your date comes at the end of the file name or the beginning.

Because of all the information you want to include in the file name, your documents may have names that create a file path that is too long. An overly long file path can also prevent you from moving the document to another location, or in some cases even emailing the file. Abbreviations can help, but be sure to be consistent. If you abbreviate Joe's Coffee Shop as JCS on one project and Joe's CS on another, they won't show up next to each other in your computer.

If you work in a fast-paced environment, set aside a blocked-out period of time each month to go through your current files and make sure they're correctly labeled and filed. As time passes, it's easy to forget which file belongs to whom and where it should go. Files can easily become lost forever, creating a huge time loss when you launch into an endless search and end up having to re-create a file from scratch. (Of course, you can always use the search function on your computer to look through a single document, subfolder, file folder, or your entire computer. After you find your missing document, check to see why it was misfiled in the first place and then correct the error.)

How far back must you keep files?

Depending on your business, you may have years' worth of files you need to keep on your computer for a longstanding client or project. How often do you call up archived or non-active information? If you keep data and detail for a long time, you may set up a system that gives you quick access to "closed" files without cluttering your screen.

You may want to try keeping the current year or the last two years in your everyday files; by the time you need to look up those files only occasionally, create a subfolder where you can combine information for each past year — then put that folder in a different area. You may even be able to move this seldom-used information out of your personal files and into your company's main folders on the server, which can keep your current computer files less cluttered and save you time.

How do you create new documents?

Do you work regularly with documents based off a template? For example, do you send out client contracts? Put together a weekly status report? Submit expense reports or check requests? Generate form responses? Think about the best system for pulling up the appropriate templates and revising them accurately and efficiently — and storing them so you can find them quickly.

If you create documents from scratch regularly, look for a way to create templates for frequently created formats to avoid reentering the same information for each version you produce.

Do you work on projects that generate multiple versions of documents? For example, do you have proposals that are reviewed, edited, and revised by numerous people? If so, you want to incorporate a system that allows you to easily track the history of changes and pull up what's been done in the past. For instance, when people save new, updated versions of a document, you may have them alter the file name by adding their initials, adding an abbreviation to indicate a certain stage of a project, or dating everything so you don't end up searching through proposals that are so old and outdated that you'll never use them again. Make sure every knows the naming system.

Are most of the new documents you create specific to one issue or one client? When you spend time producing documents for specific clients, your organization method should make it easy to call up a client and identify everything related to that client.

If you're constantly creating new documents, the job of organizing is more challenging. Your document load is heavy and constantly increasing. Consider setting up your organizational system by client or using an archive file where you store master contracts, proposals, letters, templates, checklists, and other regularly used items. You may also set up folders so these frequently used master files are easy to access.

Offloading excess by archiving or deleting

The more files your computer has to search on its hard drive the more slowly it works. As with paper files, a key part of organizing your computer is removing what you don't need to keep, including duplicate files. Electronic clutter is hard to see because unlike the physical stacks piling up on your desk, it tends to be invisible — until your computer slows or balks. I've found numerous copies of the same programs on my computer because I forgot that I'd installed earlier versions.

You know you need to archive when the icons proliferate on your desktop until it looks like the parking lot at a busy superstore. *Archiving* files doesn't mean deleting those old files; it means backing them up to a thumb drive or other storage device. Whether you have a few desktops or a large server, archiving frees up hard-drive space and speeds your computer's performance. To weed out excess, follow these steps:

1. **Search your computer to make sure that the programs installed are ones you need and that you're using the most recent versions.**

   Save the data in the old versions onto a thumb drive, cloud account, or update the program and transfer it to the new version. Then send the old versions to your computer's recycle bin or uninstall them.

2. **Create a permanent archive directory or folder and get in the habit of archiving any files you don't use regularly but want to keep.**

Always label your thumb drives or backup drives. Don't just throw them into storage in anonymous jewel cases. If nothing else, print hard copies of the disc's contents, fold the paper to the size of the case, and secure the package with a rubber band. That way, if you come back to it five years from now, you'll know what the disc contains.

Cleaning up a hand-me-down computer

You may inherit hand-me-down computers filled with old files. If and when that happens, check organization dates or last-edit dates. Often, files have been passed on for generations of employees. Instead of sending the files out to be carbon dated, do the following:

✔ Store the file in an interim file so you can research it when you have time or archive it so it's out of your way.

✔ Print out a hard copy and ask your boss or the computer's previous owner whether you should save it.

✔ Save the file on a thumb drive, and purge the file from your computer.

Be sure to keep thumb drives and other storehouses in a safe place. Buy a fire safe that's rated for electronic storage (read the label before you buy because not every safe protects flash drives). Store particularly important files, such as periodic complete system backups, in a safe deposit box. Also use multiple backups so you're well-covered for a catastrophe — if one drive is corrupt, you don't want to lose all your data.

After you've purged the excess files, periodically defragment your computer. The process helps increase the speed of your computer so the data is compressed and organized in a manner in the computer that it can find it easily.

Saving new files strategically

The Save As feature on your computer is one of technology's greatest functions — for personalization, for producing numerous letters with only minimal changes, or for tailoring presentations to specific groups without losing your original documents. When you save without Save As, you replace one file with another, losing potentially valuable information that could save you time later should you need that information for a similar situation in the future.

I had an assistant a number of years ago who never used the Save As function. When I customized a presentation based on an industry's or client's needs, my assistant typed and formatted workbooks and PowerPoint presentations and saved the customized information over previous versions of the file. In essence, she replaced every presentation with the most recent version. I lost at least a year's worth of new ideas because my assistant didn't make strategic use of Save As.

For all its benefits, the Save As option can also be your hard drive's demise if you don't use it judiciously — it's too easy to create (and store) numerous documents that are almost identical. For example, if you have a master file of a letter to customers, Save As makes it a cinch to personalize the letter from your master file. But do you need to keep copies of all your personalized letters? You may want to save the letter into the appropriate customer file, but you probably don't need to keep a copy of every personalized letter in the master letter file (unless each version is different enough from the original that you may use the new version periodically in the future).

Managing Contact Info with a CRM Program

If you're in business, you already know the profit to be tapped from existing customers. They're already yours! In countless customer service studies I've read in the last 25 years, I've seen one conclusion over and over: It takes many times more effort, energy, and time to acquire a new customer than it does to retain an existing one.

No matter what your business, the ability to contact existing customers easily and frequently — with the inside knowledge of someone who knows them well as customers — is invaluable. Add the ability to send customers personalized communications at the exact time they're in the market for your product or service, and you're in business: *profitable* business. Even if customers won't need to replace your product for many years, you may be able to offer them related items or garner a referral to their friends.

One of the most valuable tools in business is a customer relationship management (CRM) program. CRM helps you maximize the service, communication, sales, and relationship-building with prospects and existing clients — the lifeblood of any business — by providing quick access to critical customer information, whether you're selling, serving, or invoicing.

Additionally, CRM enables your office practices to become nearly paperless, especially if you have compatible software that changes faxes into electronic documents. You can even enter notes into your CRM software while you're on the phone with prospects and customers, allowing you to keep records of discussions in one centralized place, banishing sticky notes and random slips of paper. This automation saves time and money and provides practically unfettered access to documents and client files from anywhere in the world. What's more, it's kind to trees.

Looking at software and services

Most computers come with simple CRM systems. In Microsoft, it's Outlook. However, Outlook isn't powerful or customizable enough to keep more than basic client and prospect data, so I recommend ACT! (www.act.com), GoldMine (www.goldmine.com), Salesforce (www.salesforce.com), or SugarCRM (www.sugarcrm.com). These four programs are reasonably priced and readily available, and they've stood the test of time as high-quality CRM programs, so they're reasonable tools for businesses big or small. They offer powerful capabilities to customize your business data, and they also help segment your customers and clients so you can tailor your communication, service, and sales strategies to particular groups. If you need multiple users, you'll need to establish a network for the CRM programs or cloud-based versions to run on so all people in your company have access.

Unleashing the capabilities of a CRM program

I can personally testify that, having used one for nearly 25 years, a CRM can provide the following:

- Cross-selling opportunities to prospects
- Upselling opportunities to current clients
- More revenue in slower months
- Better service to current clients
- Increased referral business
- High levels of customer satisfaction
- More time for technicians to take new customer service calls

This section covers some of the ways you can use the program to make it happen.

Categorizing clients

You can use a CRM program to segment your clients, which is a tremendous strategy. All customers are important, but some are more important than others. Your most important customers

- Do more (and more profitable) business with you.
- Send more of their friends, neighbors, business contacts, family members, and associates your way.

✔ Hold strategic positions in companies or organizations you'd like to do business with, meaning they can send even more business your way.

You can use CRM to reach out to clients based on their relationship with you. You can, for example, segment your customers and clients into three distinctive categories:

✔ **Platinum clients:** These are your best customers. They're delighted with your service, are likely to send you referrals regularly, and wouldn't think of going anywhere else. CRM helps you stay in touch with them through newsletters, phone calls, or special correspondence on a regular basis.

✔ **Gold customers:** These people may not be as excited about you and your company as the platinum people, but they continue to do business with you, even if you get raves and referrals only when you ask. CRM helps identify gold-level clients and reminds you to communicate frequently — with the goal of raising them to platinum level.

✔ **Bronze customers:** These are folks who may only sporadically do business with you, switching to other sources from time to time; or they're individuals and businesses who haven't called you for a long time. You can use CRM to help you make a more concerted effort to build a stronger relationship with them.

In addition to current customers, you can also segment prospects and customize your communication with them. A strategic CRM program helps you categorize and organize your prospects as well as separate them from suspects. (*Suspects* have a less than 50 percent chance of using your products or services. *Prospects* offer you a better than 50 percent chance of creating a new business relationship.) Using the technology of a CRM effectively, you can increase the frequency and effectiveness of contact and move the prospects up what I call the *loyalty ladder* more quickly.

Contacting target groups all at once

When you group your prospects, customers, and clients, you can communicate with them with a few keystrokes or clicks of a mouse. If deliveries of your pressure washers are back ordered, for example, you can easily notify all your pressure-washer customers. Or if you're changing the pricing on the half-page ads in your magazine, you can contact all your customers and let them know. You may tell them that, beginning at month-end, ad prices go from $4,000 to $5,000 (but as valued customers, they can lock in the lower price by signing a one-year contract now).

Most CRM programs can merge information, including inserting customer and company names in both greetings and bodies of letters. This allows you to craft a generic email or business letter, but use customer and company names in strategic spots so the letter is more personalized. It also saves you from writing 20, 50, or even 300 separate customer letters.

Putting customer contact on auto-pilot

After you categorize your customers and clients, you can take the final step to saving time with a CRM: automating customer contact. The companies and people who use CRMs most effectively automate *everything*. They have documents, communications, letters and systems, troubleshooting communications, and so on in the CRM. This allows the program to find the document, write the letter or email, attach the document in a PDF file, and keep it in the current client record — all electronically. After you design an automated process (who, what, where, when, and why), the CRM does the rest. You can even set up some programs, such as ACT!, GoldMine, Salesforce, and SugarCRM, to dial the phone for you.

CRMs let you set up long-term communication systems delivered through automation. After your customers receive their 5,000 tongue depressors, an automated thank-you note goes out. The following week, you (automatically) offer a special on gauze. The week after that, you may (automatically) send a customer-satisfaction survey. You can set this system up in advance for customers, clients, prospects, and suspects in platinum, gold, and bronze groups (see the earlier "Categorizing clients" section for more on these groupings).

The CRM program can also integrate the notification for calls from different people in your company or department as well as email and faxes. You can establish a system in which each person gets his or her marching orders from the CRM. For instance, you can tell Susie in accounting to send the invoice and tell Bob in sales to make a follow-up call at 3 days, 7 days, and 14 days after the delivery; and the CRM will also generate a thank-you letter that Sally in administration can send out tomorrow. And finally, Penny in customer service gets the notice to make a call in 5 days to check in on any training needs the customer has with the new product.

Creating effective client profiles

The building blocks of a profitable customer file are standard: name, address, phone number(s), email address, and (if applicable) administrative assistant's contact info. These five or six bytes of information provide you with the start of a great customer record. To take customer communication to the highest level, however, you need more information.

The more you know about your customers, the easier it is to deter defections — times a client chooses to do business with someone else or refers business to another company or agency. That's a killer for your business: Just think of the enormous time you've invested in getting and keeping your customers!

Figure 8-1 shows a form you can use to increase your knowledge of your customers and create more personal connections with them. You can program this information into your CRM by customizing the fields.

Say you've collected this information about your customers over time and you've entered it into your CRM. The next time you come across a couple of extra tickets to the golf tournament in town, you search your CRM for customers who are golf fanatics and give them the tickets. Of course, it doesn't hurt your relationship that the tickets came from you!

Another example: You see a great article about the University of Alabama. You search for University of Alabama alumni on your customer list and email them the article. What have you invested? A few minutes of *really* listening to your customers (and you do that anyway, right?) and a few minutes of data entry. What have you achieved? You've brought your relationship with this customer to a new level and spent minimal time doing it.

If you really want to impress a customer, take great notes in your CRM and start the next call with something like the following:

- ✔ *"How did (the wedding, your party, the conference) go?"*
- ✔ *"How was Bobby's soccer game last week? Did his team win?"*
- ✔ *"What did you do with X? Last time we spoke, you said Y."*

Take a few moments of your time to note nuggets of information in your CRM, use that information to make your prospect or customer feel valued and unique, and watch your customer relationship grow and solidify.

Putting a CRM program on a server or in the cloud to maximize accessibility and backup

My rule: Everyone in the company must be able to access public information in real time at all times. All employees who serve or sell to customers need access to client documents and information. This is true for all departments: sales, marketing, administration, accounting, and so on. And you can set up a CRM program so all employees can tap into the data. Putting CRM on a server has security advantages as well.

Date: _____

Customer Profile

1) Customer Name _____
   Nickname _____
2) Company Name _____
3) Company Address _____
   Home Address _____
4) Telephone Numbers _____
   Business _____
   Home _____
5) Date of Birth _____
   Place of Birth _____
   Hometown _____

Education

6) High School _____
   Year Graduated _____
   College _____
   Year Graduated _____
   College Fraternity/Sorority _____
7) _____
   Sports _____
8) _____

Family

9) Spouse name and occupation _____
10) Spouse education _____
11) Spouse's interests _____
12) Anniversary _____
13) Children _____
    names/ages _____
    _____
14) Children's education levels _____
    _____
15) Children's interests (hobbies, problems) _____
    _____

Special Interests

16) Clubs, fraternal associations, service clubs _____
    _____
17) Community activities _____
    _____

Lifestyle

18) Favorite place for lunch _____
    Favorite place for dinner _____
19) Favorite spectator sports _____
    Favorite sports teams _____

Figure 8-1:
A sample
customer
profile.

Not only does having company data spread around on various computers create an organizational nightmare, but it also represents a security flaw — you can lose valuable customers in a keystroke. For example, if you have a salesperson who has given notice or, worse, one you've terminated, that person may have 200 customers — and all their customer information — saved on his or her computer. Before leaving, that person can easily delete every customer file in the computer.

Ouch! You just lost the history and possibly the contact information for 200 customers. You also lost customers that current salespeople were hoping to close in the next 30, 60, or 90 days. Now you have to try to reconstruct which customers the salesperson sold to, what he or she sold to them, and what the customer-salesperson relationships were like. And you're back figuring out how you can increase sales and service to these customers in the future.

If you have multiple independent computers with company data stored on each, I highly recommend that you connect your company's computers in a network run by a server. Server- or cloud-accessible CRM data ensures that your business can avoid data-loss nightmares. With the CRM program, you can immediately lock an ex-employee out of the system and have system backups to reconstruct data as needed.

Some companies may be reticent to open access to this information because of client confidentiality or simply the risk of corrupting or deleting important data. If you want to protect accounting, personnel, and other private information, you can do that with no problem. The programs offer password protection so that only certain employees can access the most confidential information. You can also set it up so employees can *see* the data but not delete or modify it in any way.

Part III
Using Technology to Leverage Your Time

Photo courtesy of Getty Images/iStockphoto

In this part . . .

- Learn how to use and leverage technology as a significant influencer of how you manage your time.

- Evaluate and explore organizational tools and apps that enable you to "go paperless" and stay more organized.

- Use Evernote for storing notes, tasks, to dos, images, articles, photos . . . basically everything!

- Tame your email beast and learn how to avoid email overload.

- Keep the time investment and the value you receive from social media in check.

Chapter 9

Leveraging Your Time with Technology

In This Chapter

▶ Choosing what application to use

▶ Communicating effectively through technology

▶ Understanding technology tools

▶ Creating a digital brain with Evernote

*I*could write a whole book on the amazing new technologies that save everyone time. There are computer programs and apps for your tablets and phones that dramatically increase organization, recall, and storage of both your personal and business needs. You can organize your time with calendar apps; make lists and memos on the fly by opening a notes app and speaking into your smartphone; and find the best prices on everything from gasoline to dog food with other apps. If anyone told me 20 years ago that I'd be able to write a message on my phone and send it halfway across the world in the matter of seconds, I would have asked what they were drinking!

But as with everything, there are drawbacks. By its very nature, cutting-edge technology is ever changing. Moore's Law states that the speed of computers doubles every two years; this can be said about most technology. In the quest for more productivity and efficiency, you must be open to learning about new innovations.

I caution you that just because something is new doesn't guarantee it's better. Everyone has different skills, so the results with any specific technology app, software, or tool can vary. Just be open to trying new things. You could be very pleasantly surprised.

Timing Is Everything: Taking Charge of Your Time

Recent advances in electronics and technology have given consumers a bevy of new tools. From hardware to software, the choices are nearly endless for ways to track your time and keep yourself on schedule. Evernote, Dropbox, ScanSnap, Google Calendar, Excel, and LastPass represent software and applications; and of course, tablets and smartphones are needed to run these programs.

The leverage you create through using current technology adds value to your life, and can also make you more in demand — you can access data and documents within seconds, have a face-to-face talk with a client across the country without leaving your office, and you can stay on top of your schedule every day.

Making choices about technology

Being successful enables you to make more choices. The person who earns a million dollars a year has more choices and freedom than someone who makes one-hundred thousand a year. The goal should be a life filled with choices and freedom, such as the choice to take the afternoon off on a beautiful day.

In the world of technology you have to make choices. Do you go with a smartphone, tablet, phablet (combination phone and tablet), a desktop computer, a laptop computer, or a combination of several devices? You also need to decide on operating system platforms. Are you on the Apple team with your iPhone, iPod, Macbook, and desktop? Or are you running a PC with Microsoft products and an Android phone system and tablet?

Unlike ten years ago, you can actually choose to use both Apple and PC systems, which I did for many years. Switching back and forth, however, can create confusion, crossover, duplication, and potentially lower productivity . . . and yes, using two systems can take up more time. Find a combination of hardware and possibly software that works for you. Knowing your systems and making wise choices can lead to huge time savings for you.

Automate rather than replicate

A large waste of time is created when you do the same tasks over again and again each day, week, or month. Automotive companies have transitioned many of the repetitive car-building tasks to machines over the last 20 to 30 years. Their efficiency rate has grown per each car they build.

There are a number of simple ways to automate your workday. Setting up an online banking system is one. I didn't embrace online banking when it was first introduced. I liked controlling my checkbook. The truth is, the amount of time it takes to pay your bills via check can be slow and cumbersome. Setting up your recurring payments — such as your mortgage, life insurance, health insurance, electric bill, cable bill, garbage service, city services, credit cards, and so on — on an automated process is easy. You certainly need to review the bills each month to ensure you have the funds necessary to pay them, but you schedule a date for the bills to be paid and voila . . . bills are automatically paid and you've saved time.

You can also set up a specific amount to transfer to your savings or investment accounts each month. The process of forced savings creates more freedom and time for you later in life. The vast majority of people don't retire well off. It's not because they failed to make enough money; they've simply failed to save any of it. The world is filled with stories of lower-income people who gave large sums of money away at their death. The reason wasn't because of their vast earned income. It was due to them having a savings system. Any online banking system allows you to be more structured in your savings.

In evaluating what you can automate, ask yourself these questions:

- ✔ What do I do each day that I can automate and save time?
- ✔ What do I do each week that is routine and can be automated?
- ✔ What unpleasant tasks do I do that can be automated?

Look around and see if there's a software program or small application that can make your life easier by doing tasks for you, or simply remind you that a task needs to be accomplished. Like yours, my to-do list each day is pretty long. If I can cut down on some tasks through automation, or give myself automated reminders on my computer or smartphone calendar, I reduce my unwieldy to-do list each day.

Communicating Effectively through Technology

In the last ten years, communication options have exploded far beyond Mr. Bell's exclamation to Mr. Watson, "Come here, I want to see you." That first telephone message took place in 1876; Mr. Bell would have never imagined the amazing devices available today that are the basis for most of communication. But what's the best medium for you? Do you want to talk? Send text messages? Create and send video? Use technology to talk in real time plus see the person with whom you're chatting? Check and respond to email? You need to determine what you want to do before you can choose your medium. And the amazing thing is that all of these communication options can be performed on everything from a desktop computer down to your smartphone.

You hold more computing power in your smartphone than what it took to get astronauts to the moon and back!

Social media options to consider

The world communicates via social media. To not be part of the social media revolution is to get left out of the communication loop with your friends and family. Facebook is a primary part of most people's days and lives (see Chapter 11). If you want to be entertained or informed, turn to YouTube for videos. For breaking news, many people are using Twitter (see Chapter 12). For photo and video sharing, Instagram is an up-and-comer.

Facebook has reached 665 million users with the fastest-growing age group being the 45-to-54 age demographic. And there are now over 500 million registered Twitter accounts. The fastest growing age demographic for this social media site includes 55- to 64-year-olds. Their use is up a whopping 79 percent in the last year.

Which social media options you choose depend on your needs. If your family is spread over many locations, states, or countries, use Facebook to keep them informed and communicate.

Getting family members involved

I have tried to get my 83-year-old father on Facebook a number of times. It would enable him to become more involved with Annabelle and Wesley, not because they are on Facebook but because we frequently post pictures and happenings of our family on Facebook. It would be easier for Dad to grab pictures of the kids for his use. He would know when they scored the game-winning goal or a life event happened. There are times I forget to email him an update or a photo. I have yet to be persuasive enough to accomplish this goal.

For pre-teens and teens, Instagram seems to be the favorite social media tool. That doesn't mean it can't be used by others, however. Instagram can be connected to many of your other social media platforms. It posts to my Facebook page, as an example.

As a parent I need to brush up on my Instagram because Wesley has hit the teen years in the last few months. He and his friends communicate frequently through Instagram. If I want to be an informed parent, it requires my technology skills in social media to be ever improving.

Using FaceTime, Skype, and other video communication systems

Because communication is more effective when you can see facial features and expressions through a video feed, I am in love with video communication technology. When FaceTime was announced by Steve Jobs midway in 2010, it changed the world of video communication forever. FaceTime has made communicating among the family of iPhone users a snap. As someone who has logged 200,000 air miles over the years, I know I can see and communicate with my family and children as easily as making a phone call. Although Skype was an option before FaceTime (that is, for anyone with a webcam or phone camera), it was less responsive and more cumbersome to use on the fly (no pun intended). If you're accustomed to a PC, then Skype is a good option. It enables you to make calls internationally, engage in video communication, and even instant message.

In my office at Sales Champions we use Skype's instant message service among our office staff, sales staff, coaches, and trainers. This creates a flow of communication instantly without geographic barriers. Skype has created apps for both Android and Apple systems so you can launch Skype right out of your smartphone, tablet, or phablet, as well as laptop or desktop. You can use Skype on more devices than you can FaceTime, because FaceTime is an Apple-specific product. Because most new laptops and monitors come with webcams, Skype has made up much of the ground that made FaceTime so revolutionary.

Engaging through online meeting platforms

I believe the future of business communication, sales, and training is online meeting platforms. The skill of delivery, sales, company trainings, and education is through online delivery. These time-saving options eliminate the need for travel, which is time consuming and a stress for the traveler. Now, meeting participants can attend from their home office, a hotel room, or even in their jammies from their living room.

The flexibility of delivery and design is amazing in these systems as well. If I'm asked a question by an attendee, I can easily pull a related series of PowerPoint slides, Word files, and other materials and begin speaking while sharing the slides. I can even upload materials and files for the attendees to review now or later. The ability to respond to the needs of employees, customers, and clients is astonishing.

The industry leaders in online meetings are GoToMeeting, WebEx, Adobe Connect, and Join.me. There are other companies that are in the online meeting environment, but these are the heavyweights. Each has varying features and costs, which makes selecting the right one for you one of the most challenging decisions. Each one has different enterprise levels as well as allowed participant numbers.

I have personally conducted more than 4,000 online meetings and trainings in the last seven years. My company has conducted more than 6,500 sessions in that period of time, as well. We are the experts in online training and education. WebEx is the industry leader in online meeting software, if you want all the bells and whistles. It has been around the longest and offers a number of versions of its system. Meeting participants need to download the WebEx software before the meeting, and they can participate on a computer, laptop, tablet, or any mobile device. If possible, use voice-over Internet protocol (VOIP) for audio.

WebEx offers the option of a video feed from your web camera as well as any participant's web camera. You can have meeting sizes from one person to hundreds of people at a time. As the host or presenter you can assign privileges to participants where they can chat, type on the screen, and use a highlighter to create interactivity. You can also share files that meeting participants can download directly from your computer or from a Dropbox account.

The participants can use their computer with or without a headset. They have the option to raise their hand and ask a question audibly, just as with a normal in-person meeting or training event. You have the option to share video, pictures, PowerPoint slides, or even whatever is on your computer screen. This allows you to have preplanned or off-the-cuff meetings and presentations. The options are limitless.

GoToMeeting has similar features to WebEx. The layout and design revolves around a panel that allows you to move it to the right- or left-hand side of the screen, unlike WebEx, which has the participant and host panels only on the right. You can limit what the participants can see, comment on, or use as with most online meeting software. All participants need to download software before they can participate.

GoToMeeting is used heavily in the GoToWebinar version. Webinars are larger educational meetings that can accommodate hundreds to thousands of people. GoToWebinar is frequently used as a free educational webinar session on a topic or problem. At the end, usually the presenter offers more complete or comprehensive training or solution for a fee. There are literally thousands of webinars conducted each day by experts to help people and also sell their services to the attendees without leaving the comfy confines of the home or office. GoToWebinar is the most-used online meeting software in this niche. The GoToWebinar software allows you to manage signups, send them reminders, create links for the sessions, deliver pre-webinar materials, and drop the scheduled webinar into their Outlook calendar, Google calendar, or customer relation management (CRM) system easily. You can also record the webinar to make it available to people that attended or couldn't make it as well. You can post the link on your Facebook page or host the recorded session on your website or YouTube.

Some experts develop a library of webinars that they market to and replay over and over again. So when they are on the beach in Bora Bora, their webinar is playing to a packed house on GoToWebinar. That's the definition of time savings and leverage! The other online meeting platforms like Zoom, Adobe Connect, and Join.me have some similar features and amenities as do GoToMeeting and Web.ex. I will share with you a few differences that might make them a better solution for you.

Join.me is the simplest of all the online meeting platforms. It doesn't require the participant to download any software. The removal of this step for the low-technology-minded user can be a big help, because all they have to do is click on a link and they are in your meeting. It can be the best avenue for a quick meeting. Join.me also has a free version so you can easily test and try without making a financial investment. Your only option with Join.me is to share your screen, unlike GoToMeeting or WebEx, which can have a cleaner look rather than a row of all the programs you have open across the bottom of your screen in Join.me. There is no video capability or audio in the free version of Join.me, and you need to be on a phone line to have audio communication. You use your cell phone or other phone line to verbally communicate.

This can be a challenge when you have more than one person with whom you are meeting. It requires conferencing people on your phone system or using a teleconferencing service. Using Join.me with a service like Free Conference Calls.com for the audio means you can have zero costs to host and hold meetings.

Adobe Connect is an up-and-coming online meeting platform. It has many of the same services — from screen and file sharing, video, recording, and participant engagement. The biggest difference between Adobe Connect and the rest is you can design the visual of your layout. You can put the video feed, PowerPoint slides, chat panel, and so on anywhere and in any size on the screen. This allows you to create different looks and experiences for different types of trainings and meetings.

Online meetings are the wave of the present and future. It's important to be able to master the delivery in whatever software you are using to communicate. Five years from now, most people and companies will say, "I wish we had been on the cutting edge with online meetings."

Organizational Technology Tools

Everyone seems to be an expert these days with something to share or sell the masses. The information marketing world is exploding with podcasts, e-books, white papers, videos, e-courses, and webinars. Being able to organize all this information with the ability to retrieve it, use it, and implement it can be a full-time job.

Whether it's pictures of your kids and family, a research paper that you wrote years ago but now need to reference, or a long-lost relative's obituary, we all need a system and set of tools to store and grab the information we need.

Building your system to find what you need fast

My first suggestion for you is to separate your personal retrieval system from your business. For example, because I write books, white papers, articles and blogs, create videos, training courses, podcasts, and many other forms of content, I need to retrieve work quickly so I can update, refresh, and rebrand it. I personally use Evernote, which I describe at the end of this chapter in the "Creating a Digital Brain with Evernote" section.

And then there's the organization app called Alfred, named after Batman's handy butler that was always ready to assist the caped crusader. This app saves you a lot of time when you need to search your local hard drive. It can even review your bookmarks and the web for information that you need. You can create your own themes in colors and font sizes to match how you learn and retrieve.

Because you work in the world of many accounts and passwords, rather than having a piece of paper with all your accounts, user names, and passwords, use LastPass. Your personal identity and passwords are something you never want to fall into enemy's hands. The only solution for most people is to use the same user name and password on all accounts. That is not safe either. The time it takes to clear your name when you're hacked is enormous. LastPass allows you to safely share passwords with others that might need access to your information.

If you're serving as project manager and leading people and projects, you might try SweetProcess. This app is a work-flow documentation program that enables you to delegate more effectively. SweetProcess emails you to create procedures, and share and track results all in one place.

Protecting your technology from catastrophe

Accidents can and do happen, especially with technology. Backing up work files and information is imperative today. Although many still perform regular backups, the need for cloud-based or offsite types of backup systems have never been more important.

There are numerous services that offer backup capability, such as Carbonite, Backblaze, or CrashPlan. My personal favorite is CrashPlan because it is easy. It also offers a forever free option, or you can upgrade for a small fee of $5 a month for individual users or about $10 a month for a family with multiple users (your data is backed up continually in real time with an upgraded account). Most people have a limited backup-plan strategy. It's not a matter of if your hard drive crashes; it's only a matter of when. When it happens, whether you lose one file or hundreds, it still causes problems.

Clouding, Dropboxing, and storing your stuff

The ability to use cloud or have documents, data, and information available on any device creates time efficiency. In cloud computing you share computing resources rather than store documents, software, data, and files on a local server or single server and system. Putting something in the cloud refers to Internet-based storage and commuting. Transferring data from your laptop, tablet, phone, and desktop is truly a "has been" action. Selecting cloud-based software and apps is the only way to go.

If you select a CRM solution for your business, using cloud-based technology is a must. The remote servers of the past don't offer the flexibility needed today. The cloud provides safety in case of lost data or files and provides access to all people and devices. It promotes sharing of information between departments and people.

Dropbox is the most-used cloud document sharing software for both business and personal use. No need to email large files anymore when you can give people access to specific folders and files. Dropbox provides strong encryption so your private business or personal files remain protected. It's easy to use, so you can set up files and folders similar to a Windows-based filing system. You can use over 300,000 apps that connect to Dropbox, enabling you to increase your productivity from Microsoft Office to AutoCAD.

For those who travel, Dropbox allows you to access your presentations, documents, and PowerPoints from the road. If you need to make adjustments and update when on the road, you can easily do that and store them in Dropbox.

DocuSign is another must-have time-saving and storage program. The ability to replicate and edit a standardized agreement can save hours of work. The faster you can deliver an agreement of the terms and conditions of service, the less likely the prospect could change their mind, have second thoughts, or your competitor outflank you. People want easy and faster service, and DocuSign fits both of those to a T. It stores all your contracts, but the best feature is how quickly clients receive them and can approve them with a few clicks of their mouse. No more printing the document, signing the document, then scanning it back into a computer to email back to the sender. It also tracks when they received the document, and when they opened it as well as completed and signed it.

Creating a Digital Brain with Evernote

Evernote can help you create a paperless environment in your office or home. You can store almost anything in it — recipes, articles, web clippings, documents, pictures, Kindle notes, meeting notes, and so much more.

Getting the most out of Evernote requires some planning and execution. You first need to set up your system (computer, tablet, and so on) to work with Evernote *notebooks* for your collected and stored notes. You can have only one notebook, but that would be like having one large filing cabinet that you dump everything in without labeling. Use notebooks for the different areas in your life. You can have a notebook for business files, personal stuff, travel, family, and financial. These are some of the notebooks you might consider.

You then create *stacks*. Think of these as a grouping or collection of notebooks. Your work stack could be broken down by client, area of responsibility, or specific project. For example, the stacks for me in my personal notebook are Wesley, Annabelle, and Joan, along with goals, books I want to read . . . just to name a few.

The final sorting method uses *tags*. These are attributes that you attach to an individual note that you create. Evernote gives you the ability to view all notes and documents based on the tags. They can be notes in different notebooks or stacks, but because of the tag you can find them easily.

Getting your notes, ideas, and thoughts into Evernote

There are a number of ways to transfer what you want into Evernote; you create a note and start to type your thoughts, ideas, or observations. You can attend a meeting, training, or class and type your notes directly in. Because cell phones are never far away, you can photograph anything and store it in Evernote. That dress you tried on but were not quite sure about buying it; you wanted to think about it for a day or two. Evernote indexes all the text from your picture so it's easy to recall it and decide that you deserve that dress after all. (Finish this chapter before going back to the store for it, though.)

You can forward any email to your Evernote address, and the email will show up in your default notebook in a matter of seconds. This allows you to tag it, then place it in the correct stack for storage. You can use your scanner to scan into Evernote for storage. You might go the paperless route once you master Evernote (although the rest of the world may not follow suit). You can send an invoice, contract, Christmas card, or invitation directly into Evernote from your scanner.

One of the coolest ways to use Evernote is with social media posts, blog posts, web pages, and online images. You can clip the online article you want to save using the Evernote extension for Google Chrome, Microsoft Explorer, or Mozilla Firefox, to name a few search engines. You can then decide in which notebook you want to place an online story or picture, and attach a tag for easy finding. Evernote extensions are available for almost all Internet browsers.

Remembering and finding things you need

It's so easy to find your stored notes in Evernote that it doesn't even include training on this in its *Getting Started Guide*. There are three basic ways to find your notes easily.

If you click on your notebook or your tags, you can look for what you want. The notebook and tags feature is set up on the left-side toolbar for easy access. This way is easiest when you have a limited number of notebooks, stacks, or tags. As you use Evernote more and continue to expand your organizational strategy, you might have to move onto another method.

Using the Evernote Search box is similar to using any search engine. You merely type into the search box what you want to find, and it pulls up everything matching your command. You can limit the search results by clicking on a notebook or tag first. This shows only the search results within the notebook or tag.

If you wanted to search all files that contained references to salt and pepper, you would type "salt pepper." What Evernote would do is pull up any notes that had both "salt" and "pepper" in them. This is considered an "and" search. If you type "Any: salt pepper" into the search, this sets up an "or" search and you get back any note that had "salt" or "pepper" in it. By omitting the "any," the default was an "and" search.

You can search tags with Evernote by using the Tag: command. This creates a search of all the tags that you type in after the semicolon. For example, you could put in "Tag: success tools," and Evernote would bring up notes or saved items that are tagged under *success tools*. You can even search for things you haven't tagged simply by using the minus sign before "tag" (such as -tag:dogs).

Evernote also enables you to save often-used searches. After you create a search that you know you'll use again, you can create a saved search and reuse it whenever you like. After you create your search, you need to get into the habit of asking yourself, "Would I use this search again?"

Chapter 10

Controlling Email Overload

· ·

· ·

Some of you may receive less email because you communicate more on social media platforms like Facebook, Twitter, or Instagram. Others of you may have gotten so frustrated with more email and spam that you vow to dramatically cut the volume of your email however you can. Whichever category you fit in to, this chapter helps you reduce, remove, and reclaim your email box.

Managing Email Effectively

If all the email correspondence you've ever received, sent, saved, responded to, forwarded, and deleted were turned into paper mail, your output alone could probably fill a U.S. Postal Office. Of course, you don't keep it all, but if you're like me, you let your email accumulate at times, perhaps until your system notifies you that your mailbox has exceeded its limit.

A good tool is only as good as the person wielding it. If you know how to use email properly, it can make your productivity output hum. If not, you can end up sabotaging your efforts to get things done. This section helps you rein in the all-too-often unwieldy paperless communication system.

Setting up filtering systems

Even militant time masters can lose hours of productive time to email — and much of that email isn't even work-related. Sometimes it's not even something you *want* to receive, yet you still have to dig your way through the sludge to see what the email is regarding.

Spam is only one factor that adds to the deluge of email you find in your inbox on a daily basis. If you're like most people, you probably authorized or even requested most of the promotional email you receive. Here are some tips to slow the flow of spam and other incoming email that clutters your inbox:

- ✔ **Unsubscribe from newsletters or mailing lists that you no longer read.** When you were starting up your organic garden last spring, a weekly email about composting tips seemed like a great idea. Now you find that you almost always delete it without opening. Time to put that idea to bed.

- ✔ **Think twice before signing on for new mailing lists.** You may appreciate a monthly newsletter about one of your hobbies. But instead of bulking up your inbox, why not add the website to your Favorites list and visit when it's convenient for you?

- ✔ **When ordering online, seek out the check box that confirms your agreement to receiving email — and *un*check it.** Called the *negative option* response, many merchants include a box on the order form that indicates, "Yes, I want to receive regular notices about your company's special offers." That box is already checked off, for your "convenience." In order to get *nothing,* however, you have to take action and get rid of that mark.

- ✔ **When visiting or leaving personal or contact information on a website, always check the privacy policy to confirm that your information won't be sold.** You can usually find a link to the privacy notice at the bottom of the web page or next to where you enter your information.

- ✔ **Install spam-filtering software on your computer.** Remember, though, that these programs typically don't remove the spam; they simply filter it to your junk folder so you can review or simply delete it.

Don't ever respond to spam. You may hope that your polite request to remove you from the mailing list will stop the mailings, but most often the opposite happens. Your reply confirms that your email address is a valid one. You may start getting even more email, and your address may be sold to other annoying spam-senders. Clicking an opt-out link can also put you at risk if the email is spam, so let your spam software do its job and leave it at that.

Separating Your Work and Private Life

It's important (and healthy) to keep your home and work lives separate. And one way to do that is to create different emails for your job and your personal correspondence. Setting up email accounts through services like Gmail is easy and enables you to have all personal emails, newsletters, and store offers sent to a specific personal account.

Just about every email service or software (such as Outlook or Thunderbird) has ways to filter all the mail you receive. Check each one for the steps necessary to make sure you see the mail you want, and reroute the spam and other unwanted mail. This is a timesaver for both your personal and work lives.

Managing multiple email addresses

You might think that using multiple emails can exponentially create frustration and confusion. If done correctly it can be a huge timesaver. It takes a little upfront design time and organization of what email to use with different people and offers.

I don't recommend forwarding all emails from different email address to one central warehouse location for email. I see many people do this, but it really defeats the purpose and efficiency of using multiple addresses in the first place. It does allow you to easily leave one of your email addresses behind if you or a sender gets hacked or the address gets sold off to a spammer.

If you are an executive, key decision maker, or entrepreneur, marketers and salespeople are targeting you. You are the big fish they want to land as an account. If your email address is posted on your website or can easily be figured out by looking at all the others posted on your or your company's website — you know what I am talking about, such as bigfish@dontbotherme.com — you are bound to get a volume of solicitation emails on a regular basis. I can't tell you how many emails a day I receive to dirkzeller@realestatechampions.com, but I know it's a lot! Those emails route to my key staff members directly. They review them, respond as necessary, and forward the ones that require my direct attention. But I have a "secret" email that only my best clients and key strategic partners have access to. This enables me to save large amounts of time when it comes to reading and responding to emails.

Organizing and storing email

Managing, organizing, categorizing, and filing your email is a practice that can serve you much like maintaining a well-organized paper filing system. Many of your email messages are probably important to you as reference, especially business correspondence. And you, like me, have probably searched in vain for that important email you know you received, oh, maybe eight months ago.

Fortunately, you don't have to print off every email and stick it in a filing cabinet. Your email program includes many valuable tools that help you keep information as close as the click of a mouse. Most email programs include various folder and filing systems that serve as a virtual lateral file cabinet — but searching and finding what you want is a lot easier with just a little experience. You can sort and store your email by a number of categories, grouping them by sender, date, project, importance, or subject. Here are just some ways you can use the features your email service or software provides:

- Set up so that certain messages — periodic newsletters, for example — automatically route to a specific folder. (This tool works on the same concept as spam blockers, except these items go in a folder you actually want to see.) With the help of filtering software, you can flag specific email addresses and automatically send them to a folder — or even delete them — before they hit your inbox. I find that most people use only a small portion of what their filtering features can do. Take a few minutes to explore your options — filtering takes very little time to set up.

- Create a new-arrivals folder, defining *new* as a day, a week, or whatever you determine.

- Establish a *dump* folder that you clean out once a month or as often as you choose.

Don't look at all the email in the dump folder before you dump them. That takes too much time. You've filtered them enough to be able to let them go.

- Make specific project folders where you can save relevant email, providing a record of all conversations for the future. When you no longer need the file because the project is long completed, you can delete it. This setup also presents a great backup system.

- Employ the search function to track down any correspondence about a certain topic. For example, if you're looking for an email outlining details for a trip to the Bahamas, you can type "Bahamas" in the search field and all inbox email with *Bahamas* somewhere within the body or subject line will come up.

Responding to email using less time

There are days where I receive hundreds of emails. This is after the filtering techniques I shared with you earlier. (And even after using a double-secret-probation email as well.) Receiving only what you need to deal with is only half the battle. You must be able to create a system that shrinks the response time and investment if you still get a large volume of emails.

If you are set to craft a long email response, ask yourself if it could be quicker to pick up the phone and place a call. You can talk faster than you can type. If you don't need documentation of the correspondence, you might be able to shave half the time off by calling and speaking rather than writing out an email.

The other option is sending a voice text or video email. I love video email! It saves time and improves the quality of the communication. If you have a webcam you can create video email quickly using a service like BombBomb. In less time than it takes to craft a medium-length email you can record the video in BombBomb. While it's finishing the processing of the video you can craft the short text subject line, cut and paste the email address to send it to, then hit the Send button. The message has more impact, and it took less time.

When responding to a long email with many questions and points of clarification, create an opening greeting at the top of the email and then instruct the person that your responses follow in red, or blue, or whatever color you choose. This enables you to avoid scrolling up and down when you craft your response and allows you to refer to the question because it's on the screen right in front of you.

Employing an email response system

During my formative years, I watched the TV show *M*A*S*H* with my family. I remember that when the wounded would come into the medical unit, the doctors would perform *triage,* the process that determined patient priority. Does this wound need medical attention now? Will this soldier die without immediate care? Will this one die even if he receives attention? In this way, the medical team could most efficiently prioritize their work in a situation of chaos.

Performing triage is an excellent way to approach your email responses. Some mail you get is dead on arrival; other messages are of interest to you but not critical to address immediately; and others need your attention right now. When you receive 100 or more new messages a day, you need a good email management system.

Here's what works for me: When I open up my mailbox, I resort to the three Ds: *delete, do it,* or *defer.* Every email fits into one of these categories.

Hit the delete

Although your computer doesn't take up any more space if you have 10 or 10,000 emails, the clutter of useless, obsolete, irrelevant correspondence in your inbox can *seem* like a mile-high stack of stuff you have to carry with you.

Keep your inbox clean by discarding any email that's unimportant or long-obsolete. As for the advertisements, forwarded jokes, or urban myths, and the string of thanks, you're-welcome, have-a-good-day, see-you-after-work correspondence, read them (or don't) and delete immediately.

Also delete without opening any email with a subject line that seems too good to be true or seems like a marketing pitch from an unknown sender. How realistic is it to think that some company has sought *you* out to offer you an opportunity to make millions? And if a deal is really so incredible, would the advertiser really need to tell you that? Probably not. Beware of any email with subject lines containing misspelled words or words with symbols in place of letters (such as *Fr** Mon!y*). Spammers do this to try and bypass spam filters.

Knowing how to delete helps everyone in your company. When employees share a network, the server fills up when everyone retains all email, which can stop the flow of inbound email for the whole company. Most networks establish a limit to the size of individual inboxes and send notices when you get close to the limit. Then it's time for some major housecleaning. Better to keep up with the cleaning rather than let it build up.

Just do it

Just down the street from my high school in Portland, Oregon, is the head-quarters of Nike, the company that coined the phrase "Just do it." That's not bad advice for email management, either. Of course, this *do it* response is critical if the matter is urgent or must be done today, but it's also a sound strategy for most other email, too. If a message warrants a response, do it. Now. Answer the question. Forward the message. Transfer the to-do to your task list or schedule. Send a response. If you need little more than a click or a minute or two to respond, file, or forward, then don't waste time by keeping it for later.

Just as with mail or papers in your inbox, the best strategy is to handle it once (see Chapter 5) and then get it off your plate.

Defer until later

For those email messages that aren't critical-care matters, it may make sense to set them aside to address after you pass through all your correspondence. So you *don't* forget and leave them buried in your inbox to be remembered too late, immediately place these email messages in an appropriate folder so they'll pop up later for your attention. Messages that fall into this category may include personal email that you want to read carefully and to which you want to take time to craft a response. They can also include flexible-timeline projects that don't have to be done today or even this week.

Actually, I just thought of a fourth D: *delegate*. It falls in the defer category. Although you can simply click the Forward button and send the message along with instructions for carrying out the requested action, the reliability of email is suspect enough that you want to remind yourself to follow up if you hear nothing back from the delegate.

Automating your responses

The ability to plan ahead with email communication saves you loads of time. If you regularly field the same FAQs numerous times during the week or day, it may make sense to craft template emails of standard responses. Place these templates in a folder where you can easily access them, and you're ready to cut and paste your reply, using the form language and making personal tweaks as necessary. For example, if you get queries from clients about the status of their projects, you may put together a standard response informing them that you're attending to their project and will get in touch with them by such-and-such a date.

Don't forget about the automated message function when you're out of the office. Set up a message with the pertinent details: when you'll return, whether you'll be checking email, when people can expect to hear from you, and who they can contact if they need immediate assistance.

Chapter 11

The Facebook Balancing Act

Social media has changed the way the world communicates, and Facebook is the leader in this form of communication. Facebook can be used for businesses to communicate with prospects; it can also be used to market yourself and your services, and converse with your past clients and sphere of influence along with personal and family uses.

Although Facebook is no doubt an increasingly important part of your life and is here to stay, it can take up larger chunks of your day than you can afford to give it. Allocating the right time, strategies, and communication systems helps you maintain the correct balance between traditional business tactics and new tech-savvy strategies like Facebook.

The Time Advantages of Facebook

The efficiency of Facebook in communicating a message to a group of people with a few minutes invested is second to none. While writing this chapter, my daughter Annabelle has been in final rehearsal to dance in *The Nutcracker* ballet. Between rehearsals that have lasted for months, costume fittings, two dress rehearsals, and three performances, my life is all about Tchaikovsky.

The advantage of Facebook is that my friends and family, many who are long distances away, can experience the annual *Nutcracker* through posts, pictures, and videos. They are able to offer instant responses and encouragement to Annabelle. This broadens her validation of herself, her self-esteem, and the enjoyment of her performance. The communication cycle is reduced by Facebook. The response cycle is reduced and response numbers increased. This creates a large time savings.

In business, Facebook has the capability to shrink the time in the communication cycle as well. You can post a white paper, e-book, or video that can be of value to your clients and customers. This helps position your stature as an expert, brings value to your client base, and can even upsell or cross-sell new products and services that you launch.

Additionally, Facebook can open your customers and clients to you as a person by giving them a window into your world at home or through outside interests. When they see you're a dad who focuses on his children, or you took a trip to hike the Pacific Trail, or you passed a marriage milestone, they get to know more about you and the trust in your relationship is enhanced. Your clients connect to you through common interests and thoughts. In sales, this is called building rapport, and Facebook creates that opportunity.

The black hole of time in Facebook

Although there are countless advantages to Facebook, there's a major drawback as well. A new study by Ipsos Open Thinking Exchange shows that the average American spends 3.2 hours a day on social media. The net result is personal face-to-face communication is out, and online electronic communication through our machine is in.

Nothing can replace face-to-face or voice-to-voice contact, though. You can't type as quickly as you can talk. I don't care how fast you can text, it's not as fast as talking. You also miss the nuances in vocal communication of voice inflection, pace, and tonality. Communication via electronic mediums has a much higher chance of error. I'm not talking about missing messages due to technology issues; I'm referring to the incorrect interpretation of the sent message. You have wasted time when you have to resend, clarify, or change the message.

You can waste time scrolling through your Facebook news feeds because you follow too many people and we want to read all their posts.

To help achieve the right balance in your Facebook use, set specific times of day to check your account. For example, check it first thing in the morning to catch up on overnight happenings. Focus on a 15-minute limit and stick to it. Then midday, take another 15-20 minutes to catch up, respond, and post a few things. This helps you stay connected and have some fun but doesn't waste time. Don't go over the time of the standard you set. In the evening, set a 30-minute use standard so you ensure family time away from the cyber world of business and friends.

Put a limit on social media

We recently had an evening at a friend's home with a large cadre of Wesley's school friends. As the parents were having conversations I observed the 13-year-olds sitting on the couches, glued to their phones. After a few minutes I asked Wesley what they were doing. He said they were texting each other, texting other friends that were not there, and posting pictures and comments on social media. In watching them for 15 minutes not one of them had uttered a word, and they were all in the same room within 8 feet of each other! I view that as a time waster and relationship building missed opportunity. If you want to enhance your quality of life and save time, limit social media time. Set specific time limits and boundaries for its use.

This event made me realize that time spent texting and on Facebook and other social media sites needs to be limited. In our home, there are no cell phones at the dinner table. That's where families have traditionally engaged in communication and togetherness, learning, and encouraging each other. When we are out to dinner we often do a quick picture, tag it, and post it if the occasion is memorable. Then the cell phones go in a pile in the middle of the table.

Which to use personally and professionally

Facebook is the most used social-media tool in the world. Using Facebook in business is a great way to build relationships and stay at the forefront of the technological world. If you have an entrepreneurial business or service business like a real estate agent, insurance agent, or financial planner, creating both a business Facebook page and a personal page is advisable. If you use both your personal and business relationships to conduct business, the line between the two can become muddled. I personally believe you need to establish both types of uses for Facebook.

Establishing a personal profile enables you to post your personal history — your likes and dislikes, photos, stories, and so on. This is the most common experience on Facebook, which now has more than a billion personal profiles. This type of profile is a one-person profile that highlights your interests and connections with others.

From a business perspective, Facebook enables you to brand your product or service. (Just a hint . . . the product or service is still *you* until you grow a larger market presence and leverage yourself through your business.) Facebook gives you numerous free methods to interact with prospects, clients, and people you know. This allows your company to connect and encourage people to like the page so they receive valuable information and updates.

Using your personal page to create business

On your personal Facebook page, you need to achieve a balance between communicating your business interests and sharing personal updates. Your personal profile should be mainly personal with a sprinkling of business information.

Your photo is one of the most important first decisions. Facebook is a casual and informal media. Your profile and cover photos should reflect that. You don't need the glamour shot, professional head shot, or air-brushed shot; in fact, it's probably better not to use those. This is your personal page, but you'll get crossover from personal contacts with whom you do business, so it's important to choose a photo that represents who you are in a casual setting, but that isn't too hobby-driven or inappropriate. Remember that your profile photo will appear in most posts, communications, and connections. Choose one that shows you as both the warm, personal person next door and the professional. The mistake I see too frequently is a picture that makes one appear unapproachable.

When you change your personal photo, it updates that photo on all the previous posts and creates a post that says you have changed your photo. By updating your photo you can express yourself and stay in front of clients and customers. You also get engagement as people comment on your new profile. This helps you stay on the minds of your clients.

Walk the fine line with business on your personal page

Too many people cross the personal/professional line. They post every new business accomplishment or offer on their personal timeline. Most of your friends don't want an overload of business invading their newsfeed. The rule of thumb is four to five personal posts for every business post you make. Err on the side of caution. If you think you may have overdone the business posts this week, you probably have.

Watch for life changes

One of the best ways to use Facebook is not posting but listening. Just review your friends' posts to see what's happening and changing in their lives. The coolest part of Facebook is how quickly you can pick up on clues and cues of change.

Before Facebook, we often heard about job transfers, marriages, pregnancies, empty-nest situations, and many other life-changing events months after they happened. With Facebook, you can be front and center when life events happen to congratulate or commiserate with your friends, clients, and past clients.

The right message or comment can lead to a wealth of new business. If you're in real estate, telling someone how happy you are about the announcement of a new child can lead them to mention that their home is now getting cramped. As their insurance agent they might feel the need to add or up their life insurance policy. You generally won't have to say too much, because your warm greeting will jog their memory about their needs. You can also private message the person if you don't want to publicly seem like you're pouncing on a lead opportunity.

Leveraging your Facebook business pages

A Facebook business page should be part of your overall online marketing strategy. Most businesses try many different strategies for Facebook business pages. Some businesses have one business page where they drive much of their online interaction. Others segment their business pages to align with different aspects of their business. Starting out, this is probably more complex than you need to get.

The keys to a powerful Facebook business page are:

- ✔ **Frequently update the content of your pages.** The more you update and refresh the information, the more your likes on your page will grow and the more people will come back to see what's new. People that have liked your page will get notified that you have made a post. By posting regularly you keep your face and message in front of your prospects, clients, sphere of influence, and past clients.

- ✔ **Create posts that lead to interaction.** Using questions to foster interaction is a way to create interactivity. When you create engaging content that gets people talking, reposting, and sharing, you know you've been successful in expanding your reach.

Posting on your business page

You should post quality content to entice new *likes* and retain the current group of followers. Before you get all fired up to promote your page to the world, gather or create good content. No one wants to like a page that has limited information and value. You don't need a truckload of posts, but you need some value that can be seen and digested. Perhaps you want to ask a few close friends and family to take a quick peek before you promote the page.

The more powerful the content, the more it will be shared. Sharing is one of the most useful aspects of Facebook. It explodes your reach exponentially.

If you're a real estate agent you should post market data to update your followers on that state of the marketplace. If you own an HVAC company, post tips on saving energy and when to change furnace air filters.

Practice consistency

A key to posting is consistency and frequency. You need to post at least five times a week. When you post, use photos, videos, or links on a handful of those posts and you will see growth. You can't set the standard for yourself that every post is earth-shatteringly brilliant. The truth is that not every post will create the attention you want. Your job is to build a voice and build a habit. When it comes down to it, success comes to people who are consistent more than it comes to the brilliant.

Find the right mix

The right mix in your posts fosters community and connection. The focus of 40 percent of your posts should be to engage others in conversation and communication. Use 20 percent of your posts to link to other content that positions you as well informed and that has value to your followers. Another 20 percent can be general business or economic news that influences the world or region you live in. The final 20 percent could be motivational or inspirational messages or sayings.

Keeping Contacts with Facebook

Facebook can be a real timesaver when communicating with people. It also creates an opportunity to learn more about your friends, customers, and clients. Businesses can save a lot of time by knowing their customers' wants, needs, and problems. It enables a business to bring out the right product or service to the customers and potential customers. Facebook provides a conduit for listening.

There are no absolutes with Facebook so you have to find your own style of posting pictures, videos, and text. Many social media and Facebook experts agree that authentic or in "your voice" posts garner the most attention and response.

To friend or not to friend . . . that is the question

Who do you want to *friend* on Facebook? That actually is not a simple question, especially if you have both a business and personal page. Are you only going to allow people you really know to be your Facebook friend? Are you going to friend someone who is an acquaintance? How about that high-school bully from years go who tormented you? What if you friend someone to later find out their posts are not what you want to see? Are you casting a wide personal friend net to transfer them to a business relationship? And then there are the political and religious posts, which are beyond the scope of this book. To learn how to navigate around controversial topics, check out *Facebook For Dummies* by Carolyn Abrahm (Wiley).

Posting from public to private

You can post to public, which means anyone within Facebook, whether you are Facebook friends or not, can view your posts. You have the option to post to a single individual, to a group (a list of people of your choice that you create), or to everyone you're friends with in your Facebook account. I share with you the use and power of the list feature later in the chapter.

Keeping people up to date with both your personal life and business can be a chore. Here are a couple of tips on how to keep up with posting and create variety for you and your friends.

✔ **Share what's up.** Don't be afraid to share about your family and what's happening. This makes you approachable and shows that you're just like your friends, clients, and prospects. As your stature in business grows, it's even more important to remain approachable. Share your likes and dislikes with your friends. If you ask questions that create interaction, you can improve your position in the newsfeed of others who answer and comment. Post about places you're going, and share pictures of your experiences, both professional and personal.

Giving out too much information about vacations and business trips can be tricky. Be smart about not giving away too much detail and having your home or office broken into.

✔ **But don't share everything.** Be careful to not post controversial political views, especially during election season. Many people can become highly charged and sensitive at this time. Be careful with religious and societal views as well. Any photo of you that doesn't align with your professional image would also be a no-no. Avoid the revealing bathing suits, the giant margarita, or the less-than-flattering hangover picture.

Use the check-in feature when you visit stores, restaurants, and travel destinations. Check-ins can create conversations or spur memories from others that will open dialogue between you and friends. The more interesting you seem in your check-ins and experiences, the wider the net you cast for posts from others.

✔ **Share your photos.** Most people prefer to see visuals rather than read text. Your photos can reflect personal shots or community involvement. Don't be shy about showing that photo of you at work on a Habitat for Humanity home, or walking dogs at a local animal shelter. Photos of local places and events create an image of you as "the man (or woman) about town."

✔ **Share interesting articles or links.** The key is sharing links that your network of friends and colleagues will find interesting. It can be notices about local events and issues, or it can be business information from *The Wall Street Journal, USA Today,* or other respected sources. This demonstrates that you're well read, educated, and on top of the business trends.

✔ **Acknowledge others.** If you've received great service, or if someone in your network has achieved success by winning an award, opening a business, and so on, acknowledge that. You're spreading the wealth of who you know to aid others in achieving their dreams.

Getting people to share your posts

In the personal and business setting, Facebook offers some time-saving advantages to communication and business through sharing. When you can get someone to share your posts, it can spread your reach to a new group of "friends" you do not know. Create posts that your friends want to share. By doing so, you get your name and business out of your circle of friends and into the general Facebook community. By writing humorous quips, posting unique pictures, and sharing timely links, you create content that others want to share — and even more want to see. Using video and photos makes the sharing go through the roof.

If you use a photo, select an interesting shot that catches the audience's attention. And along with that compelling picture, create a great headline. Many people only read the opening headline, but if it's provocative and engaging you can get them to share.

Create anecdotal stories that align with what's happening in your business or business niche. Also, think about posting general marketplace updates, funny stories, announcements of big sales, and pictures of hot new opportunities.

When all else fails, ask. The adage "ask and you shall receive" is still in play. Asking your friends to "help me out," "share if you would like to," or "feel free to share with your friends" can increase your shares, as well.

Using the list feature to manage interaction

One of the least used but most important features of Facebook is the list feature. You can create lists of people that categorize them so it's easier to listen and watch. Use the smart list suggestions in Facebook to separate some of your lists. These smart lists break your contact list down by city or high school, for example. These are helpful, but setting up your own lists is even better.

Set up specific watch lists around the type of people or business prospects you want. You can set up any type of list you want. I have lists of people who are CEOs of companies, high school friends, college friends — I even have a list for my best prospects so I can keep in front of them. Put in people who are high-level prospects with whom you interact and who have shown an interest in your services.

Watch lists make it easier for you to monitor these peoples' posts. They still remain in your newsfeed, but they also appear in the list area on the left-hand side of your Facebook page. All you have to do is click the specific watch list, and the recent posts of all the people on that list are organized on your screen. It creates a smaller more organized set of posts of people to review each day. This list approach saves you lots of time instead of scrolling through your whole newsfeed to see what a group of people you deem viable prospects posted today.

It's easy to create different lists. If you go to your newsfeed and select Friends from the left side, you can select Create List. You see a pop-up menu that requires you to name the list; then you can select the friends you want to be part of the list.

You can send posts directly to these lists as well, rather than to all your friends. For example, you can create a post targeted to the people on your list that could buy your product or service in 60 days or less. Maybe you read a great newspaper article about rising interest rates and why people should buy now. You can post the article but target it to your group. You're sending information of value to the group that is most likely to use it.

Keeping up with family

The group feature is wonderful for families. If your family is spread apart by many miles, you can easily share information, posts, pictures, and even files with each other by creating a group. If you have a family Christmas party, you can inform, invite, and create an event just for that group. You can easily receive RSVPs, assign potluck dishes, give directions, and more, all from the comfort of your Facebook group page.

Communicating through groups

Facebook helps with time efficiency through the creation of groups. Businesses use the Groups feature to create communities with their customers and clients. Their group communities create interactivity and share best practices as well as gather new ideas for products and services. When creating a group, you can invite specific people to join, or you can simply add names to your group. When someone wants to join, you have the option to accept or reject their request.

Facebook offers three types of groups: secret, closed, and open. The open group allows anyone who has a Facebook account to see who and what is being said in the group. If people can find your group through the search function, they can see all the members and posts; however, they aren't able to post until they join the group.

The closed group has become common is business circles. They allow members only to see what's posted and post their own content, past threads, and files. Note that anyone outside of the group can see who's in it. An effective business strategy is to review your key competitors' closed Facebook groups. That enables you, in essence, to see their customer list. It's a mistake many businesses make with a closed group.

A secret group does not allow anyone not invited to the group to see anything. The membership of the group is secret as well as the posts, threads, and files. If you want to set up a Facebook group, in most cases I would recommend a secret group.

Chapter 12

Twitter: Time Saver or Time Waster

. . . .

In This Chapter

▶ Following your friends, family, and others

▶ Preventing Twitter from taking over your cell phone . . . and your life

. . . .

Twitter has had an explosive impact on how we communicate with others. The number of active monthly users of Twitter is just short of 300 million. Twitter users don't send messages, they send tweets. A tweet is an expression you have in a moment. It can be an idea or thought. You can include text, photos, or videos in your tweets. You are limited to 140 characters so brevity is essential.

There are over 500 million tweets a day shared on Twitter. They are shared in real time so communication is instantaneous. The most famous tweet was the photo of Ellen DeGeneres and friends at the Oscars. It had over 2 million "favorites" and more than 3.5 million retweets. A retweet is when someone shares someone else's tweet with their followers. A favorite is when someone wants to acknowledge your tweet. It would be similar to a "like" on Facebook. Anyone can gain a following on Twitter that enables you to communicate short messages to a larger group of people than just your grandmother. Just as with Facebook's Like button, tweets collect favorites from your followers and people who see the retweet. You can also include hashtags (#) so Twitter can better categorize or assign a topic to your tweet. This allows an ever-widening audience to see your musings.

Deciding Who to Follow

If you decide to use Twitter, you need to decide who to follow. Celebrities generally have the largest number of followers — singer Katy Perry has the most followers with more than 61 million people reading her tweets. But

Twitter isn't all about the rich and famous. Although few of us would ever develop that level of devotion to our 140-character communication, just about anyone can have a Twitter account.

Twitter and time management can be mutually exclusive, though. The challenge is paring down the number of people you follow; you could be reviewing an endless stream of tweets all day and night and never get anything done. The overwhelming interruptions could dramatically reduce your ability to stay focused and productive. Limit yourself to a small group of select people at specific times (see "Preventing a Twitter Takeover" later in this chapter). If you are following 50 to 100 celebrities, you could be reviewing more than 100 tweets a day on top of your business contacts and friends and family. Because each interruption shifts your focus from what you are working on, by the time you refocus, several minutes have passed, and the lost productivity is exponential. When making the decision who to follow, consider sticking with four categories of people you want in your life.

It's easy to waste time both online as well as offline. Spending too much time communicating online can reduce productivity and mess up your time management abilities. Social interaction through social media can be productive and fun. The skill and strategy of setting up effective social media boundaries of the type of people you invest your time with online and offline can dramatically influence your utilization of time and success in life. People do influence how you feel, act, and what you believe. That's why monitoring your four categories of people and applying them to social media benefits you.

Because your mood, feelings, and interactions with others play a role in success, your career can hinge on those who you let influence your thoughts and actions. That's true, whether you're an executive, administrator, salesperson, or entrepreneur. There's Twitter trash that can invade your mental space . . . and you must avoid it. If someone you are following on Twitter is dumping negative tweets . . . next.

Keep your mindset positive and directed toward success and achieving your objectives. Henry Ford said, "If you think you can or you think you can't, either way, you're right." Ford knew that your belief and mindset will help produce the results that you desire. Staying positive, every day, is one of the hardest parts for most people. That is why limiting access to people who don't help in that effort, be it online or offline, is paramount.

I adopted a rule when I started my professional career that I still use today, especially in social media realms: Hang out only with people you can learn from, profit with, have fun with, or people you can teach. Those four types of people help you construct an abundant life. The complainers and lemon-suckers will only pull you down to their level. There is an age-old question: How do you keep a crab from climbing out of a bucket? Answer: You just put in another crab; when one tries to crawl out, the other will pull him back down. Some people are like that even in their tweets.

Those from which you can learn

Follow people who have something to teach you. If you have a career field, select people you respect, maybe who are more successful than your. Key questions to consider include:

- Are they more successful than I am?
- Have they achieved what I want from my life?
- Are they innovative in their thinking?
- Are they highly educated in school-smarts or street-smarts?
- Do they represent a system in action or thought that I might learn and follow?

People I follow include Brian Tracy, Seth Godin, Rick Warren, Bill Gates, and John Maxwell, to name a few.

Those with which you can have fun

This is probably the largest category of people you might follow on Twitter. Although celebrities and athletes can be part of your "fun" list, you can also include personal friends who are fun, engaging, and have quirky observations in life. Everyone needs people around them who have quick wits and are able to share it online. Some people know how to find the coolest pictures and put the right captions on them to create big belly laughs. There are others who find videos to share or create funny videos. I've got lots of personal friends who are really fun, but I think one of the funniest guys on Twitter is Jimmy Fallon.

Those with whom you can profit

Selecting people in this category can be difficult. Who could you partner with, do deals with, or create new products and services with? There can be crossover between your learn-from and profit-with lists, but you may have never met some of these folks. For example, I learn a great deal from Seth Godin; he's an innovative thinker and observer of marketing and business. And although I don't know Mr. Godin personally, he has helped me make a lot of money using his ideas in my business to increase sales and marketing.

The greatest gift

I recently had a call with one of my clients. He talked about how his life had changed and how he had increased his sales more than 1,000 percent since we started together. He went into detail about the challenges and objectives and how he overcame them. Then he went on to describe in detail the three buyers who purchased from him in the last week. After 30 minutes or so, he stopped and realized he had been talking the entire time about how much he had accomplished and how his life had turned around. He was embarrassed to have spent so much time describing the excitement that was going on in his life and had failed to ask how I was doing. He began to apologize for being insensitive. I told him not to be concerned, that I received more enjoyment hearing about how he has reaped the fruits of our work together than from anything else.

There is no greater gift in life than the ability to teach and change someone's life for good. There is no greater honor than to share in the transformation of someone's life. I truly receive no greater joy in life than hearing these stories. That is true if those stories are in person or online.

Those you can teach

When you choose to learn from someone you follow, he or she has to be willing to teach. Teaching is the greatest joy in my life (maybe yours, too) because I love to watch people grow and prosper. When you become someone who teaches, you'll find that it dramatically improves your skill level in that particular subject. I know more about sales and success from teaching and coaching for the last 15 years than I learned in my entire sales career. There also is a great joy in the teaching process. Become successful in any field and you will be able to share in that joy. As you grow and advance your objective should be to get skilled enough in what you do so you can share it with someone. I certainly feel blessed for the honor of being able to teach and positively impact people's lives.

Preventing a Twitter Takeover

Twitter has an app that can be downloaded to any cell phone with an Android or Apple operating system and can make sending and receiving tweets more efficient. At the same time, however, it makes Twitter accessible 24/7/365. You can create your own settings and preferences so that your phone isn't constantly blowing up with Twitter tweets.

When using Twitter, you must invest the time to determine which mentions, replies, interactive notifications, followers, favorites, updates, or even specific people are important to you. Sign into your Twitter account, go to Settings, and then select your mobile tab. From there, you can select your options for text notification. My rule is, when in doubt leave the notifications off. For more information about Twitter and how to control your settings and preferences, check out *Twitter For Dummies* by Laura Fitton, Anum Hussain, and Brittany Leaning (Wiley).

After you set your notifications and preferences, you can also set restrictions for yourself! Limit yourself to specific times and duration when checking your Twitter account. Consider allowing yourself a guilty Twitter pleasure only after you're ready for work; or reward yourself an hour before going to bed.

Chapter 13

Creating Effective LinkedIn Strategies

In This Chapter

▶ Attracting quality connections and recommendations

▶ Networking on your schedule

*L*inkedIn is a business-oriented social network, used mainly for professional networking. It's supported by nearly 260 million users in over 200 countries. LinkedIn enables users (workers and employers both) to create profiles and connections with each other. It can save you a lot of time with interacting, following, and learning from others in your organization or even experts in your field.

More efficient than your old Rolodex, LinkedIn keeps you in touch with those who support your career or who can help you advance it. If you find yourself out of work, it can be a huge timesaver. You can use this organized network to help you leverage your connections, relationships, and business friends to land on your feet. This chapter takes a look at effective LinkedIn profiles as well as how you can best use your time on LinkedIn.

Creating a Link-able Profile

Your profile on LinkedIn is the key to being seen, found, and connected to. And with LinkedIn, the larger the group of contacts you have, the more associations you can generate. Your connections and network strategy should be focused on quality and quantity. To attract a lot (quantity) of pertinent and reputable people (quality), you have to have a compelling profile.

When people search for you in LinkedIn, your well-constructed profile increases the chance they will find you and want to contact you. Your profile communicates key information about you, although it's not a resume or an autobiography. A well-constructed profile conveys your value. It clearly articulates the brand of "You Inc." Your profile should contain your education, experience, key skills, past positions, and interests.

Creating a personal profile

Your profile highlights your experiences and accomplishments. As part of this, you can attach files, videos, presentations, and anything that presents you in a favorable light. Be creative in this section. You want someone to gain a clear perspective of you and the benefits in hiring or associating with you.

Start building your profile by entering your name, profession, and other pertinent information. You can add your city, state, education, even a picture (I talk about that a little later on in this chapter). After you click Create My Profile, you can start getting to the meat of your story.

Sharing your experience

The Experience section of LinkedIn gives you several ways to showcase your work involvement. Too many people view this area as a resume format, but the truth is that you can go into more depth on LinkedIn as opposed to your resume. The conciseness and bullet points of a resume need not apply; however, there must be alignment with your resume so your job titles, work history, dates, companies, and so on are all consistent. Frequently an employer will compare your resume and your LinkedIn profile. This more thorough approach also has search engine optimization (SEO) benefits as well, meaning that an employer uses key words to search out people with your types of experiences. The search engine benefits won't exist if you have not inputted the information for it to find. Use all possible variations of search terms. How many ways can you describe being a manager?

Note that an employer may also use LinkedIn to review your connections as well as do background checks and reconnaissance on you.

When listing company names or school names, use every possible option from full name to abbreviation. I went to Willamette University, so I like the full name along with WU. List both the full names as well as commonly referred names of any company you've worked for or with. If United Airlines was a previous employer, like it was for my wife, Joan, it would be advantageous to use UAL, the common abbreviation. You might even include the stock market lettering as an abbreviation as well.

Your skills need to be clearly and concisely presented. As already mentioned, many potential employers use LinkedIn to search for people with specific skills. Again, this is the case where clarity and specificity create an advantage.

Along with information about you, LinkedIn provides a way for business contacts and friends to "endorse" your work and skills. (Note that you can do the same for your friends and colleagues.) Your connections can validate your professional skills and accomplishments, which always looks good to an employer. If you state on LinkedIn that you can tame wild tigers, and 15 people give you endorsements, you just may be the tiger tamer that Tigers Unlimited is looking for! So encourage co-workers and colleagues to endorse your skills, and always do the same for them.

Picturing yourself on LinkedIn

Your picture is one of the first things your colleagues and potential employ- ers see in your profile, so select a shot that reflects your professionalism. Leave the family photos, your pets, and exotic locations on Facebook; LinkedIn is for business. The type of head shot and smile you feature can lead to a higher level of credibility and trust. Choose a picture that shows a well-groomed and happy individual with tons of experience and potential . . . someone who would be an asset to any company or for any assignment.

Defining LinkedIn Goals, Objectives, and Connections

To be efficient with your time in any area, you must have clearly defined goals and objectives. The same is true for a LinkedIn account. Are you trying to increase your stature and credibility in your chosen field? Is your objec- tive to protect from long-term unemployment? (More than 80 percent of com- panies use LinkedIn as one of the resources for recruiting.) Do you want to use LinkedIn to gain involvement in a specific community? Start by defining you goals, objectives, and what you want from LinkedIn.

Are you looking for a fun way to connect with others professionally? LinkedIn is primarily a business network, so it might fall short of that objective. Another business service organization like Rotary might be better suited for that need.

With the connections you build, more is better. You never know when making a new connection will pay off in new business, new ideas, or a better job opportunity. The goal should be a high-quality connection with diversity. You want connections, not only in your field but in complementary fields as well. If you're in pharmaceutical sales, any doctor in your local community or territory would be a worthwhile LinkedIn connection, as well as anyone in parallel industries — for example, medical devices, imaging equipment, even medical software. Certainly anyone that is in pharmaceutical sales management would also be a valid connection. Don't limit your connections just to the medical field. There are literally hundreds of sales job similar to pharmaceutical sales in the broader sales market.

Use the tools on LinkedIn to expand your connections. The first and easiest is to use your contacts in your email accounts, whether in Outlook, Gmail, or most others. By using people who are already in your database, you can increase your number of connections rapidly. Using your school affiliation is another excellent resource to create connections.

Establishing Your LinkedIn Schedule

When using any social or business network, having a system that you use to track your time is essential. Even with all the positive opportunities LinkedIn provides, it's like other social media platforms — it's one tool in your business strategy tool belt. Creating a schedule can mean the difference between spending hours a day surfing LinkedIn — which could lead to you needing a new job — and not checking your profile for months.

New articles, studies, and information are posted frequently on LinkedIn. This can be a deep resource in your field, the field you would like to enter, or just general knowledge of business and success. Establish a schedule of reading at least one quality article or information piece on LinkedIn each day, which creates an opportunity to visit the site on a daily basis and check your connections. Even 10 minutes a day repeated consistently over time can add thousands of connections to your network in a short period of time.

And don't be shy about posting articles yourself! If you're respected in your field, or simply have new and creative ideas you'd like to share, write an article and post it for all on LinkedIn to read. This is another way of finding new connections.

Being prompt in accepting invites to be added to someone's network shows courtesy as well as an indication you take your profile seriously.

The two-check system

Institute a two-check system for checking your social media, LinkedIn included. If you institute the two-check system, you stay on top of your LinkedIn network without losing productivity in other areas. The two-check is as it sounds; check twice a day. Not at random times, but at the same time each day. I suggest you do the two checks in your time schedule that has lower value. For example, I'm at my best in the morning, so I usually delay time of my social media checks until later in the day when my brain is not as sharp. This gives me the maximum use of the direct income-producing activity time.

Meeting weekly to check for success

Investing 30 minutes a week to review and check your strategy and results on LinkedIn is important. By having a success meeting each week you can plan what to share with some of your groups, what to write, what to report, and what to do to increase your reach in building connections. Learning how to join groups and post articles in beyond this chapter, but you can learn more about LinkedIn from *LinkedIn For Dummies* by Joel Elad (Wiley).

You can also see who has viewed your profile in the last week. Are these people who are potential additions to your network? Send them a request to join your LinkedIn network. Are they possibly representatives from companies or recruiters looking for a quality employee? A large number of corporate recruiters and executive headhunters use LinkedIn to find qualified people.

Part IV
Confronting Challenges to Time Management

Five ways to manage work interruptions

1. Be realistic. Interruptions at work are going to happen, so build a handful of minutes into your schedule each day for them. Never schedule your time so tightly that you can't handle the unexpected.

2. When interruptions occur, try to keep them as short as possible. You can always ask your coworkers or clients to send you an email or schedule a time for a phone call.

3. Prioritize your daily to-do list; after the interruption, train yourself to go back to where you left off.

4. Put a note on your door or on an outside wall of your cubicle that you're in the middle of a project and can't be interrupted.

5. Minimize your own distractions — turn off your email notifications; set up a timely outgoing voicemail notice and don't respond every time the phone rings; disconnect from the Internet if social media sites are too tempting; turn off the ringer on your phone so you don't hear text messages coming in.

Find out how to shut out the noisy and stressful world around you, as well as how to dismiss disruptive thoughts at www.dummies.com/extras/successfultimemanagement

In this part . . .

✔ Learn how to handle unexpected time management obstacles; reduce stress and increase productivity.

✔ Realize that procrastinating and overscheduling are time vampires that are hard to eliminate, but can be tackled with determination.

✔ Discover how to communicate effectively and enhance your productivity.

✔ Learn the secrets to warding off interruptions, whether they come from the phone, email, text, social media, co-workers, family, clients, or bosses.

✔ Keep meetings with coworkers short and sweet and save everyone a little time in the process.

Chapter 14

Communicating Strategically to Get Results — Fast

*W*hen communication goes awry, the impact is often subtle, though no less time-consuming and expensive. For instance, in a recent survey by a temporary agency, employees estimated that 14 percent of their work week was wasted by poor communication. That's more than 5.5 hours per week — and more than 290 hours per year! Studies also show that managers spend 80 percent of their time communicating, and that 80 percent of work mistakes are due to miscommunication.

Communication is as important today than it ever has been. And we have so many different ways to contact and communicate with each other — from text messages and email; to social media and group chats; to online meeting options such as Skype, GoToMeeting, and more. The ways we can reach out and touch someone seem endless today.

Everyone makes real efforts to get messages across to family, friends, colleagues, business associates, and supervisors. But as these figures illustrate, many of those messages fail because they're unclear, inaccurate, or too long. And for every message that doesn't succeed, you waste time: repeating, redoing, reworking, and reorganizing. In this chapter, you discover how to head off those problems by choosing your medium and using it effectively, keeping your message direct, and asking the right questions.

Choosing the Right Medium for Your Message

Whether you realize it or not, you communicate in three main ways: words, tone of voice, and body language. When you communicate with someone face to face, you can employ all three forms of communication, dramatically increasing your effectiveness and speeding your way to the desired outcome. Skype and video conferencing services allow you to use all three mediums. When you communicate over the phone, you use only two — tonality and words — and when you communicate via email, text, social media, or instant message, you're down to only your words. So despite the speed and efficiency of email or text, sometimes a face-to-face meeting, electronic conference, or a phone call is the best way to address and resolve a situation.

How you decide which medium is most appropriate for the information or for your topic of discussion depends largely on the complexity of the information you're sharing as well as on the nature of the topic of discussion. When you have to communicate by email or text or telephone rather than in person, you need to make these channels work for you as much as possible.

Communicating face to face

As companies expand, merge, spin off, morph, and spread their influence throughout the world, an increase in meetings seems to be one of the side effects. And you can't outrun meetings simply by getting transferred to a remote office. Advancements in audio and video conferencing make even telecommuters vulnerable to meeting overload.

The purpose of a good strategic meeting is to communicate goals, identify objectives, seek counsel and advice, share knowledge, solve problems, and gain cooperation from others. Although I concede that sometimes just having face time with a group of co-workers brings value, it's not a good enough reason to hold a meeting. You may be better served to build camaraderie in another way.

A key skill in this new technology age is the ability to run video-based meetings on WebEx, GoToMeeting, or Google Hangouts. The value of being able to plan, organize, and lead collaboration when people are in remote locations will be commonplace in the future economy.

The value of the meeting, whether physically face to face or online face to face, needs to clearly meet or exceed the costs. Identifying the costs can provide a strong motivation to reconsider the *need* for a meeting when so many other communication options are at your disposal. My formula for evaluating the time cost is a bit more complex than simply adding up the hourly salary for all the attendees. I also figure the following:

- ✔ Time invested in preparation for that meeting.
- ✔ Time for the meeting host to design the agenda, goals, and objectives.
- ✔ Time to coordinate and communicate meeting details to all participants.
- ✔ Time required for traveling to the meeting, whether people are coming from across town or across the continent. This is certainly a cost for a physical face-to-face meeting. For online meetings you might have travel as well, but most people can attend online meetings from any location.

After I add up all investment of company resources for even an hour-long meeting, the labor costs alone are often in the thousands of dollars for a typical meeting. So before you call a meeting, make sure that face-to-face communication is absolutely required to do one of the following:

- ✔ Solve the problem
- ✔ Make a decision
- ✔ Share information
- ✔ Plan and facilitate a project
- ✔ Launch action

Apply your *necessary* test to standing meetings as well. Sure, your department holds an update every week: same time, same place. But if you find that week after week, everyone drones off status reports or presents information others already know or can get in some other way, reconsider the value of the weekly commitment. If there isn't a significant reason to hold your meeting this week — or any week — come up with a better, quicker way to communicate.

Countless studies have pointed out the power and effectiveness of face-to-face communication. Face-to-face communication is best for situations where tone of voice and/or body language is crucial in determining how to respond. Here's some of what you can effectively do in a meeting:

- ✔ Present or sell new ideas
- ✔ Deal with emotionally charged concerns
- ✔ Carry out personal or professional evaluations or disciplinary actions

✔ Discuss complex topics that may require explanation or clarification

✔ Handle controversial situations that generate back-and-forth discussion among a group of people

✔ Communicate when there's a chance that meaning may be misconstrued

✔ Discuss sensitive or confidential issues

For instance, if you're in sales and you sell a complex product or service such as MRI machines or consulting services, a phone call can help you book an appointment, but you should make the sale through a series of face-to-face meetings. Or if you're breaking up with your boyfriend of two years, meeting face to face to explain why you're kicking him to the curb is more acceptable in breaking-up etiquette.

If you're hesitant to call a meeting but it fits in one of the preceding categories, consider whether you can keep the meeting small or dovetail it into an existing meeting.

Vocalizing your message over the phone

In my opinion, the telephone remains one of the greatest time-saving communication devices ever created. Certainly, the phone offers advantages over face-to-face encounters because you don't have to drive to get to where the other party wants to meet. You also avoid some of the technology issues with online meetings, such as inexperienced attendees, non-native technology participants, slow Internet speeds, and attention issues such as boredom or multi-tasking. And although many people feel email has overtaken the telephone call, I prefer the phone call because it's more personal, more interactive, and more adaptable. Here's why the telephone is tops:

✔ Calling can bring a discussion to a quicker conclusion. You can get instant feedback and response from a phone call.

✔ The phone reduces chances that the other party will misinterpret your words. You get a chance to correct misunderstandings in real time rather than hours or even days later.

✔ You send a more personal sense of warmth and caring; and you get to use your tone, volume, and selected words to convey meaning via your voice. Email, text, or instant message, on the other hand, allow readers to filter the communication through their current attitudes toward business, life, and you — without your input.

Should the person you're trying to reach not answer the phone, leave a voice message — don't hang up and try a different means of communication. Voice mail offers myriad advantages that email, text messages, and messages taken by other people don't:

✔ With voice mail, your message will be delivered verbatim. And because you're not leaving the message with a person, an overzealous assistant won't screen it out.

✔ Because you can speak faster than you can type (or even text), voice mail is faster than email.

✔ Your message won't get zapped by the spam filter or mixed with the hundreds of other email messages your addressee receives daily.

Numerous studies show those in the millennium generation prefer text communication. You might text a short version of your message, and ask them to either review the voice mail message or call you back.

See the "Corresponding Clearly and Confidently via Telephone" section later in this chapter for tips on leaving effective voice messages. And if you're in sales, be sure to read my book, *Telephone Sales For Dummies* (Wiley), for valuable advice on increasing your phone sales results.

Putting messages in writing: The joys (and perils) of email, text, and instant messages

As with all seismic tech changes, email has its infinite blessings — and its bitter curses. Email can help you get more work done, but it can also distract you from working. Younger readers may have only heard about the days when business correspondence was conducted through the mail. But those old enough to remember a time before computers and voice mail recall that the only way to get an immediate response from a colleague meant a phone call — and I'm not talking text-messaging. You had to actually talk to them!

It's hard to imagine a time before email. Sometimes, when I've just firmed up a speaking engagement with a client in Asia after one day of emailing, I can't fathom how I ever got anything accomplished! Even within my own staff, I can shoot off several projects, answer questions from a dozen employees, review a critical proposal from my top manager, send my sales team an updated status report, and forward a couple of resumes to the HR people — all without lifting my fingers from my keyboard.

Indeed, the email explosion has been one of the most significant advances in the world of work in the twenty-first century. The speed with which email communicates and the breadth of its reach, the efficiency in the ability to store, respond, forward, copy, follow up, and conduct business online is beyond momentous.

But for all its advantages, email is often misused in ways that result in inefficiencies, misunderstandings, and added time. Be sure the message is right for email; some subjects are better handled by phone or face-to-face, where you can gauge responses as you're delivering the message and add information through tone of voice and/or body language. Email is ideal for the following:

- In straightforward situations that require a simple, direct response
- When you need a written record of communication
- When the recipient needs to see attached documents, reports, and articles
- When you need to forward information to multiple parties
- When you're unable to reach a person by phone
- When dealing with non-English-speaking people who have heavy accents that diminish understanding
- When the person you need to speak with is long-winded
- When time differences are an issue

I have clients in the Middle East and Asia, which means that while I'm busy working, they're either done with their workday or sound asleep. Email allows me to keep our business deals flowing without getting up really early or staying up late. I send off my queries to them and get their replies the next morning.

Email can be particularly dangerous in situations where your response is strong or emotional. Who hasn't received an email or voice message that riled them up to the point of pounding out a ferocious email response? In most cases, this situation only ends badly. The blessings of email can also be its curse: Its immediacy gives little time to reflect and process. *Never* send an email when you're still angry, whether to your colleague, vendor, boss, or political representative. Give yourself adequate time to completely calm down before shooting off an emotional message.

That said, I'm all for using the process of writing an email to work through anger. The exercise helps you work off some of that emotional energy and serves to clear your head and think through your reaction and response. But where I put a stop to it is in clicking the Send button. Go ahead and write your email response — I suggest you do it offline so you don't inadvertently send — and then park it in your draft folder until you cool down some. If you reread it the next day and still feel justified, go ahead and send. But if you review and blush at your vitriol, you're saved the embarrassment of apologizing for your outburst.

Email: A little less conversation

Research shows that the nonverbal methods of communication are far more important to the message you put out than the words you use. Consider these stats (and check out the following figure for a visual of the communication breakdown):

✔ The words you choose deliver 7 percent of your message.

✔ Your tone of voice delivers 38 percent of your message.

✔ Your body language delivers the remaining 55 percent of your message.

When you communicate via email, text, instant message, social media, or private message, you lose the 38 percent of your communication that's transmitted by your tone of voice during a face-to-face conversation; and you lose an additional 55 percent of your message because your recipient can't see your body language — and you can't see your recipient's. Compared to face-to-face communication,

email shortchanges you of 93 percent of your total communication! The 7 percent that's left is totally dependent on the effectiveness of the words you select.

Whereas many social media platforms have a plethora of emoticons, these fun images don't usually align as well as your ability to convey your own emotions. When you use text, instant message, or other immediate forms of electronic communication, you are down to 7 percent effectiveness in the words you select. The speed of communication is a clear advantage in text and instant message. These clear advantages of responsiveness and instantaneous communication are reasons to use text or instant message. Your communication has higher deliverability than phone or email. People tend to review their texts faster than email or voice mail. The ability to weigh the pros and cons of each method of communication to select the right one for the situation is a skill to develop in the new communication economy.

Basic Communication Skills: Being Direct and Succinct

Your high school English teacher was right when she told you that length and quality aren't necessarily synonymous. Just because someone's lips move and sound emerges doesn't mean communication is taking place. To ensure that your audience fully receives your message, invest time upfront crafting your correspondence. Plan out questions, presentations, and even short conversations.

For impact, build your message with as few words as possible while still getting your meaning across. Keep the message short, sweet, and to the point. This section tells you how.

Cutting out the clutter in your language

Many people are uncomfortable about following a direct approach, so they fluff out their communications with superfluous information or wrap the salient points in a veil of irrelevant niceties. The problem with this fluff is that it extends meetings and phone calls, confuses important issues, and turns a fellow employee's quick stop by your cubicle into a 25-minute tale about how the weather rained out her kids' soccer game last night. You don't have to do away with social pleasantries — in fact, you shouldn't — but remember what you're trying to accomplish and what your time frames are. Gab is only as useful as it is meaningful.

Being direct doesn't mean being curt, cold, or negatively opinionated — it means that you're clear, concise, and professional, and that you convey a constructive and supportive tone, not a confrontational one. The distinction sounds subtle, but it matters greatly when you're aiming for the most time-effective response.

Don't try to impress others with your use of obscure words, phrases, and unnecessary technical jargon — it only blocks communication and wastes time. The result is confusion, hesitation, misunderstandings, and alienation from the receiver. Hearers may become quiet because they don't want to admit they don't know the meaning of the words you're using. Using simple and straightforward language to communicate complex ideas will make you look smarter and more gracious every time.

Including the essential stuff

To maximize your time (and everyone else's), shoot for a succinct message but don't sacrifice crucial information in the interest of brevity. Ask yourself these questions as you craft your message: Who are you giving information to? What is important for this person to know? Then answer those questions — and don't be afraid to ask others whether you've missed anything. When you communicate directly, you let people know

- ✔ What situation you're facing
- ✔ What you want or need
- ✔ What you expect the receiver to do and what the standards of measurement are
- ✔ What the time line is

Just saying no

One of the most crucial parts of being direct (and managing your time well) is saying *no* when you need to (and when doing so is appropriate). If you're swamped at work, for example, and someone asks you to volunteer to decorate the office for the holidays or to serve on the Thanksgiving celebration committee, the best response you can give is, "I'd really like to help, but maybe next year. I'm seriously under the gun right now to finish Project X. But please ask me again next year."

If a simple *no* would put you in bad favor, such as when your supervisor asks you to take a side project that you don't have time for, ask your supervisor for help in reprioritizing your work so you can make the deadline instead of responding with a flat, "No way. I have too much to do." That way, your boss sees your commitment to getting the job done, but she also knows that you're realistic with your time commitments and value your own well-being enough to set some boundaries.

Notice how the following statements improve by adding this specific information:

- ✔ *"As a company, it looks like we need to do a little better."* (Compare: *"Our goal is to improve corporate results by 6 percent by the end of the third quarter."*)

- ✔ *"You all know what you have to do, so go out and do it!"* (Compare: *"Let's work together to cut travel expenses in each of our areas by 2 percent by year-end."*)

- ✔ *"There's a lot to be said for making our goal."* (Compare: *"We outdid ourselves this year. We exceeded our goal by 7 percent! Let's see if we can exceed our goal by 9 percent by next year. If we do, you'll all earn a 3 percent bonus!"*) (Now, *that's* communicating!)

Fostering Camaraderie When Meeting in Person

Almost all business situations — whether one-on-one conversations or group meetings — benefit from a beginning that's dedicated to creating or strengthening relationships. That's simply good business. Teamwork is what makes the business world go 'round, and good teamwork is built on positive interactions with colleagues, clients, and co-workers.

Use a little small talk to get people comfortable with each other and prime them for conversation. Some safe starters for any meeting or conversation include the following phrases:

✔ *"How was your trip?"*

✔ *"Did you have any trouble finding our offices?"*

✔ *"Is it still raining (snowing, sleeting, hailing, hot, cold) out there?"* (I know — everyone always talks about the weather, but that's because the weather always provides a safe opening gambit!)

I advise only a few minutes of conversation starters.

Use small talk only with people who have some sort of relationship with you — a current customer, client, employee, or friend. Don't ever use it with someone new. If you use these conversation starters with new sales prospects, for example, all they can think of may be "salesperson and what is he selling?" Not exactly the opening that you want to project!

During your conversation, read others and take your cue from their behavior. For example, avoid pursuing personal information if the other person is obviously uncomfortable. It's okay to let people be themselves — after all, you're working for positive relationships, which means different things to different people.

Be sure that your body language is inviting and open. Smiling can warm up the communication with the other person.

Corresponding Clearly and Confidently via Telephone

Obviously, body language isn't front and center when your conversation is via telephone, but you do need to keep in mind how your body language affects your tone of voice and ability to focus and convey a sense of energy. Here are some options that can help you project your body language into the telephone conversation:

✔ **Use a headset.** A phone headset offers a number of advantages:

• It reduces fatigue because you aren't holding a phone to your ear.

• It allows you to stand and move your body while you communicate.

• It leaves you free to take notes and record important information that you can review later.

✔ *Warning:* Do *not* get the cheapest headset you can find. Inexpensive headsets usually have such poor sound quality that the person on the other end can't hear you clearly. This defeats your purpose. Spend what it takes — possibly a few hundred dollars — to get a headset of sufficient quality.

✔ **Smile.** A smile will help your attitude and the delivery of what you're saying.

✔ **Stand up during the conversation.** Standing up helps you to use your body language to reinforce what you're saying. The listener can't see you, but when you're standing, more energy flows through the phone. You have more confidence and conviction, which make their way into your voice. If you really can't stand up, at least sit on the front edge of your chair with your back straight and shoulders back.

If the person you're trying to reach can't or won't take your call, you can get a lot of information from assistants and front-desk people by asking questions — reconnaissance can help you make a sale or get the info you need later on. You may also consider dialing the wrong number — either one higher or lower than the number of the person you're trying to reach; if you reach a person who will internally transfer you, the person you want to reach may be more likely to pick up the phone.

If you get voice mail, don't give up and send an email. If you have the option of using voice mail, take it. It's more effective and possibly less intrusive than an email, text, or out-of-the-blue private message on social media platforms. Leave a message so the listener gains the full effect of hearing your voice. Properly used, voice mail can stand in for a personal visit from you in a lot less time. You can easily come up with a basic voice mail template you can customize, especially when you have enough insider information to tailor it to your recipient. Here are some guidelines for a productive working relationship with voice mail:

✔ Keep your messages to 15 to 30 seconds.

✔ Be prepared. Have a script in hand; if you stumble, mumble, and bumble your message, you're worse off than if you leave no message.

✔ Launch the call by identifying yourself. State your name, company, title, and phone number.

✔ Because of the unreliable reception quality of voice mail, speak with greater clarity. Relay information slowly and carefully.

If a recipient has to replay a message several times to decipher it, he or she probably won't. This is especially true when leaving your telephone number. You must speak it slowly and at least twice. You know your phone number by heart, but the recipient doesn't!

✔ Ramp up your energy level to deliver your message with passion and enthusiasm. (If you sound like a sleep-aid commercial, delete and repeat!)

✔ Smile when you leave voice mail messages. Even if it's the 50th message you've left today, don't let your recipient know it.

✔ Take advantage of voice mail features, such as replay and re-record functions.

Writing Effective Emails

The advent of email has forced everyone to focus on keeping communications brief, if only because so many people dislike writing and typing. That's all good. But as short and straightforward as email messages seem to be, they're also dangerously deceptive and easy to misinterpret. Studies indicate that more than 50 percent of those who use email say their business correspondence is misunderstood.

There's no getting around it: Email often leads to misunderstandings. For instance, a message from your boss may translate as curt or even displeased to you, when in reality he or she was simply rushed. A remark that would pass as playful humor in person can come across as an insult in writing.

In this section, I explain how to write a clear, effective email that minimizes the potential for misinterpretation.

Crafting a clear and targeted subject line

Your Aunt Edna, of course, always opens your emails, with or without a subject line. But a potential customer or business contact is flooded with messages from advertisers and with other highly expendable email. You have between 25 and 35 characters to persuade the recipient to move your correspondence from the B pile (or the *delete* file) to the A pile. Make your email a keeper by tagging it with a standout subject line after you write the body of the email. Pull out a phrase or series of words that sums up the message.

As you decide what to write in the subject line, keep in mind that this line has two purposes:

✔ To tell the recipient the purpose of your email

✔ To pique the receiver's interest enough to command attention from the slew of email he or she is sifting through

In sales and marketing, one tactic I employ is to use a *page-turner* subject line: an unfinished thought that can be completed when the recipient opens the email:

- ✔ "Just one week until . . ."
- ✔ "Our clients have increased sales by 84 percent . . ."
- ✔ "Don't miss this tremendous . . ."

Spam software programs identify some key words and phrases and block any email containing those words in the subject line. Steer clear of the following words and phrases (and their relatives):

- ✔ Incredible
- ✔ Free
- ✔ Limited time only
- ✔ Money
- ✔ A friend gave me your email address

Keeping an eye on composition

The subject line gets readers to open the email, but as with people, wine, and birthday presents, it's what's on the inside that counts. Here are some tips for composing the body of your email.

Looking at structure and length

Emails are most effective when they're short and to the point. If recipients have to scroll, the odds increase that they'll miss some of the information toward the end or feel so overwhelmed that reading your missive is a task they shift to the back burner. That's why many experts suggest that email messages should be about four paragraphs long or less — definitely no longer than a screen full. If you find you have more to say than will fit on the screen, consider these alternatives:

- ✔ Use another mode of communication.
- ✔ Send the message as an attachment, including a paragraph of explanation within the email.

If you know for certain that you must include all information in the body of an email and that you need more than four paragraphs to house it all, remember that the first and last paragraphs carry the most punch. To make effective use of your presentation, follow these rules of thumb:

- ✔ Be sure that the most important information is in the top part of the email.

- ✔ Include a call to action earlier in the email rather than at the end, where it typically goes. The reader may not make it to the last paragraph.

- ✔ When you receive an email that warrants forwarding — or one that you want to copy someone else on — delete the trailing chain of discussion so only the issue at hand remains.

- ✔ Use bullet points rather than narrative to call out the critical points for the reader.

What if you're on the receiving end of a litany of questions in email form? Simple: Hit Reply (with history) and craft a short paragraph that explains that your responses are found below. Then respond right after each individual question — within the original message — in a professional but standout color so the original sender clearly and easily sees your responses. I frequently use red, blue, or black for my color — and if need be, green. This setup helps senders avoid scrolling up and down from their questions to your responses.

Maintaining a professional level of formality

Because of their immediate nature, email tends toward the informal. Between friends and family, dispensing with punctuation, salutations, and even correct spelling may be acceptable. But in the world of business, it's a huge no-no.

Although you may have congenial enough relationships with co-workers and even some clients, my advice is to keep *all* business correspondence formal. These messages reflect on your professionalism and may end up printed out and passed around or forwarded to other businesspeople. Just like dressing for a job interview, it never hurts to keep it formal.

Treat an email the same as you would a paper letter, and follow these tips to maintain your professional appearance:

- ✔ Use conventional salutations and closings: *Dear_____, Hello _____* and *Best regards, Sincerely,* or the like.

- ✔ Don't assume your recipient knows lingo or abbreviations common in text messages and online chats — leave them out. Abbreviations, single letters, and misspelled characters may only confuse recipients to the point they ignore the message.

✔ Steer clear of *emoticons,* those sideways facial expressions created from punctuation keys.

✔ Keep vernacular and slang out of the email.

✔ Don't use all capital letters. In email vernacular, capital letters indicate shouting. True, the recipient doesn't hear you shout, but it's difficult to read long tracts of copy in uppercase.

✔ Always close with your name, as if you were actually signing a letter.

✔ Run spell-check.

Reviewing your writing

Email produces copies of your writing that you usually can't retrieve after you send it into cyberspace, so make sure everything you write is exactly as it should be. To ensure that you don't accidentally overlook any errors or omissions and that you'll get the response you're seeking (if any), follow these bits of advice:

✔ **Allow yourself time to put written communication aside; then come back to it to see it as a first-time reader would.** Email is a lot like a tennis match, with the Reply button serving as the ball. It's a good idea to take that button out of the game and allow a little more reflection. Have you covered everything that needs to be covered? Time spent upfront, honing your communications, can save you more "expensive" time later in the project. As for your own email messages, try putting them in the draft box and coming back to them later. This can help you catch any language that comes off as snippy, short, abrupt, or offensive.

If you're in a rush to get out a lot of correspondence, go ahead and whip through them all at once. But stick them the draft box and return to each with fresh eyes before launching them.

✔ **Have a co-worker — preferably someone not involved with the project — look over your memos and email.** Are there unanswered questions?

✔ **Proofread your email for spelling and grammar errors by using spell-check *and* reading through your email one last time before sending it.** Making typos and grammatical errors is common in email, primarily because the communication is so fast and immediate. Again, in a business environment, you want your correspondence to reflect your high level of professionalism. Although you may not get a pay cut for misspelling a few words, others may note your lack of attention.

Preparing for the send-off

Before you hit that Send button, review your recipients and give your sending options one last review:

- ✔ **Give the urgent-message flag a rest.** Avoid the boy-who-cried-wolf syndrome: When every single message you send is marked *urgent,* well, you know what happens. Don't use the flag unless you need a response in 24 hours or less.

- ✔ **Don't overuse the carbon copy (Cc) function.** If you need to include others, terrific, but keep the list of Cc's only to the people who really need to know. If someone has only peripheral interest in the discussion, leave that person off.

- ✔ **Use the blind carbon copy (Bcc) for large email sends.** The advantage of Bcc is that you're not sharing your list of contacts. With the explosion of spam, everyone needs to protect privacy, and people who have your address have that obligation as well. By using the Bcc feature, no one other than you knows who has received your correspondence.

- ✔ **Mark it *private*.** With most corporate email systems in companies, you're able to send an email privately. If the message is confidential or sensitive, be sure to make it *private* — for the recipient's eyes and your eyes only. Ask the IT department in your company how you can send private email throughout your division or department.

Asking Targeted Questions to Get Results

The key to finding out what you need to know more quickly is asking the right questions. No matter what your job is, good questions direct your communication through the veritable maze of issues, challenges, and distractions that pop up whenever two or more people get together to exchange information and solve problems.

When you pose strategic questions, you guide the conversation to make the most of the time spent. You also gain insight that influences how effectively you can move forward. Don't be afraid to ask as many questions as necessary to completely understand the situation. And don't stop asking until you have a clear picture of what's expected.

Maybe you learned as a child that asking too many questions was impolite or intrusive. Not in business situations! By focusing on other people and keeping them talking, you gather more information — information that can make you more effective. If, for example, you're in sales, ask questions that center around the prospect's DNA[2]: *desire, need, ability,* and *authority*. To shrink decision time, ask more questions. Before you discuss products, services, or solutions, construct a clear image of who this person is and what he or she needs.

Of course, you can't ask questions willy-nilly and expect to get the information you need. You have to ask questions that get results, which I help you do in this section.

Determining what sorts of answers you need

Whether you're in management, administration, sales, service, human resources, or any other facet of business, preparation is essential. Your communication is far more fruitful if you think it through beforehand. To improve your chances of success, envision how you want the conversation to go before you initiate it. What's your ultimate goal? What information do you need to do the best job in the least amount of time? What specific questions must be answered? What are the potential stumbling blocks or choke points?

Amazingly, many people link organization and advance planning to mechanical communication. But *planned* is not *canned*. You expect the pilot who flies your plane from Los Angeles to Sydney, Australia, to be well-prepared before take-off, right? You take it for granted that he or she has checkpoints along the way. Without proper planning, the plane could end up thousands of miles from Sydney because it was a few degrees off at the beginning of the journey. It's just as easy to be off-target in important conversations.

There's a fine line between preparation and creative avoidance, otherwise known as *procrastination*. (See Chapter 16 for more on the topic of procrastination.) Five or ten minutes is typically plenty of time to organize for an important call. If you're spending a half hour to an hour preparing for calls or conversations, chances are you're putting them off rather than preparing for them.

Starting the flow with open-ended questions

The most valuable questions early in any dialogue are open-ended questions, ones that require more than yes-or-no answers. Open-ended questions allow you to gather information, thoughts, ideas, observations, opinions, and comments. You reach agreement much more quickly and easily through open-ended questions.

When you ask open-ended questions, you force dialogue and trigger the flow of information. Starting your questions with *who, what, where, when, why,* and *how* narrows the focus, defines the standards, gives you insight into what others are thinking, and outlines expectations. Here are some sample questions:

- **Who?** Who should I consult about this? Who else will be involved in the final decision? Whose standard do we need to meet or exceed? Who else are you considering for this job or position or project?

- **What/which?** What's the best way to approach this problem? What new product are you offering? What's the deadline? What are the specific standards of performance? What's my number-one priority? What has moved this project to the front burner? Which priorities should I shift to accomplish this project? What else should I know about before I begin?

- **Where?** Where should we go from here? Where does this project fit into our strategic objectives?

- **When?** When can I expect an answer? When do you want to review the first part? When should we meet to review my progress? When are we meeting with other key people?

- **Why?** Why do you think this problem keeps recurring? Why is this change, project, or new procedure coming up? Why did you give this opportunity to me?

- **How?** How can I help you? How does your product compare with other products we offer or with other products we've offered in the past? How will this help you, our department, or the company? How will this help me advance? How would you go about tackling this project, challenge, or issue?

If you have answers to these questions, you can achieve the desired results faster — and ensure that they meet everyone's expectations. That's a powerful combination: better time management and more successful results.

Narrowing the focus with closed-ended questions

Many experts in time management, sales, customer service, and management tell you to avoid closed-ended questions. I disagree. A correctly placed closed-ended question lets you take a reading: Are you progressing toward your goal? Are you moving in the right direction? Are you earning your customer's business?

A closed-ended question — one that can be answered with a simple _yes_ or _no_ — serves as a temperature gauge that tells you whether to turn up or turn down the heat. If you don't use closed-ended questions to test your progress, all you're doing is gathering more and more information without moving toward a conclusion. Here are some examples of good closed-ended questions:

- Is this what you envisioned when you delegated this to me?
- Do you believe our product is right for you?
- Do I need to run this by anyone else?
- Is the timing right for a salary increase?

Limited and strategic use of closed-ended questions can save time. However, if you don't follow a closed-ended question with another open-ended one, the dialogue often dies there. Follow that _yes_ or _no_ response with another open-ended question and keep the conversation moving.

Pinning down maybes and other conditional responses

Sometimes open- or closed-ended questions need clarification. This is especially true when you receive not a _yes_ or _no_ but a _maybe_ — what's known as a _conditional response_.

Maybe is probably the most misunderstood response in the world. Depending on your level of optimism, a _maybe_ can mean _yes_ or _no_. If you're like Eeyore in _Winnie the Pooh,_ you assume the _maybe_ is a _no._ If you're a bouncing Tigger, you may take _maybe_ for a veiled _yes._

In fact, a _maybe_ is a _maybe_ until it's clarified. To do that, ask simple, direct questions that elicit a concrete response; if you're still unclear, ask direct follow-up questions until you get the definitive response that you need. The following are some examples of questions that can help you pin down "maybe" responses:

- What does that mean exactly?
- Under what circumstances do you see yourself using our service?
- Under what conditions would you consider _____ for this project? How did you arrive at your conclusion?

✔ So if I did ____, would that change your decision to a *yes?*

✔ Would you ever see yourself giving me that opportunity?

✔ Under what conditions would that be?

Don't be too quick to rush to take the next step without pinning down the *maybe* first.

Achieving a positive tone

No matter where you are in the questioning process, remain positive. Negativity can increase the time it takes you to mend gaffes, or it can stop the process altogether. A negative approach puts others on the defensive and squelches your ability to gather information. Asking positive questions, on the other hand, communicates that you anticipate a positive outcome. You're focused on the future, learning from your mistakes, and ensuring that you don't repeat them.

How do you put a positive spin on your questions? Here are some examples:

✔ *"What would you like to see improved?"* instead of *"What didn't you like about ____?"*

✔ *"What should I have done differently?"* or *"How could I have done better?"* instead of *"What did I do wrong?"*

Preparing to listen

People like to talk about their favorite subjects: themselves. That's good! When people talk about themselves, you glean valuable information about them, their business, how they make decisions, what's important to them, their business relationships, their goals, projects, spouses, kids, pets — in short, what they think and feel about pretty much everything. You can also discover their needs, wants, and desires. What motivates them? If you identify their challenges, you can create opportunities to help them solve their problems. You may even discover new business or career opportunities.

After you ask questions, remember to actually *listen* to the responses. If you're talking, you're not listening; and if you're not listening, you're missing important information, spending additional time following up by phone and email, and frittering away minutes and hours you could use to work on your real goals. There's wisdom in the old adage that you "have two ears and one mouth for a reason." If you listen twice as much as you speak, you reduce the time you invest with others to achieve results for them and for yourself.

What's my motivation? Getting input from your key actors

The point of a dream question is to help someone envision a better time and place where results are improved, goals are achieved, and problems and challenges are reduced. When you supervise people, asking dream questions gives you unique insight into their motivations and goals. The upshot? Connecting their tasks to what they want in life can increase their production during work hours. Some examples of good dream questions include the following:

✔ Where do you see yourself in five years?

✔ What are your long-term goals for your department?

✔ What are the most challenging issues you see, now and in the future?

✔ If you could close your eyes and make one problem disappear, which would it be?

Bonus: When you ask questions and engage people by getting them to talk about themselves, you're considered a brilliant conversationalist. If you want to get invited to more galas with the movers and shakers in your town, ask terrific questions — and really listen to the answers.

Chapter 15

Defending Your Day from Interruptions

*W*ithin the past two decades, people have embraced communication technology. But in many ways, these miracles of convenience have robbed workers of their ability to control their own time. Multiplying points of access — voice mail, email, instant messaging, audio and video conferencing, social media, texting, and of course, the cell phone — can shackle you like a house-arrest ankle bracelet, sentencing you to a life-term of perpetual availability. Business colleagues can track you down on vacation, and friends can interrupt an important client presentation. I'm not sure I'd describe this as *progress,* but it's inarguably a fact of modern life.

Consider this: Every one of these interruptions — no matter how small or insignificant — robs you of at least 5 *additional* minutes of productive time. Whether your spouse calls and talks to you for 30 seconds or 30 minutes, you can subtract at least 5 more minutes from your day. And then there's the text from a friend about last night's date . . . by the time your focus is rechanneled again, you have just lost another 5 minutes. Tally up 20 to 40 interruptions over the course of your day, and you lose nearly 2 to 4 hours of productivity — and that totals to the loss of 36 to 72 hours a month!

Distractionitis is the scourge of time-block adherents; the fastest way to render a time block or even a whole day useless is to not deal with distractions well (see Chapter 5 for more on time-blocking). So now's the time to gain control of the interruption game, whether you're at risk from wandering bosses and colleagues, demanding clients, or the technological tools that can slice through your best defenses. I show you how in this chapter.

The Fortress: Guarding Your Focus from Invasion

Being successful in time management and adhering to your time-block schedule happens through controlling access: You need to limit the frequency of the interruptions you allow. Recognize that I use the word *allow* here. You're the one who controls your time and allows other people and situations to pull you away from your goals, dreams, objectives, and time-blocked schedule. You're in control, and you're the master of your time.

Think of yourself as the castle guard: Your workplace is a fortress, one that must be protected in order for it to remain a happy and productive place. Your best strategy is to establish an impenetrable wall between you and interruptions. In this section, I explain how to protect yourself from invaders on foot and how to disconnect from the electronic devices that can cut through your physical defenses. Finally, you discover how to screen your calls so only the essential information gets through.

Protecting your domain from interior intrusions

The biggest interruptions in your workday frequently come from within. Your co-workers pose a great threat to your effective time management. What's doubly scary is that you don't always recognize your colleagues as threats. Hey, these folks are on your team — they're the good guys, they're *there* for you! However, it's important to recognize the signs of danger from time-wasting co-workers. If not, you're at risk of falling to friendly fire.

The modern work environment is often designed on an open-office, open-door, and open-exchange environment. Workers are connected through instant messaging, and employees text with co-workers in the office as well as out in the field. The days of working remotely and virtually are here to stay. The physical proximity of working in an office can be a help or hindrance. Few if any employees are granted an office with a door, and most workers are parked in open cubicles, often with partitions that do little to block views (and definitely not the noise) of co-workers. It's supposed to manifest a more unified effort and team spirit, I guess. But it doesn't do much to protect you from your teammates' intrusions on your time. Unfortunately, the same open-door philosophy that allows employees to drop in on their supervisors at will is often carried throughout the workplace, so co-workers may stop by to talk about a mutual project — or the office football pool.

The following sections look at the traditional work-space environment and how you can work a little more intrusion-free.

Creating virtual barriers

When you have little in the way of a physical barrier, defending your border from invasion becomes a challenge. But it can be done — just because you don't have a door to keep people from entering your space doesn't mean you can't create *virtual* barriers when you're unavailable:

- ✔ **Communicate subtly through the posting technique.** Put signs on your office door or cubicle letting others know you're busy.

  The best action you can take is to post a do-not-disturb sign outside your cubicle, perhaps indicating the critical project you're working on. Your co-workers and supervisor may be more sympathetic to your plight if it's a project they're familiar with.

- ✔ **Verbally communicate your schedule to others so they know when you're unavailable for interruptions.** I call this *communicating the standard.* For repeat offenders, the posting alone won't work. You have to explain to them verbally and with authority that you don't have an abundance of time.

- ✔ **For electronic invaders, set your status to "away" or "invisible" on instant message.** This way, you're less likely to receive a message. Or sign off from your messenger. For some people you just need to close off access points. For that Facebook friend who has nothing better to do but message you when they see you online, sign out or change your settings to reflect you are offline.

- ✔ **Threaten to put them to work.** If you're in sales, for example, inform the would-be interrupters that you're prospecting and that if they interrupt, they have to come in and make calls with you. That'll usually stop any salesperson from the interruption because he or she won't want to join you in the prospecting quest.

Set your unavailable time for the hours before 11 a.m. It's uncanny, but the world seems to start delivering problems to your doorstep just before midday. I've dubbed this phenomenon the *11 a.m. Rule.* If you set your "closed" hours prior to 11 a.m., you can get your important stuff done before you start to hear the buzz of trouble brewing outside your cubicle wall.

Scheduling time to manage and interact with your staff

If you're a manager, you walk a fine line: It's important to be available to staff to address issues and offer encouragement, but a manager who loses control of the border may discover that the flow of employee communication is akin to a circus parade with a never-ending line of elephants connected by trunks and tails.

Fortunately, you have a few additional ways to keep those elephant invasion forces at bay, preventing in-person interruptions while maintaining your role as a teamwork facilitator and employee go-to resource. Both management techniques center on blocking time in your schedule to interact with staff so you put constraints on the open-door policy. Creating specific time blocks to interact with the staff allows you to shut your door and focus a greater percentage of the day so you follow your schedule more readily. The times before and after lunch — when you're likely between projects — are excellent for open-door hours.

Creating an open door of specific appointment times for your people, whether they are physically present or work remotely, can help you be more effective with your time.

Here are some options to approach this scheduled time for interaction:

- **Making the rounds:** A popular preemptive tactic that managers have followed since the first workplace self-help books came out, *management by walking around*, puts the time control back in the manager's domain. It suggests that making the rounds on a scheduled basis allows you to establish your availability and deflect those interruptions that could otherwise come later. Instead of getting snagged on the way to get a cup of coffee, *you* proactively seek out your staff, asking how their projects are going or if they have any concerns or issues you can help with.

   A good manager can make the rounds as well with virtual staff members. By setting a time to call, text, or instant message remote team members daily or weekly, you can open up communication but also limit and control the time. Most virtual or remote staff members feel somewhat disconnected from other parts of your team; however, the regular check-ins, even by instant message, can create a lifeline of connection.

   Setting your rounds for the morning is a sound strategy, though it's a good idea to wait until everyone gets settled in at their desks, computers, and remote work areas, and the caffeine kicks in so they can respond to your "How's that proposal coming?" with some clarity.

- **Having employees come to you:** Establish your scheduled interaction time as open-office time for staff to drop in. Or require employees to make appointments to meet with you during that time.

One danger in setting up specific drop-in hours is that it puts you in a state of waiting. You may not get any takers of your time, but your ability to focus on any other work is more challenged because you're expecting to be interrupted at any moment. To avoid this, I've implemented scheduled-appointment hours in my office. I still set aside the same time block to be available to my staff, but I insist that they make appointments. They can't just stop in without notice.

You can require whatever advance notice you're comfortable with — 15 minutes or 15 hours. That way, if some of the time goes unbooked, you can schedule something else in that slot. You can choose to limit these appointments in length — 15 minutes, a half-hour — and you can require that employees explain what they want to talk about when they schedule so you can be prepared.

See Chapter 22 for more guidance if your job involves managing others.

Scheduling time offline

Used effectively, the use of the telephone, text, instant message, social media, and email can enhance performance, increase productivity, boost profitability, and expedite career growth. But there's a flip side: Because modern communication allows for easier interruptions, it creates a greater loss of production, performance, profitability, and advancement than ever before. And to a certain extent, these easy forms of electronic communication have taken many people hostage. Do you feel compelled to open all email immediately? Do you feel obligated to respond to a text or instant message within moments? Do you jump on to the next email even before you've responded to or resolved the previous email? Just as with cell phones, the fact that you *can* be reached easily and at any time seems to dictate that you must be available to anyone — all the time.

When you stop to open each and every email as soon as it arrives or answer the phone every time it rings, or the ding of the text or instant message, you are, in essence, *multitasking,* trying to perform one or more tasks simultaneously. And as I frequently point out, multitasking is just not time-efficient.

To keep your focus, set aside time — daily or several times per week — during which you simply do not take calls, respond to text or instant messages, check email, or allow other interruptions. Such prescheduled segments ensure blocks of concentration, a tactic certain to raise productivity and lower frustration. If you're concerned about being unavailable for too long of a time, then limit these periods to one or one and a half hours, with time afterward to return messages.

Letting email wait in your inbox

I am a firm believer in working offline. There's no way I can resist the temptation to check my email every time my computer tells me a message has arrived. The interruptions of texts, instant messages, and social media would take over my day. During your offline time, turn off your email notice, mute your cell phone, or disconnect from the Internet. Schedule your email, text, and social media time, and devote a reasonable time block to take care of it. Then turn email those programs off so you don't see the You've-Got-Mail icon on your computer or hear the ding in your ear until your next scheduled email session.

Or compose all your own email correspondence in your word processing program, and when you've completed, reviewed, tweaked, polished, and made sure each message says exactly what you want, you can go online and send those email messages. If you compose your email in a word processing program, you gain yet another advantage: This tactic serves as a safety precaution — you won't inadvertently shoot off a critical email before you're completely satisfied with it; no more "recalls."

The toughest decision you may face is whether to check your email messages and social media first thing in the morning when you fire up your computer. Wait and knock out a few priorities first? Or open it up and relieve the suspense — and possibly get waylaid by some marauding issue you feel compelled to pursue? It's your choice — do what works best for you. But by staying offline for the bulk of your workday, you're likely to stay focused on the tasks at hand and get much more accomplished.

Stopping the ringing in your ears

Let your voice mail or assistant take phone messages. Voice mail is your not-so-secret weapon for dodging phone interruptions and taking back your time. If your system has a do-not-disturb button, push it or put your ringer on mute and you won't be tempted to ponder who called. If you're an executive, forward the calls to your assistant for a time or ask the receptionist to let your callers know that you're in an appointment and will call them back.

Additionally, give yourself times when you turn off your cell phone. The most brilliant innovation with these amazing devices? You can turn them off! Without missing a message, you can continue with your conversation, errand, or work without distraction and get back to the call when you're through. Of course, you may already protect yourself against uninvited interruptions by limiting who you give your cell number to. But unless you're awaiting an urgent call from your kids, your boss, or the state lottery commission, you can likely afford a period of off-time while you attend to important tasks that require your full concentration.

Screening interruptions before letting them through

You may need to make sure certain types of information can get through to you, even while your barriers shut out everything else. The solution is to screen your calls using caller ID or to have your assistant screen your calls for you.

If you're the boss, you're the wizard who turns business transactions into gold, and your assistant or receptionist operates the drawbridge, keeping out those who attempt to foil your efforts. Your administrative staff needs to adopt the gatekeeper philosophy. The first step is to set your business up as a fortress, making it hard to get in to see the royalty — *you*.

The administrative staff has total control of the drawbridge that grants access to the fortress. They should have a militant approach to allowing people access to you. You need to clearly identify to your staff who is to be granted access and who is not. Only a few people should pass easily through the gate; the rest should be screened thoroughly to see whether another team member can assist them first.

Arm gatekeepers with the tools necessary to identify and keep out intruders and the knowledge to recognize for whom to lower the drawbridge. Their role in managing access is instrumental to your productivity and that of the department. A properly armed assistant is able to

- Answer most questions from callers and eliminate the need to talk to you

- Capture enough information so that you're prepared with a response, which means a shorter interaction when you do get back to the individual

- Schedule an appointment for you

- Know which issues or requests require your immediate attention

- Take messages from people who must talk with you

Taking a message is more than just noting the caller's name, phone number, date, and time of the call. A highly trained assistant finds out the specific reason for the call and tries to handle the question right there on the spot. This is one of the biggest time-saving techniques of all. If unable to handle the situation on the initial call, the assistant finds out the answer and then returns the call.

If it's absolutely necessary for you to speak to the caller, set a specific time when you'll return the call, effectively making a mini-appointment for the return telephone call.

Those who don't have a loyal staff can turn to technology. What a miraculous invention, caller ID! By glancing at the phone number ID on your receiver, you can determine in a second whether it's a call you want to take. Not only is caller ID helpful for screening out unsolicited telemarketing calls, but you can also use it to determine whether a call is critical to take *now*. And at work, if you're on a roll on that big proposal and you'd only take a call from your boss, your phone helps you make that decision.

If you're working from home, you face some unique challenges in handling phone calls (they don't call it *tele*commuting for nothing!). Not only do you have to contend with more calls from the office (if you were there, you could at least put up a do-not-disturb sign on your door), but you also catch all the solicitation calls you'd miss if you were out of the house during the day. Plus there's a strange phenomenon at work for telecommuters: Both friends and business contacts seem to feel more comfortable interrupting your workday when you work from home. Then you add all the instant messages, texts, and social media in the mix. It can be harder to work from home because the lack of administration staff members that screen and protect you from time-wasters.

Limiting phone interruptions from loved ones

In some cases, family calls are the primary source of telephone interruptions. Have a frank talk with your family members about when it's appropriate to call you at work.

If you have young children, you know how they want to tell you all the cool things that happened during the course of their day, well before family dinnertime. You likely expect and welcome these calls. Certainly you want to set opportunities for them to reach you, but it's good to establish boundaries at the same time. You may, for example, ask your kids to call you and fill you in on their day at a certain time — say, after they get home from school or in the case of preschoolers, after lunchtime. Same goes for your spouse or partner.

Warning: Most job environments allow for some personal-call time, but few are tolerant of employees who receive calls throughout the day. That type of phone interruption can undermine your productivity, not to mention your career. At work, you really don't need the kinds of emotional distractions that'll dramatically affect your performance and productivity for the next 30 minutes, an hour, or even the rest of the day. Calls from family can move your mind to home even though your body is still at the office.

Caller ID for telecommuters is even more effective if you have two separate lines, one for work and one for personal calls. That way, you can tell by the ring which is which. When you're "at work," you can choose to disregard the personal line — and if you're sitting down to a family dinner, you can ignore your work line with a clear conscience. Only my work number rings into my home office. I can't hear our personal residence line, so it doesn't distract me. A second phone line is a small monthly investment that helps me manage my time and increase my productivity.

Secondary Defenses: Minimizing Damage When Calls Get Through

If you set up the defense mechanisms and blocking techniques I cover throughout this chapter, you can avoid more than 90 percent of the interruptions that most people experience each day. But no matter the system or strategy you use to protect yourself, telephone interruptions are certain to penetrate your defenses. When this happens, your best strategy is to accept it and go with the flow. Okay, so an interruption slipped past your perimeter: Instead of expending effort to repel the breach, just deal with it. A negative attitude or reaction is likely to cause more damage and waste more time than simply resolving the matter that made its way to you.

The most effective technique to help you adhere to time-blocking is to plan for the distractions that'll undoubtedly come. You may use the preemptive strike technique, which allows you to deal with distractions from others on your terms. In this section, you discover a few plans for handling the phone calls that make it through to you.

Delegating the responsibility

When the call penetrates your defenses, attempt to delegate the call to someone who can handle it for you. Inform the caller that you're booked, buried, under a deadline, committed, or heading into a meeting — and that you're shifting the responsibility for the call as the fastest way to resolve the problem or challenge. Assure the caller that you're bringing in someone qualified to help.

You also convey a strong reassurance when you explain that the other person is better equipped to resolve the situation. Often, especially if you're the boss, clients and business contacts want to talk to *you*. When you confess that you aren't the best person to fulfill the request, you're more likely to gain the caller's confidence that you have his or her best interests in mind.

Shortening or condensing the conversation

When a call does sneak past the fortress guard, your best defense is to bring that call to a close as quickly as possible. Your focus has been broken, and it'll require five minutes from the point you wrap up the call to regain your momentum. You want to keep the conversation short so you can get back in the groove.

Inform the caller upfront how much time you can offer. You may, for example, explain that you're in the middle of an important project and have only ten minutes available. You can also plead an appointment — and if you've implemented the time-block schedule (see Chapter 5), you've blocked out your day, your claim is true.

Some people feel uncomfortable about cutting calls short in this way, especially with clients or prospective customers. Giving the caller a time limit feels abrupt. But it doesn't have to. Here's one way your speech may go:

"I know we can resolve your problem, but I have an appointment in ten minutes that I have to keep. If we can't resolve the problem to your satisfaction in the ten minutes, then we can set a time to talk later today to finish up."

This approach still gets you off the phone in the allotted time but gives you an out. The customer can also feel better that you're offering more time. I've used this technique for years with high-maintenance clients. Rarely do we need the additional conversation, but they appreciate my offer all the same.

Rebooking discussions for a better time

If now's a bad time to handle the call, then reschedule. The caller certainly doesn't know your schedule, and it probably never occurred to the caller that this could be a bad time. Offer a brief explanation — you're in a meeting, on your way to an appointment, or simply tied up at this time. Then without allowing time for a response, offer two options of when you're available:

"I'm not able to give your situation the full attention it deserves at this moment. Can we schedule a phone meeting for this afternoon after three or first thing tomorrow morning?"

By offering options, you give back some control to the caller. If you've been caught without your day planner, give a general time, such as Wednesday morning or Thursday afternoon. Then don't forget to transfer the call appointment to your planner.

Handling Recurring Interruptions by Co-Workers

Being very clear on your personal boundaries is essential with your co-workers. However, there's a fine balance between being viewed as a hermit, loner, or outcast and conveying your commitment to your job and the deadlines that you've been given, so you have to approach the confrontation with finesse.

Especially if the interruption outbreak is a department-wide epidemic, suggest to your supervisor that the team get together to talk about solutions. By coming together as a department or work group, each individual is more likely to take ownership of the situation. Call a team meeting to discuss workflow, distractions, and interruptions. As a group, you can brainstorm solutions and come up with a strategy that everyone can buy into. Because you're all making a commitment in each other's presence, everyone is more likely to honor it.

Time-wasting co-workers fall into a few categories, each of which can cause you interruptions that are detrimental to your career. You first have to figure out which category the offender falls into so you can respond in a way that'll effectively remedy the specific situation. In this section, I preview four of the most common colleague categories and some signs to watch out for. These individuals may be hard workers, possibly overburdened, and very productive. Unfortunately, they sap a lot of their productivity from their co-workers, often disrupting others in the office to seek assistance, whether it's emotional support or actually trying to pass off specific tasks.

The colleague with nothing to do

Face it: In most companies, the division of labor is rarely parceled out equally — not fair, maybe, but it's a fact of life. For you to survive with your time intact, you need to recognize who's not carrying his or her share of the work. Why? Because to add insult to injury, these are often the same people who sabotage the efforts of those who do the bulk of the work by interrupting their productivity. These folks often pop into your space, flop into a chair, and strike up a conversation about anything and everything.

If you get interrupted by someone who clearly doesn't have enough to do, ask her what she's working on. What are her priorities and deadlines? Inform her of yours and ask for her help. Asking offenders to help or to work sends most of them the other direction to their own cubicles — voila!

The colleague who just doesn't want to work

I may be in the minority on this view, but I think people who waste time on their company's dollar are stealing a portion of their paycheck from their company. Workers owe the company that pays their salaries and benefits their best efforts for the whole time they're working. The people who lumber along, encourage others to waste time, take two-hour lunches, and generally don't give their best effort have a character flaw. The problem is that you can't help these individuals a whole lot. Your boss needs to be the one to lay down the law.

Make sure your own responsibilities aren't at risk. In time-management terms, give a few minutes, and someone will take an hour. That means you can't sugarcoat the issue with co-workers. You have to be direct and firm, noting (with a smile) that you don't have time for frivolity. Better to confront your co-worker than miss a deadline and be viewed as not trustworthy of performance under pressure. Don't allow someone else's agenda to diminish you in the eyes of your boss.

If all else fails, go to your boss for help. If the time-waster is influencing your performance, then your boss will want to know. Be careful not to create a link between your frustration in telling the lazy co-worker she's lazy and talking to the boss. Give yourself a few days between each discussion so you reduce the chance of backlash.

The employee who's wrapped up in his world

Some people are excited about everything in life, especially their family and outside interests. They're constantly talking about their weekend, their date last night, their favorite team, and their family ad nauseam. Their focus is so scattered and their excitement is so high that they're almost like a Dalmatian jumping at your feet for attention. The real challenge is that like a Dalmatian, they don't get the subtle hints you drop that you're busy. It's as if you have to hold them still, bring your face to theirs, and say, "I am busy!" nose to nose. Be direct.

The person who treats work as her sole social outlet

Some people have such a limited life outside of work that they want to know all about yours. They live vicariously through your life experiences, from dating to family to your weekends past or future. Short of being their dating or activity secretary, you need to limit the interaction. The lunch hour is usually a bad option for talking with these people because it can wipe out time before and after lunch as well as lower productivity, but if you want to help them get their lives in order after work, go for it.

Dealing with Interruption-Oriented Bosses

In most companies, probably the biggest offenders who interrupt the staff are people in supervisory positions. In some ways, this is understandable. These folks are presumed to have an inside track on corporate priorities and often have to call upon staff to change gears and redirect their efforts. It's no surprise when the director whips into your cubicle, announcing that you've just been tagged to take on the company's latest and greatest new program — and you're to put anything else on the back burner. However, that's a far cry from the boss who sidles into your guest chair and launches an hour rant on executive office demands, reduced budget, and upcoming weekend plans. Or the one who drops in every 15 minutes to ask you how you're coming on that report that's due in 3 hours.

Most bosses aren't out to find ways to deliberately disrupt their employees' work. More than likely, they're focused on their goals — whether those goals are meeting sales quotas, completing a project on time, reducing costs, or maintaining production. And in their quest to meet those goals, they're often simply not sensitive to others' need for focus.

Enlisting the cooperation of your direct supervisor can be a bit touchier than confronting a co-worker with your interruption issues. It may take some more diplomacy and tact, but it can and must be done. Meeting with your boss to discuss your time-block schedule or to ask your boss to help you with your schedule is a good opening salvo. Get your boss's commitment not to interrupt you during a certain segment of your day — it can pay large dividends for you both.

The seagull manager

It's hard to gain control of the seagull manager. These types of managers do the aerial attack of interruption by flying over, pooping on everyone, and flying back out. Their bombing run of new ideas, changed priorities, and emergency deadlines is ever-changing because their organization and skills in management are lacking.

This type of manager is generally young and inexperienced in management and motivation. These managers can also be overly aggressive and unrealistic about the results that can be achieved in a specified time frame. The truth is that in my younger days and even once in a while now, I can put myself into that category.

With seagull managers, your best bet is to play up to their desire to achieve. Point out that you understand the importance of the department pulling together to help meet these goals. Confirm with your boss that the work you're currently involved in is in alignment with those goals. (You may uncover that it's not — and that may be the reason for your boss's repeated interruptions.)

If you get an affirmative, however, you then have an opportunity to ask for your boss's help in assuring that you fulfill your role in the process. The talk may go this way:

> *"I want to do everything I can to help meet our goal. As I understand your expectations, I need to devote at least X hours of uninterrupted time each day to this work. To make sure I'm investing that time on the right tasks, would you like to meet briefly to go over what I plan to accomplish during that period?"*

With a response like this, you establish that you're on board with the boss's agenda and you assume an implied agreement that he or she believes that your work should be uninterrupted. But by asking for the boss's advice on your approach, you soften your declaration and offer an opportunity for the boss to reaffirm your need for uninterrupted time.

The verbal delegator

The verbal-delegator type of manager can really gum up productivity and performance. In my experience with skilled staff members, delegating small projects, small tasks, and deadlines works better through writing. The verbal delegator often delegates because something popped into his head and he wants to move it off his plate because he doesn't want to think about it again. He moves into some subordinate's world at that moment, regardless of schedule.

Your best solution is to try to turn the verbal delegator to a nonverbal delegator. To do so, urge your boss to put any work request in writing. This ensures that you get the directions straight and avoids the risk that the boss will double-assign a task. The icing on *this* cake is that you reduce the number of interruptions. If your supervisor has to put the order in writing, he's sitting at the computer writing up an email rather than buzzing you on the phone or stopping in your cubicle. If you're working with a boss who's still in the information cul-de-sac trying to find his way to the information highway, then use written request forms instead. You can use something as simple as the example in Figure 15-1.

Request Form

Date: _____

Request:

_____
_____
_____
_____
_____
_____
_____
_____
Figure 15-1: _____
Written _____
request _____
forms clarify _____
details and _____
reduce Requested By: _____
interrup- Date To Be Completed By: _____
tions. Completed By: _____
Date Completed: _____

Working with Intrusive Clients

Most businesses have customers of some sort — and most embrace a philosophy of placing a high level of value on their customers. From department stores to fast-food drive-throughs, most companies follow some iteration of "the customer is always right."

That said, you know that to provide the best service to each customer, you have to seek some balance. If the squeaky-wheel clients take up more than their share of your time and resources, you won't be able to give the attention to other deserving customers. Although all customers and clients are important to a growing and thriving business, some *believe* they're more important than others — even if they aren't. Some customers just require more attention, and they often manifest those feelings by being more disruptive. Their interruptions are simply cries for attention — they want to be valued and appreciated.

The truth is that some customers and clients really do have more value than others to the company. Their revenue to the company is larger. They buy products and services that have higher profit margins. They're more influential in the marketplace as your advocates in sending you more business through referrals. To assume that all customers and clients are alike is a naïve approach.

When dealing with intrusive clients and investing large amounts of time, make sure they're worth it. If they're high maintenance, they must be also high revenue and high reward. In the following sections, I tell you how to handle customers who want attention.

A little attention goes a long way

I'm amazed at how taken for granted customers and clients are in today's business world. Expressing appreciation packs a powerful professional punch. When was the last time you were thanked or told, "I appreciate your business," by your attorney, doctor, dentist, accountant, realtor, dry cleaner, gas station attendant, grocery clerk, barista, or food server? Just that simple act stands out significantly as a positive interruption for clients.

A preemptive strike can reduce the interruptions you may entertain from some of your more high-maintenance clientele. Here are a few strategies for making your customers feel appreciated and — at the same time — reducing interruptions from them:

✔ **Send a handwritten thank-you note for their business.** Then send one again any time they upgrade, add to their order, or increase their business with you.

✔ **Remember their birthdays.** Send a handwritten card or small token.

   A terrific service for mailing cards is Send Out Cards. You can program a business follow-up plan for key clients or even your nephew's birthdays for years in advance with a few clicks of the mouse.

✔ **Call them on a regular basis.** How frequently you should call depends on the business, the client, and other particulars. But a check-in for no other reason than to make sure everything is going okay racks up a lot of points.

✔ **Deliver added value.** Forward articles of personal or professional interest. Alert customers to resources, products, and services that may or may not be related to your business interests. This gesture conveys that you value the relationship beyond business motives. (See Chapter 8 for tips on keeping client information with a customer relationship management [CRM] program.)

Another technique is calling customers back and telling them that they're so important that you squeezed them into your schedule or that you called them first. This technique is extremely effective when you return a call before the appointed time. If you informed them on voice mail that you'll be calling them back at 11 a.m. and you manage to get your priorities done early and can start calling the high-interruption clients back at 10:30 a.m., they'll think you walk on water.

Setting clients' expectations

Educating customers about your availability is important. Let new customers know your schedule and the best times to reach you as well as how to leave a message when you can't be reached. As part of this education, you also want to establish how quickly they can expect a response from you after they leave a message: Within 24 hours? The same business day?

What you're trying to avoid is the person who calls you back five times that day because you were in meetings. With every call, the client gets more frustrated you haven't called her back. Or worse yet, she reaches you on the fifth call before you're walking into your most important meeting of the day, creating the worst interruption of your life because she unloads on you and ruins your focus.

Creating reasonable expectations is key in good customer relations. Taking 24 hours to return a client's call may be reasonable — but it won't seem that way if the client expects to hear from you within an hour.

As for existing clients and customers, be sure to update them whenever your availability circumstances change. If, for example, your work hours are changing — maybe you're switching to part time or a four-day work week — notify customers of the schedule revisions and your new availability. Depending on the importance of the client and the immediacy of the situations you deal with, you may even want to let customers know when you're on vacation or on a business trip in which you can't be reached.

You can also reinforce wait times through your voice mail message. By leaving your availability and response details as part of your message, callers are more likely to recall and retain. Here's an example:

> *"You've reached Dirk Zeller. I am out of the office today, Tuesday, September 2nd. Please leave a message and I will return your call by end-of-day Wednesday, September 3rd. If you need immediate assistance, please call so-and-so. Until then, make it a great day!"*

I've set the scenario: The caller shouldn't expect a return call from me today. And in fact, because I'll be returning to an inbox filled with calls, email, and correspondence, I may not be able to get back until as late as the end of the day. I've offered, however, a backup plan if the situation is more urgent. This should satisfy virtually anyone who calls.

Don't be tempted to include "If it's an emergency, call me on my cell phone" unless you're prepared for lots of interruptions. After all, isn't *interruption* exactly what you're trying to avoid?

Chapter 16

Overcoming Procrastination

. . . .

In This Chapter

▶ Recognizing procrastination before it slows you down

▶ Understanding when putting something off is good

▶ Taking action to stop procrastination in its tracks

▶ Taking advice from recovering procrastinators

. . . .

Much of my work today — writing, developing far-reaching sales programs for clients, and putting together and presenting training workshops — involves long-term, complex, multi-staged projects that require great investments of research, development, and time. And with business booming, I can't afford to get behind.

And I don't have to — not when I can conquer those tendencies to put things off. In this chapter, I show you what procrastination is and how to recognize it. Not all procrastination is bad, however, so I help you see the difference between good reasons to postpone action and mere excuses to put something off.

But most importantly, I provide tools and tactics to help you overcome that debilitating paralysis that keeps you from getting started or the attacks that slow you down or stop you mid-project. One of the most important principles in overcoming procrastination is to take the first step — so go ahead and get started.

Staring Down the Source: How Procrastination Takes Hold

Although many people believe that they postpone the unpleasant when they indulge in procrastination, fact is, putting things off carries a lot of emotional unpleasantness. Boiled down to its purest form, *procrastination* is simply deferring or delaying action. But of course, it's not nearly that simple. Understanding what provokes procrastination and how it affects you is the first step in overcoming the impulses that keep you from moving forward.

Recognizing procrastination isn't always easy, especially when your time of reckoning is a few weeks or months away. You may simply believe you're waiting until the right time to get started. Here are some indications that you may be putting off what you shouldn't.

Calling on short-sighted logic: "I have plenty of time"

It's easy to justify the idea that you don't have to start on a project when its completion date isn't for some time. Perhaps your tax returns don't have to be submitted until April 15, and it's the middle of January. True, you still have time, so you don't need to put "file taxes" at the top of your priority list at this point. But you should pull your documents together at least 30 days before the deadline. If you use an accountant, you may need even more time to have meetings and research a few deductions to get the proper documentation. Procrastinators, on the other hand, tend to cling to this logic way past the point of manageability. Frequently the procrastinator who says "later" in January is scrambling to get in the extension form at 11 p.m. on April 14.

Avoiding the unpleasant: "I don't want to think about it now"

If you just discovered that you hold the winning lottery ticket, you wouldn't delay calling in for your reward. Who feels conflicted about winning money? But putting off tasks that are unpleasant, that are difficult to accomplish, or that you feel conflicted about is human nature. Consider these examples:

- ✔ You delay turning in the expense report for your recent business trip. Tallying up receipts is such a bore.

- ✔ You put off having the birds-and-bees talk with your preteen.

- ✔ You've ignored keeping up with your quarterly statistics for weeks.

- ✔ You rearrange your office and clean your desk instead of picking up the phone and starting on your sales calls for the day.

When someone faces a situation that requires confrontation with others, the tendency is also to procrastinate. Most humans — talk show hosts excluded — seem hard-wired to avoid disagreements with others. Sometimes, however, what may have been a small confrontation turns into a major confrontation because it builds over time. Say, for instance, Boy meets Girl. Boy and Girl go out. Boy decides he wants to go out with someone else. Boy keeps putting off "the talk" with Girl because he knows it'll be uncomfortable. But every time Boy postpones until the next date, he has a miserable time with Girl and adds even more guilt and discomfort.

Or take the case of delaying a disciplinary action with an employee. When you avoid that conversation, the employee's behavior may continue or become even worse. In some cases, it can lead to cause for dismissal. But most companies require that certain steps be taken to resolve issues before termination, and documenting disciplinary actions is one of those steps. Because you haven't followed the process, you're in the middle of an unavoidable and ugly conflict that you can't quickly resolve.

Triggering your fears: "What if I screw up? And what if I don't?"

Sometimes putting something off stems from more than poor planning or overcommitment. Many procrastinators are unsure of themselves and their abilities. They wait until the last minute to complete projects because that way, if their work isn't well received, they can tell themselves it was because they didn't have enough time to finish the project to their satisfaction.

I know of one woman who was thrilled to have finally gotten her first book deal with a well-known publisher. She had a reasonable schedule for a nonfiction title — six months — but three months passed and she hadn't produced more than the book's introduction. After some soul-searching, she recognized that she was delaying her work because she feared that if the book were published and no one bought it or she got a bad review, that would mean she'd failed.

You can just as easily procrastinate because of fear of success as fear of failure. Fearing success and how it may change your relationships and friends is real. Many people don't reach outside their comfort zones because of what their parents, siblings, and Uncle Ned will say. In some circles, becoming too successful may cause you to leave some people behind.

Success also can affect your spouse or significant other. I have a sister-in-law who feels that all wealthy people did something wrong or unethical to acquire their wealth. Being vocal about views like this can make family events uncomfortable.

Paralyzed by perfection: "I'll wait till the time is right"

Sure, you want to do the best job you can. But procrastinators often use their quest for perfection as an excuse to delay. As a close cousin to fear of failure (see the preceding section), the desire for perfection can paralyze you. If you spend too much time checking facts, trying to select the perfect words or phrases, or rewriting a paragraph numerous times, you're probably doing so at the expense of other more important things. Frequently, procrastinators try to avoid and delay challenges, like projects that are mentally taxing or big-picture tasks. They rationalize that they're not in the right frame of mind, are too distracted to give it their best, or are waiting for inspiration to strike. The danger here, of course, is that by procrastinating, you push yourself into a corner and, without adequate time, do a job that's far less than perfect.

A bit of perspective may lead you to the root of the problem, because procrastination is often a symptom of something that's troubling you on a subconscious level. Perhaps consider why you feel the need for things to be perfect. Have you always felt the need for perfection, even as a child? Could you have learned this behavior from circumstances in your childhood? Is your current or previous boss a perfectionist?

I'm not saying you shouldn't try to do an outstanding job. You should absolutely strive to make every task and project a masterpiece — whatever it is. But be careful not to use it as an excuse to postpone taking that first step. Doing your best with the resources you have is truly the goal in life. Use your time, skills, mental capabilities, and actions to help you avoid being paralyzed by perfection. Also, keeping the 80/20 rule in mind can help you move on to the next project or goal (turn to Chapter 5 for more on the 80/20 rule).

Sabotaging at mid-process: "I've earned a break"

Although most people are stricken by procrastination before they take their initial steps, the urge to put off completing a project occurs frequently, too. The more complex and lengthy the task, the greater the odds are of losing momentum, getting distracted, and giving up before you reach the end.

I admit that my procrastinitis hits me mid-project. Starting something new revs me up. I love launching a training course or working on a new project with a client, and I tend to dive in with enthusiasm. That's always why writing the first half of a book is significantly easier than the last half.

For information on how you can keep moving forward, see the later sections "Motivating yourself with the carrot-or-stick approach" and "Maintaining Your Motivation as You Press Ahead."

Looking for thrills: "I work best under pressure"

Many people who claim to work best under pressure are merely procrastinators in disguise. The first thing to do is to figure out whether you really work well under the pressure of tight deadlines. Noted behavioral expert William Marston, who is credited with the creation of the DISC (Dominance, Inducement, Submission, Compliance) behavioral system and assessments, indicates that only one of the four behavioral systems thrives on pressure and deadlines. I know through studying Marston's work and personal experience that most high-dominant behavioral style individuals do work best under pressure. The truth is from Marston's research and others, high-dominants are only 18 percent of the population, so the chance you fit that category is about 1 in 5.

You can get a rush from working in a state of high productivity and hitting the deadline. You feel a sense of accomplishment in knowing that most of your colleagues couldn't have pulled it off. The problem with forcing yourself into those situations is that once in a while, you get burned by not hitting the deadline or by crashing as soon as you cross the finish line.

If you are curious as to your behavioral system and how it can influence you time-management systems and strategies, we have a free DISC assessment that you can take to create greater awareness. You can go to www.saleschampions.com/freedisc and take a less-than-10-minutes series of questions. You will also receive results, tips, and strategies to be more effective.

My best advice is to do some of the planning for your projects when you get them. Invest the time in planning out the steps even if you don't have the time to complete them. One of the benefits is that you'll be sure of the time, resources, materials, and help you'll need to pull off your project. This planning enables you to accurately gauge what you need so you get fewer surprises when you put your whole effort in motion.

And if you still feel you need more deadline-driven excitement in your job, perhaps your boss will reward you with more responsibility — and a raise to go with it.

Knowing Whether to Put It Off

Postponing action isn't productive when it holds you back, costs you time and money, and results in a negative outcome. But sometimes, putting something off is the best course of action. The challenge is knowing when it's right to procrastinate. This section helps you sort that out.

Poor procrastination: Considering the costs

With procrastination, the bottom-line loss of time, money, and productivity is enormous — enormous to you, to your company, to your country, and to the world. A global tally of the cost of procrastination is more than a little overwhelming to take in, but the negative impact is clear in closer-to-home examples, too. Here's what poor procrastination costs you:

✔ **Money:** Consider the impact when you pay your bills late: You get dinged with a late fee, which can be as much as $25 or more. If you do that half the time, you rack up $150 per year. And that's not factoring in the increased interest (compounded daily) you pay.

Now crank it up a bit. When you routinely pay your bills late, your credit rating isn't so hot. So when you apply for a mortgage or home equity loan, you don't get the best interest rate. You may not even realize how much that fraction of an interest point can make over your 30-year mortgage. Your habit of procrastinating can cost you as much as $50,000 over the loan's lifetime!

✔ **Quality:** Putting things off until the last minute means you have less time to do the job than it probably warrants. Some of you can boast pulling an A out of such an experience. But most people, if they're honest, confess that the eleventh-hour cram session doesn't bring them their best grades — or a meaningful understanding of the material. So as you try to cram ten days into five doing a job you're not comfortable with in the first place, you lose even more sleep, work even more fatigued, and — surprise — your paper is returned to you for major rework.

✔ **Time:** When you put off a task, you spend a limited amount of time actively choosing not to start your project. And then there's the time that the thing you should've been doing but weren't takes up residence in your mind, even though you're doing other things. It still counts as time invested in the task you're putting off because it's affecting the quality of whatever else you're doing in the moment.

✔ **Your well-being:** The responsibility doesn't go away simply because you put off doing the job, and you end up carrying the guilt of not doing what you know you should. The stress of the work ahead and the not-doing it causes both emotional anxiety and physical stress, from loss of sleep to stomach problems to depression. In short, procrastination feels lousy.

Wise procrastination: Knowing when to hold 'em

 The secret to successful procrastination is to do it deliberately, based on the time that you have and the status of the tasks. Take a look at what's on your plate and choose the tasks that are least time-sensitive and least at-risk, and then postpone them for a bit. In other words, allow yourself to procrastinate — but give yourself a deadline by which to complete those tasks. This section covers tasks you can afford to — and probably should — procrastinate on.

When haste could cause harm

Many tasks or decisions that require action are critical and must be accomplished in a timely manner. But when making the right decision is important, opt for procrastination if haste could result in a damaging outcome. When you feel pressured to make a choice or are forced to take an action you're uncertain of, in most cases, putting it off until you're clear-headed and can think through your decision is a good use of procrastination.

Here's an example: The salesperson offers you a hefty discount on those super-insulating windows — but it's only good at the time of the offer. Defer until tomorrow, and the price goes back up by 20 percent. You're torn. The salesperson assures you that the company is highly rated and the product is the best quality. You know you need new windows, but you hadn't planned to buy them until the salesperson knocked on your door.

In this case, your instinct to hold off is a good one. The windows and the deal are probably legitimate. But you haven't had a chance to investigate this opportunity as carefully as you should to ensure that you make a wise move. Trust me: This is probably not your last opportunity to buy those windows at a special price.

When the timing isn't right

Sometimes, the key to success is timing. You may have an important objective on your to-do list: It may be something that's critical in helping you achieve your goals. But your instinct to put on the brakes may be because the timing isn't right — the time and energy you'd put out is far greater than what you'd get in return.

Maybe you delay putting your house on the market — it's a bad time to sell, so why invest the time and energy when the likelihood of selling at the price you need to is minimal? Or perhaps you need to put in some time in the evening to prepare for a meeting in the morning. But the baby is sick, and even if you ignore his distress or leave your spouse to handle it, you're distracted and worried.

The point is that you can't possibly be as productive or accomplish as much when the timing isn't right. You may end up investing a lot more time and energy — and not get the return you hoped for. So do the best that you can; you need to invest the time necessary so that you're prepared enough for the meeting but also give the necessary assistance to your family. Learn to recognize those times that you're swimming against the current, and then stop and re-evaluate your priorities and change direction if needed.

When the task isn't critical

You're loaded down with projects and commitments, all of them important and none of them offloadable. Heck, you're not procrastinating — you're *drowning.* In situations like this, procrastinating can be a survival strategy. You just need to decide which items to put off.

If you have to put off doing something because of time limitations, make it one of the routine day-to-day tasks. These are the low-value, low-reward actions that produce limited results, something you can most likely delegate to someone else. Be cautious about postponing the growth and big-picture aspects: Even though they tend to be more long-term in scope, if you don't stay on top of these issues, the consequences can be significant.

You can put off less-important to-do items in your personal life, too. For instance, say you have to accomplish the following tasks: Do your taxes by next week, finish an important presentation for work in a week-and-a-half, paint the guest room before your in-laws come next week, and talk with your travel agent about your trip to Bali this summer. You may choose to put off painting the guest room because it's not critical to your in-laws' visit (they'll be just as happy with smoky-blue walls as moss-green ones). Or you can postpone the meeting with the travel agent because you have more time to accomplish that than you have for the taxes and the presentation.

Laying the Groundwork: Altering Your Mindset and Instituting Discipline

Everyone has three weapons in the arsenal for fighting procrastination. Call upon these formidable forces, unleash their power, and reclaim control of your time:

- ✔ **Decision:** First, it's important to recognize procrastination when you see it and admit that you're guilty. At that point, you can take action to squelch the urge. Decide to begin the steps to stay on course with your obligation. In short, make a commitment and hold fast.

- ✔ **Determination:** Determination is the push that gets you through the late hours, the long days, and the uncomfortable places that make you want to put off your obligation. It's the commitment to see the task through to completion and on time. Although determination is often an innate sense of responsibility, it's also a habit that you can learn, and constant practice keeps it working.

- ✔ **Discipline:** Just as you use discipline to train yourself in other areas — picking up a sport or taking a class; sticking to a time-management plan and schedule-planning system; going on a diet or undertaking an exercise plan — your vigilant effort to keep on course with your commitments can serve as a major motivator. Approach your procrastination with the same focus: Discipline yourself to get started and stay on course.

The following sections name a few alternate routes to keep you on track so you arrive at your destination — on time.

Motivating yourself with the carrot-or-stick approach

The nature of human beings is to move away from pain and toward pleasure. In setting up a prioritization plan, you can use the carrot-or-stick approach to drive yourself toward accomplishment. When you feel the urge to procrastinate, maybe what you need is a carrot dangling in front of your face — an incentive to keep pressing on. Hey, it worked when you were a kid: "If you clean your room now, you can stay up tonight and watch monster movies." On the other hand, some folks respond better to reminders of consequences — the threat of the stick. For them, the promise of a reward gets no reaction, but avoiding negative consequences scares them into action.

Here's an example: You hate working out — it means you have to get up earlier to get to the gym, work up a sweat when you could be getting another hour of sleep or enjoying a latte and the newspaper. But keep in mind the end result of your choice: the awful feeling of being overweight or out of shape, ill-fitting clothing, high blood pressure, and low stamina. On the flip side is the pleasure of a fit physique; boundless energy; and a stab at a longer, healthier life.

A work-life example is the salesperson who drives herself to put in two hours of prospecting calls each day (instead of just one) by reminding herself that a higher commission check, management recognition, and a grander family vacation are the rewards for the effort. If she neglects this effort, consequences await her: a poor performance evaluation, lower income, more effort to make up for sales shortfall, and perhaps even termination.

Seeking reward

If anticipating the pleasurable consequences of tackling an action you don't really enjoy motivates you to perform it, then focus on those positives. And if rewards help, shower yourself with them. If the vision of a latte and your favorite scone gives you the get-up-and-go to take care of your task, go for it (after you finish the job, of course!). Or if a vacation moves you toward finishing an onerous freelance project, set a date for when you'll book the trip, and follow through when you wrap up the project.

Whenever motivation lags, pause to remind yourself of your incentive upon achieving success. Consider tacking up an enticing photo near your most tempting place of hesitation. The photo can be any number of things: A place you want to go, a person you want to spend time with, someone with qualities you'd like to attain, and so on. If your reward for a freelance writing project is a Caribbean vacation, for example, tack up a photo of a tropical setting or beach along a sparkling blue ocean right by your computer.

Avoiding consequences

If you're more leery of the results of neglect than excited about a reward upon completion, ask yourself about the consequences you'll face if you fail to complete certain steps toward your goal, and remind yourself of them as often as you need to.

If you find that consequences are your surest motivators, make sure you focus on the immediate ones. Unfortunately, when consequences are delayed, the human response is to delay positive action. Skipping your workout today won't give you a heart attack tomorrow — so why not sleep in a little longer? Putting off your prospecting calls today won't reduce your paycheck this week. Because skipping these steps toward your ultimate goal doesn't immediately produce pain, it's easy to (wrongly) convince yourself that there are no consequences.

You can set up new, unpleasant consequences if you have trouble focusing on the long term. Several years ago, two of my clients struggled with procrastination. They'd fill out every last page of paperwork, sharpen their pencils, and arrange their paper clips before they'd begin their important work. Striving to be recognized as employee-of-the-month didn't motivate them, so I tried something a little unorthodox: I had each of them write a $500 check and send it to me. One client made the check out to a political party that he absolutely abhorred and would never contribute to; the other salesperson made out the check to a competitor. If they didn't break through their procrastination, I'd have permission to address and mail those checks. As expected, I never sent those checks. Their desire to avoid violating their political beliefs or giving money to their biggest competitor ensured their daily move through the valley of procrastination. If you opt for this plan, you can have a boss, friend, or even your spouse hold the money.

Recognizing excuses and shoving them aside

Procrastination is definitely in your control, but some influences in your life certainly seem to affect your inclination to procrastinate. And when that happens, the tendency is to make excuses, to blame someone or something else.

Resisting peer pressure

It's a fact of life: Co-workers, friends, acquaintances, and family all seem to conspire to tempt you away from what you *should* be doing. But on some level, when you want to avoid an obligation, you're looking for those opportunities to postpone, and it's great to have someone else or some situation to blame.

Say, for example, that your friend tries to talk you into taking the day off to go to the beach. You have a big presentation coming up the next week and you need every minute to prepare beforehand. But it's a painfully tedious process, you're dreading the presentation, and the last thing you want to be doing is writing yourself a speech. Sounds like a great opportunity to procrastinate. But here's where discipline comes in.

When another person encourages you to forsake your work, before you submit to the pressure, acknowledge that you're likely using this person as an excuse. Then remind yourself what you need to do to meet your priorities now. Here's the real question: Is taking time off with your friend bringing you closer to or further away from your goals?

Seeing whether outside forces really do prevent work

Sometimes, you may feel like you're forced to procrastinate due to some external factor beyond your control — weather, traffic jam, power failure. Trust me — I know the feeling.

Recently, I was working on a chapter of this book at home. The weather was beautiful and I longed to join my family outside. Suddenly, the power went out. Although my laptop was still working fine, I didn't have access to the Internet, which I needed for some fact-checking. What a perfect excuse to stop work and call it a day! Okay, fact is, I didn't *need* Internet access to continue working on my chapter. I knew I could make good progress, even if I couldn't tie everything up. I just wanted a reason to justify putting off the chapter until later.

In situations like this one, step back and assess the situation. Ask yourself the following:

- ✔ Is there another way you can accomplish this task?
- ✔ Would the quality of your work be compromised if you were to complete the task under these circumstances?
- ✔ Can you at least take some action to stay on track?

In my case, I had to confess that I could indeed continue to work on my chapter — and that I really did want to finish it that day. Although the quality of my work wouldn't be affected, I wouldn't be able to finish the chapter without online confirmation of a few things. I also knew that rain was in the forecast for the next day. So I determined to make myself forge ahead, writing as much as I could for another hour. Then I planned a break to get together the fixings for a family cookout, followed by another hour of work before I fired up the grill.

Granted, in certain situations, you have no choice but to put off your task. If you're poised to cut the grass and a sudden downpour soaks the lawn, you have to postpone the chore. But be sure that you're not manipulating the situation so that you have an honorable excuse to do what you wanted to do, anyway.

You have some options when you really can't make progress on the task at hand:

- ✔ Move to the next most-important task on your list and come back to the most-important one later.
- ✔ Trade time off. Take a break this afternoon but plan to work later this week during your previously scheduled afternoon off. Or choose to get up earlier later in the week to make up for it.

Give me a break: Putting off procrastination

Sounds counterintuitive, I know, but sometimes putting off procrastination is the proverbial hair of the dog that bit you. That is, a little planned procrastination can solve a larger procrastination problem. As soon as you become aware that you're procrastinating, don't beat yourself up; instead, allow yourself to procrastinate — but just not yet.

Here's how it works: Identify the ways you're likely to put off working on your project. Then, instead of fighting a losing battle with your willpower, tell yourself it's okay to do those activities — after you put in a set amount of work on your project.

Suppose you're trying to get a good head start on a paper for a class, but you've been putting it off for almost anything else that comes along: a lunch date, a shopping errand, even a TV show. You can plan to run that errand — *after* you spend a half hour getting your notes in order and reviewing your outline. Chances are, by the time you look up at the clock, you'll have spent an hour or longer and have made a lot more progress than you anticipated. You may decide to keep on working, now that you're engrossed in the task. But even if you do break at this point, you'll have gotten more done than had you simply quit earlier. The psychological edge is likely to help motivate you to make even further progress.

 When postponing your procrastination, give yourself fairly short time commitments. Tell yourself you'll just spend a half hour or an hour on the project before you allow yourself a break. This is more likely to keep you on task than if you commit yourself to three hours of work. With that time commitment, you may end up procrastinating on your procrastination of procrastinating — uh, I think.

Conquering Dreaded Tasks with Sandwich Tactics

Sometimes what's on your plate seems so big that you can't sink your teeth into any of it. In these cases, taking things apart may be the best way to make progress, stay on track, and put away that project. Here's the breakdown.

The eat-the-crust-first approach: Starting with the tough job

One extremely successful technique to move beyond procrastination is to tackle the toughest job first. Or if you're working on a single, big task, take on the most difficult aspect of it before the rest.

I advise coordinating this tough-stuff-first effort so that you start it first thing in the morning, a time when most people are at their peak in terms of energy, intensity, and focus. If you conquer the most difficult task first, your day will be a lot more productive.

To ratchet up your results further, start the prep work for the toughest tasks the night before. In Chapter 5, I share how you can set the stage and make quick work of even your most challenging projects. When you prepare well for your effort, you won't spend 30 minutes just getting ready to go.

If you get stuck on the big task, you can regain momentum with the salami approach or Swiss-cheese approach, which I outline next.

The Swiss-cheese approach: Poking little holes in the task

When biting into a major or complicated task seems overwhelming, start with the easier pieces — the aspects that you know you can complete quickly and with little effort. In this way, you poke holes in the project, making lighter work of the steps that remain after you polish off the manageable aspects.

For example, suppose you're facing your kitchen after a dinner party: dishes piled to the tops of the cupboards, leftovers cooling in their serving dishes, the sink clogged with kitchen scraps, and the roaster pan caked with burned food and tenacious grease. The job is more than you can fathom at midnight. You're tempted to turn around, go to bed, and hope the kitchen fairies come in the night to transform your kitchen into its former spotless self.

Or you can tell yourself you'll do one simple thing before you turn out the lights: maybe put away all the food and scrape the scraps into the compost bin or garbage disposal. And then when you make short work of that, you tell yourself that filling up the dishwasher with at least one load won't take that long. When that's done, you decide you can at least rinse and stack the other dishes. By the time you poke these holes into the project, not too much is left. Even if you give up at this point, the task that awaits you in the morning isn't nearly so formidable.

The salami approach: Finishing it one slice at a time

The salami approach is a great tactic for those long-term projects in which the deadline seems so far away that you convince yourself you don't need to start yet. So you don't resort to cramming at the eleventh hour, take the time immediately to cut up the project into bite-sized pieces. These slices should be small enough that you can schedule them day-by-day or at least week-by-week.

The number of ways you can slice and dice a large task are many, but here's one option for breaking it down:

1. **Set time aside to plan the project completely so you can begin working on it and cut it down to size.**

2. **Create an action order of what needs to be done and when.**

   Creating a time line helps you segment the task into pieces.

3. **Figure out what materials you need for the task.**

   Collect all the materials and make them ready and available.

When I begin my book projects, the publisher gives me a certain amount of time, usually several months, to complete the manuscript. I know from experience that I can't look at the project as a single huge step; it's too daunting. So I break it up. For example, if I have six months to write the book and it's 24 chapters long, I break down the project into chapter slices. So instead of "write book in six months," it's "write chapter this week." Or it may be "write ten pages a day this week" or some other breakdown that's meaningful to me.

The discard-the-garnish approach: Getting it off your plate

Often when you order an entree at a restaurant, the dish may include some sprigs of parsley or an orange slice in addition to a side or two and a drizzle of some fancy sauce. It makes for a pretty presentation, and it's edible, too. But unless you're really hungry, those items are often still on your plate when the bus person clears off the table.

Just as with a restaurant meal, you probably have a few commitments on your plate that aren't really a key part of your responsibilities. Take a look at your schedule and see whether some of these tasks are mere garnishes. You then have choices:

✔ Remove them from your plate.

✔ Give them to someone else.

✔ Save them until you finish everything else.

Maintaining Your Motivation as You Press Ahead

Everyone has struggled with procrastination, and many still do. I have yet to meet a person who doesn't battle with the temptations of putting off those obligations that seem too big, too hard, or just plain no fun. Recognizing your tendencies is the first step toward recovery. By following the strategies I outline in this chapter, you can make remarkable progress in overcoming the procrastination.

Staying on the right course, however, is a never-ending vigil. Use these maintenance tactics to do so:

✔ **Keep your expectations realistic.** Before you beat yourself up for your woeful procrastinating ways once again, take a look at your schedule and first figure out whether what you're attempting to accomplish is realistic. Have you accepted an assignment you're not qualified to take on, or is too much expected of you? Have you committed to an absurd deadline?

Again, when you begin to feel overwhelmed by your workload, this may be an indicator that you'll slip into postponement mode. So do whatever you can to get over being overwhelmed. It may require some adjustment in expectations — your co-workers', your boss's, or yours.

✔ **Handle the big stuff and delegate the rest.** When you find that too many obligations and projects are demanding your attention to the point that you're putting off making headway on any of them, it's time to lighten your load.

After you examine your workload and identify what's really important to your job or your career goals, you know what to attend to first. But instead of putting those smaller or less-important tasks on the back burner, see whether someone else can take over for you.

✔ **Prevent clutter overload.** Another sign that your procrastinating proclivities may soon raise their ugly head — or already have: Your office or home is cluttered with a confusion of papers and files, your email inbox contains more than a week's worth of unread mail, and you've lost control of your schedule.

You can't maintain control of your time or stay on top of your obligations if your life has become so disorganized that you can't keep on top of your work and home. It's no wonder you're procrastinating — if you have a project in all that mess, you don't even know where to start.

You may be on overload. You may have too many projects at once. At any rate, it's time to clear your head and your desk. Take a day once a month or a few hours to purge, file, respond, and clean up. (See Chapter 7 for tips on clearing your workspace.)

✔ **Focus on maintaining a healthy balance.** Both your work life and your personal life are important to your well-being. Keep an eye on the scale to be sure that these different areas are in balance. If you get weighted down at the office, you lose energy and perspective, and procrastination — both at home and at work — creeps in. If family issues take over, you risk your performance at work. When one aspect of your life gets out of whack, do everything you can to regain balance.

Chapter 17

Coping with a Time-Wasting Boss

. . . .

In This Chapter

▶ Helping your boss meet deadlines

▶ Protecting your personal time

▶ Working with and reforming a procrastinating or workaholic boss

. . . .

I entered the work world prepared to be impressed by those running the show. Surely everyone out there knew more than I did, worked as hard as or harder than I did, and provided employees with everything they needed to perform superbly and eventually be promoted themselves. After all, that's why the boss is the *boss,* right? However, I've since discovered that although many good bosses are out there, not every manager or supervisor is an employee's dream, and even decent bosses can be poor time managers.

A boss who manages time beautifully can help make your career. But if you report to an inefficient Hindenburg of hot air or even a boss with only average time-management skills, you have three choices:

✔ Deal with it, knowing that your opportunities for advancement are likely to drop because other teams and departments can outproduce you. No matter how hard you work to overcome it, this situation reflects poorly on your skills and abilities. In addition, stress takes its toll on both your potential advancement and your mental and physical health.

✔ Move on, either to another department or position within your company or to another company altogether. If you switch companies, though, you may also leave behind benefits, vacation and personal time, and possibly a company that's a good place to work.

✔ Gently and unobtrusively help your boss provide the tools you need to do your job in the timeframe that you need them. Accomplishing these goals lowers your stress, improves your work life, multiplies your advancement opportunities, and enhances your value to the company. That's why this chapter helps you examine the impact your boss's work style has on your productivity and ability to manage your time. It also tells you how to outline and implement an action plan to improve that work style if unnecessary.

Fulfilling Your Objectives to Help Your Boss Meet Hers

Whether you like it or not, your boss's time is more valuable than yours. Delegating activities to the lowest-paid competent person — someone who can complete assignments as well as the boss while freeing the boss to focus on higher-level tasks with more expensive price tags — is a basic business practice. Your goal is to supply your boss with more time. The more you take on, the better it is for your boss and for you. Ideally, your pay increases and your opportunities for advancement are directly tied to how valuable you are to your boss, how well you support her, and how much you contribute to the department.

I coach salespeople around the globe, and I have a lot of sales clients who are in real estate, insurance, and financial planning. Top performers in these fields have assistants who work for them, and I tell the assistants that one of their primary jobs is to keep their bosses on task — that is, prospecting — daily. Many salespeople put off prospecting and try to stay busy with other tasks. I tell the sales assistants that the best way they can spend their time is to help their bosses prospect with greater consistency.

The best bosses have already assessed themselves and their staff and are using the information to minimize team weaknesses by maximizing everyone's strengths. You, of course, may not have a "best boss" — or you may simply have a good boss who lacks this ability or hasn't yet figured out how to use it to full advantage.

Workers often expect perfection from their bosses, and vice versa. Begin by understanding that you and your boss are both human and that you both have weaknesses. That said, determining how your boss operates makes life easier for both of you and is essential to your success.

Sit down and look at your boss as objectively as possible. Start with some of the same general questions your boss answers when she completes your performance appraisal, and listen for conversational clues whenever you speak with her:

- What are your boss's long-term goals? It's usually safe to assume that most people are looking for more: more money, more prestige, more challenge.
- What are your boss's strengths?
- What are your boss's weaknesses?
- What is your boss's greatest frustration?
- What's the best use of your boss's time?

After you assess your boss's situation, try to pinpoint ways you can better support your boss. Doing so leads to a well-oiled working relationship with your boss and greater productivity for you both. (And assessing someone's performance is a good skill to have on your résumé — you'll use it when *you're* the boss!) Ask yourself these questions:

- How can you help alleviate your boss's frustration?
- How can you help your boss spend more time on tasks that only she can do?

Maintaining Personal Boundaries

Part of being a responsible employee includes setting boundaries for yourself, both in regard to the allocation of your work responsibilities as well as in your work-life balance. That's not to say, however, that you should be on the defensive with your employer. The objective is to maintain a positive working relationship for all — you need a healthy balance between work and personal time in order to function most effectively, and at the same time, you need to make sure you're a valuable, dependable, hard-working resource for your employer.

Sometimes, you may find yourself in a situation where your employer fails to acknowledge your need for work-life balance — this is often the case when you're working for a workaholic. Most workaholics think everyone else operates the same way they do. If you don't, they may feel your level of commitment doesn't match theirs because your hours at the office aren't at the (sometimes unbelievable) levels theirs are.

You can expect to work longer hours once in a while, depending on deadlines, but don't let yourself become the office whipping boy and regularly work longer hours just because your boss does. Here are some solutions:

- **Communicate reasonable expectations.** Figuring out how to defend your boundaries is about communicating reasonable expectations so you don't get burned out. At the same time, you want to convey support and a willingness to go the extra mile. But your goal is to make working overtime the exception rather than the rule. Here are some ways to tactfully discuss schedule concerns:
    - "I have X projects to finish by the date you've given me. Is there something you want me to drop or put off so I can take on this project?"
    - "I appreciate your confidence in me, but I know if I take on this project, my other responsibilities and commitments will suffer."

- "I can do that, but I'm afraid I can't finish it until middle of next week. Is that all right?"

- "I have a number of key projects in the queue right now. Can we talk about what's most important in the next two or three weeks and balance that with what I can realistically do in that time?"

✔ **Clearly establish boundaries around your personal time.** Most workaholics continue to impose unless you actively defend your off time by having something planned. Treat family events as you would any work appointment (see Chapter 4). T-ball games, ballet classes, church activities, and even family dinners are appointments not to be missed. The workaholic boss doesn't need to know more than that you're booked — and unavailable.

WARNING!

You may not be able to avoid being on call, at least once in awhile, for a workaholic boss. You can't always be booked because your boss will see your unavailability as lack of commitment. To offset this perception, you may want to share details of your prior commitment, such as, "Bobby's soccer team is playing the most important game of the season, and he'd be crushed if I weren't there." Other times, a simple "I already have plans" or "I'm committed" suffices.

✔ **Know when to say no (gracefully, of course).** You don't need to take a Miss Manners class to discover how to say no. All you need are a few tried-and-true phrases. Here are a few of my favorites:

- "I'm committed to going to (such-and-such athletic event, birthday, or recital), and I can't miss it. I promised my (son, daughter, wife, grandson, granddaughter, third cousin twice removed)."

- "I wish you'd brought this up a few days ago. I've committed to going to the symphony, and we've already paid for tickets." Or "I'm sorry. Our family is taking an underwater basket-weaving class. We've looked forward to it for months."

- "Let me get back to you tomorrow — I need to check with the family to see what's planned."

Preparing to Discuss Your Concerns with Your Boss

If all else fails (or if your job is rapidly becoming intolerable), you may want to have a serious conversation with your boss. If you're frustrated and getting more exasperated daily, approach your boss soon. Waiting until you're ready to explode with rage won't help your cause. Prepare by writing notes, if it helps, and then just do it.

Identifying concerns and gathering supporting evidence

Assignments usually come from the top down, and how your boss hands off those responsibilities can have big effects on your schedule. One of the most frustrating situations in business is working for a boss who procrastinates, dumping several to-do items on your lap at once, or one who's a workaholic, expecting everyone else to push the work through. If your boss's procrastination, disorganization, or overdeveloped drive for advancement (which may have landed your boss in his position in the first place!) is affecting your work or putting your career in jeopardy, try applying the following techniques:

1. **Identify the problem, figuring out the who, what, where, when, how, and why of the issue.**

   Look at where you're losing the most time, and list specific examples that illustrate your points. Where do you notice the biggest problems? In planning? Advance notice? Overcommitment? Poor organization?

   Also make sure that *you* aren't part of the problem: Are you taking responsibility for solving some of the problems yourself? Or are you waiting for someone to tell you in detail how to complete every step of the project?

2. **Gather supporting facts.**

   If your workload is unmanageable, try keeping a time sheet for a few weeks. Perhaps your boss is a performance bottleneck because he's unrealistic about what can be done in a given time frame or because he can't say no to new projects. Document hours you work on various projects and include the time you spend on generic administrative tasks, such as project-related telephone calls and email. Then, instead of saying, "Boss, I don't have time for this new project," you can point to your time sheet and say, "Look, Boss. There are 40 hours in a work week; to complete my current assignments, I'd have to work 80 hours per week for the next four months. The numbers have spoken, Boss. Something's got to give!"

3. **Describe how these problems inhibit your job performance and efficiency.**

   Bring up how putting things off causes you and others in the department to deviate from the company's mission statement and core values. Or explain how disorganization forces you to waste time with more frequent stops and starts to the project, along with more interruptions of your boss's time because you have more questions throughout the project.

4. **Devise a few viable solutions.**

   Regardless of your boss's strengths and weaknesses, he appreciates successful solutions. Staff members who point out that the company or department is underserving customers, losing sales to competitors, or wasting company dollars are a dime a dozen, but true problem-solvers are rare. If you have a favorite among solutions you propose, make sure to let your boss in on it — and be enthusiastic. If you're right, it could earn you a few feathers in your cap and set you on the road to more responsibility and a tidy salary increase.

Consider the following solutions:

✔ **Can system and procedural changes improve existing processes?** Talk about time frames and work flow, supporting your ideas with industry figures and statistics if you can find them. Show proof of typical turn-around times.

   Use specific examples. Cite examples of past projects when work flow, deadlines, and quality expectations were well-defined, and show how the work produced was excellent. Focusing on policies, procedures, and time lines is less personal and therefore less confrontational.

✔ **Would you benefit from brief, fairly frequent meetings with your boss?** Consider recommending that you touch base more often. Meetings don't have to last 60 or even 30 minutes. Ask your boss to meet more often so you can "better align your work with his priorities." Then use the meetings to keep ahead of the land mines that lie ahead.

   Your enthusiasm may also boost your boss's confidence enough to act on your suggestions. Over time, as your boss gains confidence in your ability to make mid-range decisions, those decisions (and lower-level ones) will be delegated to you. You win twice: Your boss has fewer decisions to put off making, and you have more autonomy.

Keep your expectations realistic. Don't expect your boss to change. Do expect to be hit, at least occasionally, with fallout from his work style, and do what you can to work with it so you can meet your own objectives.

Reflecting on your boss's behavior style

Before broaching project and schedule concerns with your boss, think through the discussion thoroughly and plan your focus. Your boss has a particular behavioral style that dictates how she reacts to events and situations. If you're knowledgeable about your boss's behavior, you can open the lines of communication and discuss how and why she makes decisions. Then, and only then, can you prepare for the roadblocks and one-step-backs that come up in any project and deal productively and positively with your boss throughout the process. Essentially, your boss's behavior patterns revolve around the dimensions I cover in the subsections that follow.

You can use what you know about your boss's values and behavior to frame the conversation in a way that gets your point across. For instance, if your boss is task-focused, position problems in terms of task accomplishment ("Boss, in order for this project to surpass customer expectations by X date, I need the following specific information: A, B, and C."). If you report to a people-focused supervisor, couch your questions in softer terms ("Boss, I'm feeling frustrated by the way this project is going. Can we talk?").

In addition to getting an overall perspective of your boss's behavioral pattern through the sections that follow, one formal way to get a clearer picture of yourself and your boss's basic tendencies is to take a validated behavioral assessment. I've made an assessment available at my website (www.saleschampions.com/DISC), and you and your boss can take it for free.

Focusing first on people or tasks

Is your boss people-oriented — warm, persuasive, engaged with people, and relying on feelings and connections with others to get things done? Or is your boss more oriented to facts, figures, and task lists? Here's how these types compare:

- **Task-focused managers:** These people may take time to talk to subordinates about issues and challenges *only* if the problems are seriously blocking progress. This can be frustrating because without direction or corrections, you and your co-workers may feel you're spinning your wheels, doing the wrong things the wrong way (only to have to redo them later). The communication you have with a facts-and-figures boss is usually labored, infrequent, and impersonal. On the pro side: Task-focused managers don't often interrupt. If you know your boss is task-oriented, understand that she's driven by deadlines, results, and accomplishments. That doesn't mean your boss doesn't *like* people; it means that she focuses first on tasks and then on people.

- **People-focused supervisors:** These bosses spend more time communicating and cultivating a feeling of teamwork, and deadlines are often fairly fluid. Although you may feel good about your relationship with these bosses, the amount of work getting done is often compromised: Highly interactive managers can be walking, breathing interruptions.

Following rules and procedures

Does your boss bend the rules or follow them absolutely? If your boss is strictly rules-oriented, expect quick changes to be limited.

Some bosses follow rules so closely and consistently that, in reality, the rules are ruts. Rigidity in today's rapidly changing business world sounds a professional death knell. A boss who lacks responsiveness to change won't be your boss for very long in the future. That rigidity can also put your job and career in jeopardy.

On the other hand, if your boss tends not to follow rules, follows them only sporadically, or allows employees to bend the rules to achieve desired results, you have other issues. If this approach has set you and your fellow employees up for a fall, you may be able to help your boss understand that some rules were made for good reasons and that sometimes following the rules gives you and other employees better control of your time and energy, allowing you to work more efficiently.

Facing problems and challenges

Is your boss risk-seeking or risk-averse? Does your boss solve problems aggressively, approaching them fearlessly and expecting success? Or is she cautious and deliberate?

Expect more changes, interruptions, short deadlines, and performance demands from a risk-seeking boss. How well you work with a risk-seeker depends on your own work style and preferences. Does this type of up-and-down, stop-and-go make you crazy or cause you to shut down? Are you willing and able to handle lots of projects going at once? With the risk-taking boss, that's what you get.

The risk-seeker's opposite is the risk-averse boss, with whom problems and challenges usually come at a slower, more controlled pace. If your boss is risk-averse, you probably won't get hit with ten things today that have deadlines of yesterday. However, the challenge is that a risk-adverse boss is more inclined to fight change and protect the status quo. When change is imminent, then the time left to make the change will be shorter because so much energy was invested in the-way-we've-always-done-it.

Planning and tackling new projects

How does your boss respond to new projects? Does she chunk them into smaller, more manageable tasks, plan and delegate well, consult a calendar, and assign interim deadlines? Or does she leap ahead without planning, get stressed out, and then move from planning to implementation and back to planning again? Maybe your boss is a combination or is a complete maverick in how she approaches new assignments.

Handling pressure

How does your boss handle pressing deadlines or work overload — with grace or blowups? When pressure increases, is she paralyzed, frustrated, curt, lethargic, and unproductive? Or is she energized, challenged, positive, encouraging, and determined to meet deadlines and exceed expectations?

Pacing work

How does your boss pace her work? Does your boss work at a steady and predictable pace, one project at a time? Or is your boss more of a binge worker, varying the tasks themselves as well as the speed and intensity of work, laboring without break for days or weeks, then slowing down, and then gearing up again?

Not surprisingly, the volume of work you get from a steady worker is easy to manage and plan for, but the volume of work from a binge boss arrives in bunches. Binge bosses often commit to too many projects because they have unrealistic expectations of what can be accomplished in a given time.

Taking responsibility and responding to missed goals

If goals, quotas, and standards of performance are set aggressively, then people in the company won't hit them all. Your boss can affect how many are achieved by deciding how lofty the goals, quotas, and performance standards will be. That's where there can be a disconnect. When goals aren't met, what does your boss do? Does she make excuses or look for scapegoats? Blame the marketplace, other departments, employees, the competition, or unfair pricing? Or does she work alongside employees to figure out solutions by trying new ideas, approaches, and strategies? Does your boss engage everyone to solve problems and overcome challenges, or is her preferred style more autocratic?

You've probably already stumbled across your boss's ego. Can you tell your boss that she's wrong (or even suggest it) without bringing down a hailstorm? If you can, your boss's ego is probably healthy and intact but not out of control.

Initiating and Fostering a Win-Win Discussion

Envision the conversation about your boss's time management from start to finish. Imagine the meeting as a calm, productive, successful exchange of information in which neither you nor your boss is unduly upset. Practicing the meeting in your head helps the actual meeting come closer to what you've envisioned. You may still face some bumps, but you may be surprised at how smoothly the meeting goes. Athletes use this technique to prepare for competitions, and it works equally well in difficult interpersonal situations.

As you enter the conversation, think positive, but be prepared for a negative reaction. No one likes to be told, even gently or indirectly, that he or she lacks skills or is causing problems. Here are some tips for a productive conversation:

- ✓ **Approach your boss in private.** Your boss won't hear a word you say if he's losing face in front of others, regardless of whether they're peers, superiors, or subordinates. I suggest setting an appointment with your boss to discuss a large issue like this. Don't do it in the course of your normal daily or weekly meeting; your boss already has an agenda set for that meeting, at least mentally.

- ✓ **Explain your concerns in a cool, calm, encouraging manner.** Keep the dialogue work-centered. Tell your boss how delaying affects your job performance and outline what you could accomplish if lead times and decisions were more timely — or whatever the case may be.

Frame your discussion in a positive *I* mode, using I-statements rather than you-statements, to make the discussion go more smoothly ("I could get more work done if . . ." or "I could help you so much more if . . ."). Avoid telling your boss how you feel, and stay away from personal attacks ("If only you'd . . ." or "You should be more/less . . ." or "I hate it when you . . ."). Though your feelings are involved, you're discussing a performance issue.

Avoid nagging your boss. Remaining encouraging for extended periods of time without becoming impatient or critical can be difficult, but try. Nagging can put your job at risk.

- ✓ **Present possible solutions and solicit some from your boss, even if you think you have the solution nailed.** People buy into solutions more fully if they've helped develop them. Ask what you can do to help. Offer to take some items off your boss's plate so he can devote more time to decision-making.

- ✓ **Close the discussion by assuring your boss that you're a team player and that you want to do the best job for him, as well as for the company and its customers.** Be clear that you want to support your boss's goals and objectives, not undermine them. Tell your boss that you realize your advancement is linked to his and that your job is to make your boss look good. Ask your boss to help you do that to the best of your ability.

Watch other employees in your department. Does anyone seem to handle your boss's ego more capably than anyone else? Study that person's technique and try it yourself.

Irreconcilable Differences: Knowing When to Move On

If you find that your work style is drastically different from that of your boss and it's impossible for you (or your boss) to adjust, you may have to bite the bullet and look for another job and a boss whose time-management style is more in tune with yours. If you've checked yourself and can honestly say you're doing everything in your power to make the situation better, accept that your job may require you to take on more responsibility than your job title, skills, and even your experience warrant.

A few years ago, I hired Clara as my assistant. Although I explained my work style to Clara before she came on board, she spent the first six weeks on the job trying to change me. (I fall into the risk-taker category: I have lots of projects, ideas, and deadlines going at all times.) Finally, after weeks of frustration, Clara told me she needed materials four weeks in advance of a speaking event or she couldn't guarantee that my workbooks and presentation slides would be finished. I tried to adjust my work style to meet Clara's request for additional time, but in the end, we agreed that our work styles were incompatible, and Clara left to find employment elsewhere.

Chapter 18

Mastering Meetings with Co-Workers

*I*f you regard meetings as a massive waste of time, then read on. You're in good company if meeting invitations cause your stomach to tie up in knots and your blood to pressure to climb a little higher. That feeling may arise because you know you'll walk out with more projects on your already overflowing plate. Or because your day is so packed with to-dos that squeezing in one more commitment is certain to push you over the edge. Or because you know from experience that you'll find yourself a prisoner of the Meeting That Wouldn't Die.

The classic face-to-face meeting is still the gold standard for meetings; however, modern technology gives meetings a broader definition and us the ability to use different modalities to accomplish person-to-person connection, brainstorming, and problem solving. We now have the capability to meet via Skype, WebEx, GoToMeeting, Adobe Connect, Google Plus, and countless other web-based options. These new technology platforms expand on the classic face-to-face and phone-to-phone interactions of the past.

Sadly, meetings with colleagues, co-workers, and corporate minions — as well as appointments with clients, customers, vendors, and so on — are an important part of business life. Meetings aid in the communication of critical issues, stimulate needed action, and help measure and maintain progress. But far too often, the meeting is overused, confused, and abused, leading to gross inefficiencies and wastes of time. I can't help you make meetings go away, but I can offer strategies to tame them from wild time-predators into a manageable and even productive part of your job.

Your meetings may be ones that you set and manage, or they may be appointments that someone else is eager to arrange with you. The initiator starts out with a little more control of the situation simply because he or she is setting the appointment, but just because you're the invitee doesn't mean you have to relinquish control or time. Regardless of whether you're leading the meeting or simply participating in it, this chapter gives you valuable strategies and tactics that you can use before, during, and after meetings to make them more valuable and less time-consuming.

Devising Objectives, Listing Attendees, and Crafting an Agenda

When I'm the one calling a meeting, I adhere to a strategy, supported by research, of investing twice the time in preparation as the length of the meeting. If the meeting is scheduled for an hour, I put in approximately two hours. This section explains how you can best fill that prep time.

Clarifying the purpose of the meeting

Before you schedule a meeting, get your arms around the big picture and consider all the specifics. Begin your preparations by starting with the goal and working backward. What outcome do you desire for this meeting? How are you most likely to arrive at that outcome?

At first consideration, you may think that if you're the one asking for the meeting, you automatically have a good handle on why you need to meet. Sure, you may know that you want to get to the bottom of the service problems you're having with your office supplies vendor, but chances are you have a ways to go before you've crystallized the situation and how you can to resolve it.

So give the purpose of the meeting careful thought. Start with the motivating factor for the action. Is it to get to the bottom of the service problems with your vendor? Really? Do you just want to understand the problems, or would you rather clear up the problem at the conclusion of the meeting?

Be clear with yourself about what you want to walk away with. Put it into as precise a framework as possible, identifying the action you seek and when you want it accomplished. The questions you ask yourself before the meeting really increase its effectiveness and efficiency. Here's the need-to-know info:

✔ What's the problem or goal?

✔ How do you want it resolved or accomplished?

✔ What do the parties involved have to do to make that happen?

✔ When should this action be accomplished?

Look at the difference between the following two statements of purpose; the second includes the proper amount of detail:

"Hi, Mary. I'd like to meet with you to discuss the problems we've been having with your service department."

"Hi, Mary. We've been having some issues with prompt service calls from your company for the past three months. I'd like to meet with you so we can clear up any barriers that may be causing this problem and get back on track with on-time response within the next two weeks."

Often, while working through the process of clarifying the purpose of the meeting, you may discover other ways to address the issue you want to meet about. This exercise may help you realize that a phone call or other action can resolve the situation — without holding a meeting at all.

Meeting overload in the United States

Is the United States a nation on a fast track to meeting meltdown? Have meetings overtaken the world of business like some invasive corporate kudzu? Consider these findings:

✔ The average professional employee spends approximately 1.7 hours per day in meetings, according to 3M Meetings Management Institute.

✔ Executive employees spend close to 50 percent of their time in meetings.

✔ In any given day, more than 17 million meetings are underway in the United States.

✔ The most productive meetings take less than one hour, but the average meeting length is two hours.

✔ In a survey by Microsoft, participants felt that 71 percent of the meetings they attended were unproductive.

✔ In a survey conducted by MCI Conferencing, 91 percent of the participants admitted to daydreaming in meetings, and 39 percent had actually dozed off during a meeting.

✔ The same survey showed that 73 percent had brought other work to a meeting.

Creating a guest list

For the most effective meetings, keep the size to as few people as necessary to accomplish the goal of the gathering. Numerous studies show that five to eight is the ideal number of participants for a productive meeting. Of course, the subject matter often dictates the number of people who attend a meeting, but I agree that as soon as the number of attendees climbs above eight or ten, the return on time investment begins to decline rapidly. In addition to taking more people away from their primary duties, the larger number increases unproductive discussion.

The individuals invited should be able to represent others and assume the responsibility of communicating the results of the meeting to those people. Don't invite someone just because he or she would be offended not to be included.

Given a limited number of meeting participants, you want to make sure that everyone who *must* be at the meeting is invited. Depending on the purpose and topic of your meeting, consider these criteria when making out the guest list:

- ✔ Have you included people who have the information or answers to critical questions?
- ✔ Did you invite those in a position to authorize decisions required to move ahead?
- ✔ Have you considered representatives from each of the departments or areas that will be affected or play a role in the outcome of the meeting?
- ✔ Did you include someone who can take notes and communicate the details of the meeting to attendees and others who aren't part of the meeting?

  Official *minutes* — a detailed chronological record of everything that happened during the meeting — may not be necessary, especially if meetings involve few participants. But at the very least, you should invite someone you can assign to take notes. I suggest giving that responsibility to someone else so the host can focus on shepherding the meeting to its productive conclusion. Here's what the notes should capture:

  - • Key discussion points
  - • Significant concerns or unresolved questions
  - • The action items and all details surrounding them

While considering the right people to invite, give some thought to the *wrong* people as well. Don't weigh down the invite list with *redundants* — people representing the same area or interest. When you have a choice of two people, consider their communication styles and which candidate may be more compatible to the meeting environment: the co-worker who likes to hold forth with filibuster-length pronouncements or the colleague whose contributions add value to the discussion?

Holding informal, preliminary mini-meetings

Setting up a meeting to discuss a meeting? Okay, before you declare me certifiably insane from meeting overload, hear me out: Prep work is all about keeping the meeting as short and focused as possible. The better you prepare, the more you accomplish in less time. So yes, if a quick mini-meeting improves the outcome of the big meeting (such as if the project you're working on is complex or if you'll have multiple presenters at the meeting), it's worth the effort.

Here's how it works: Say you've set a meeting with eight co-workers to talk about a project that involves multiple departments. You anticipate some of the attendees may resist the proposals you plan to present. Instead of walking into the meeting and spending some or all of it defending your program or deflecting criticism, meet informally with just a couple of the participants at a time; getting feedback from people you trust is a helpful way to fine-tune your planning. Share with them a preview of your intent for the meeting and ask for their feedback — even proactively ask them to play devil's advocate and point out what they think some of the challenges may be. That 15 minutes or so that you spend with each key person helps you identify the curveballs that would've been thrown your way during the meeting — you can now prepare a response to them. And believe it or not, you've gained support from those attendees. Because you sought them out for their input, they're more likely to support your plan, particularly if you take their concerns into account.

Mini-meetings are best set for a week in advance. This allows you to adjust the agenda, revise your presentation, and be better prepared for reactions. Face-to-face meetings are advisable when possible, though they aren't always practical, so use your best judgment. You don't have to schedule a formal meeting; stand-up conversations or quick sit-downs in your office or theirs work well. (Chapter 14 provides insight on choosing the best medium for your message.)

Meetings can also be impromptu or extemporaneous. Although those can be effective, even a little organization will lead to substantial time-management savings in a more on-the-fly setting.

Here is an abbreviated process to follow for those situations:

- ✔ Who are the "must attend" people?
- ✔ Who will be the designated scribe for the group?
- ✔ What is the most significant problem for which we need to find a solution?
- ✔ How can we commit to specific take-away actions that we can monitor for results?
- ✔ What is the check back or review time frame?

Putting together the agenda

A tailor-made agenda allows you to proceed in the most direct path with the fewest distractions. Here's the process you follow to ensure that your agenda provides all the pertinent details:

1. **Create a detailed outline for the meeting.**

   Although the purpose of the meeting determines the agenda, all agendas contain some consistent elements:

   - An agenda begins with greeting and introducing all the participants as well as reviewing housekeeping issues, such as the length of the meeting and who's taking notes.

   - It reviews the goals, ensuring that everyone understands the purpose of the meeting and what the expected outcome is.

   - At the conclusion of the meeting, the *action items* cover any follow-up activity expected of the participants.

Components of the agenda need to be specific. Don't just have an agenda that has "old business" and "new business." List the projects and discussion points as well as any interim decisions that need to be made. Be sure to use a format that identifies main topics, subtopics, and then action points in outline format. Providing detail helps spark ideas and conveys to the attendees that to get through everything, the conversation has to keep moving.

Try to keep the agenda to a single page. Like a résumé, you want to communicate that there's substance but not overwhelm the readers with so much detail that their eyes glaze over.

2. **Clarify which items on the agenda are reports or presentations and which are discussions.**

   Make these notes in the margin of the document for all to see.

3. Assign a time limit for each agenda item.

Printing it on the agenda helps participants adhere to the times. Again, you can place this info in the margin so all attendees know the expected time you're granting to this issue.

Say you're discussing the launch of a company-wide environmental initiative. A solid agenda may look like the example in Figure 18-1.

 Send out the agenda a few days before the meeting, giving invitees at least a day to review it. This allows them to request that you add to or change the agenda based on information you may not have had. It also gives you a heads-up if any items have sparked a bit of controversy — you're better prepared to head off problems if you're aware ahead of time.

Meetings tend to be conducted more collaboratively in today's business world. There is a goal of sharing and using different points of view, experiences, and skill sets to craft broad-based or more-complete solutions. This method creates more expansive buy-in to solutions from all parties or departments. This collaborative approach requires time and some flexibility on the part of the meeting leader.

Sample Meeting Agenda

I) Greeting and Introduction (5 minutes)

II) Overview of meeting (5 minutes)
        a. Length of meeting
        b. Roles of participants

III) Summary of what is to be covered and review of the goals (10 minutes)

IV) First Item (15 minutes)
        a. The problem or goal
        b. Possible solutions
        c. Who needs to be involved?
        d. What do they need to do to make that happen?
        e. When should it be accomplished?

Figure 18-1:
A meeting
agenda
outline
to follow
(adapt
time slots
according to
your needs).

V) Second Item (15 minutes)
        a. The problem or goal
        b. Possible solutions
        c. Who needs to be involved?
        d. What do they need to do to make that happen?
        e. When should it be accomplished?

VI) Closing/Q & A/Action Plans (10 minutes)

The collaborative efforts could be viewed as a reduced need for an agenda, but the opposite is actually true. There still must be a leader for the meeting, and specific agendas, goals, and objectives are required. Open discussion and brainstorming can lead to lower productivity, more chit-chat, and venting rather than staying focused on problem solving.

Scheduling the Time and Place

Smart scheduling can go a long way toward maximizing time effectiveness when setting up business meetings. Issues such as *where* and *when* to meet can determine whether a meeting takes a huge chomp or a small nibble out of your day.

How far in advance of the meeting you send out the invitations depends on the type of meeting that you're holding. If this is a once-per-year, all-company meeting, then 6 months in advance may be necessary. If this is a two-person check-up meeting, 24 hours to 2 days may be enough. If other people are presenting and you need to allow more lead time so they can prepare, you may need a week. As with all decisions, use your best judgment.

Finding a good time slot

For internal meetings, the best time to schedule them is before lunch or before the end of the day; with lunch or home on the horizon, people tend to be a bit more efficient and less likely to drag down a meeting with wandering discussions, lengthy oratories, and micro-debate. Be careful, though, *how far* before or after lunch you hold the meeting. Here's some advice:

✔ **Schedule meetings for mid-morning or close to lunch, not first thing in the morning.** The most productive time for most people is early in the morning. That's when most people have the highest level of energy and focus. My view is that most internal meetings in a company don't require that level of focus. Employees need that time to tackle the priorities for the day.

✔ **Schedule meetings mid-afternoon or near the end of the workday, not right after lunch.** Many people suffer from a little lethargy in the early afternoon after the midday meal. After the body is fed, the brain is more focused on digestion than discussion. Better your attendees spend this slow time answering email or dealing with paperwork than dozing off in the middle of your meeting.

For meetings, don't make the mistake of doing a pitch-in — pitch-ins tend to drift into recipe discussions. I'd even advise against having lunch brought in. Why? Somehow in these situations, the food seems to take over. There's always someone who didn't get what they requested, and others whose orders are mixed up.

If your guest list is small, you're meeting with an outside vendor or a client with a service problem, or you need to be off-site with other managers or employees of your company, you may find that a business lunch is best. Lunch meetings can be very productive. The meeting leader can introduce the topics, present reports, or provide updates while the rest of the attendees are attending to their pastrami and potato salad. No one's distracted by hunger, and the eating part is usually fairly short before the lunch stuff is cleared away and everyone gives the meeting undivided attention. Also, being off-site has its advantages in lowering the distraction factor — office emergencies tend not to find you as easily. One caveat of lunch meetings: The more relaxed environment may lead to a longer meeting, so be sure to weigh your priorities before scheduling.

Considering the location

If all the attendees are in one place, your choice about location is simple: Meet wherever you have the space and resources you need. Most companies have a few conference rooms of varying sizes, so meeting space is rarely a problem. Choose a location that's large enough for your group, and make sure any equipment you need is available.

You don't have to hold a meeting in a traditional location if other options are available. For instance, if you're meeting about problems on the production line, you may meet in the plant for a walk-through before sequestering yourselves in a quieter spot. Do choose such a location with care, though — the location you choose needs to foster a good environment for achieving the objectives of the meeting. Your goal is to schedule and run a meeting that's as efficient and short as possible. If the logistics get complicated, you defeat your purpose.

If you're the invitee, ask whether you can have an agenda in advance so you can better prepare. Review the agenda in advance, and based on the topics and subtopics of the meeting, determine what relates directly to your job, customers, and department.

If you're not leading the meeting, you still have responsibilities before, during, and after the meeting. If everyone comes prepared, the value of the

Choosing alternative meeting options

As business is increasingly conducted on a global basis, face-to-face meetings are rapidly becoming the exception rather than the rule. And that's a good thing. It reduces the expense and time of travel, not to mention the heavy carbon footprint on the environment.

Although nothing can replicate a face-to-face encounter, video, telephone, and Internet conferencing technology continue to improve so that a meeting with colleagues scattered around the world is literally as easy as pressing a button.

A number of teleconferencing companies, such as Sparks Communications and Excel Conferencing, facilitate such global exchanges. Services vary from company to company in quality, security, recording, and a host of other features. When choosing a teleconferencing service, think about features such as these:

- ✔ Digital recording, so you can capture the conversation and share it with others; some services offer that service for a nominal fee

- ✔ Multiple codes, so you can conduct more than one conference at a time using a universally known company-wide phone number

- ✔ A security feature to announce all attendees before they're placed in conference, keeping out uninvited guests and preventing eavesdropping on proprietary calls

Another way to expand your capabilities is with an online conference service such as Skype, GoToMeeting (www.gotomeeting.com), WebEx (webex.com), join.me (www.join.me), or Google Plus system and its Hangouts feature. These services enable you to operate a PowerPoint presentation from a centralized location and control a slide show on hundreds of computers around the world. On all these except join.me, you have the option of live video of multiple people for your people who are tech savy. If you are worried about background noise, you simply mute the call, and only the people who dial in with the host code or codes can be heard. That allows you to be interactive without the risk of having someone ruin the call for others, alleviating the problem of background noise from 500 people. It also allows you to screen questions because you're the only one who sees them.

Through voice-over Internet protocol (VOIP), the audio portion of these services is easy to use. The ideal option in meetings and events that include many attendees is to use headsets on properly formatted desktops, laptops, or event tablets to be able to access and interact. The use of a speaker and mic in your computer does work, but can create unwanted noise depending on how private and quiet your location is for communication. During setup, the facilitator or presenter can mute everyone or allow the participants to make comments freely. A quick tip — if you're concerned about background noise, open-channel communication allows all ambient noise to be heard by everyone. So if someone's dog is barking in the background, or their 3-year-old has a meltdown, your meeting will be disrupted.

If you are using a service like GoToMeeting, WebEx, or join.me for the first time, open the meeting early so your attendees can easily sign in up to 30 minutes before the meeting starts. Generally, attendees want to sign in about 10 minutes early to get settled in. Most of these platforms require the participant to take a few minutes and download some software. First-time users may need to conduct a microphone and speaker test. These two steps can take up to 5 minutes and delay your meeting, if not done ahead of time.

After the invite and meeting access sent, encourage participants to download any needed software and take care of mic and speaker checks a few days prior to the scheduled meeting. That way, when meeting time rolls around, everyone is ready to go.

There are a vast number of tools available for enable collaboration and interactivity within these online systems. These tools include slide and screen sharing, annotation tools, whiteboards, chatting, and typing options. The more involved and interactive you make the meeting, the more effectively this can replace face-to-face meetings.

When meeting participants haven't attended online meetings before, it would be wise to ask them to conduct a technology check. This task can take 15 minutes where you demonstrate

how to use the annotation tools and emoticons, how to raise their hand, and how to use pointing arrows, microphones, and chat panels. If there's an option to use a web camera, you can help them navigate that tool, too.

Video in these online platforms is starting to gain speed. I highly recommend the use of webcams to create a more personal feel and interaction. WebEx, GoToMeeting, and Google Hangouts create wonderful options for small groups to use web cameras for video communication. As in face-to-face meetings, you can then see facial expressions. This helps you better understand the attendees' buy-in and engagement.

Many of these platforms also notify the leader, presenter, or moderator of the other attendees' attention to the meeting. When leading an online meeting, I know instantly when an attendee has opened another web browser to view the sports page, stock quotes, or search for today's Dilbert cartoon. I can then nudge them back into focus.

meeting increases while the time you spend at the meeting decreases. Here are some general questions to review and even craft responses for:

- ✔ What are the most important agenda items as they relate to your job?
- ✔ Have you found specific solutions to the issues that'll be presented?
- ✔ What do you have to share to help the department, your company, and your co-workers for each agenda item?
- ✔ Are you or your department having problems that relate to the issues on the agenda?
- ✔ Can you take on projects that'll help out and advance your career? Which projects?

The Day Of: Running the Meeting Well

The secret to holding a productive meeting that eats up the least amount of time is half in the planning and half in the organization and facilitation. If you're the meeting initiator, it's up to you to grab the old bull by the horns and stay in the saddle. If you're not the one holding the reins, help the meeting stay on track by only bringing up issues that align with the agenda. If an open dialogue time is part of the meeting, save your off-the-agenda problem for then. You may even go to the meeting initiator in advance to see whether your item can be placed on the agenda.

Being on time, prepared, and engaged is the best help that any attendee can give to the meeting leader. If the meeting has openings for discussion on issues, then chime in with something of value. My best advice is to be brief, bright, and concise. You win more points and respect if you're prepared and on point rather than rambling. If someone else uses the meeting to talk about nothing, help the leader guide that person back in the fold, perhaps by pointing out that time is short and that the meeting is running over. The more you can support the leader, the better the meeting will flow and the less time it'll take.

Arriving early for setup

Everyone's suffered through this scenario: The meeting host starts his presentation and the PowerPoint presentation won't work. There's a problem with the laptop connection. The videoconferencing equipment is down. So you wait while someone runs to get the tech people to fix it. The minutes tick off and you're ticked off at the host for wasting your valuable time.

Here are some ways to make sure your meeting's ready to go:

✔ **Get to the meeting room early to test out all the equipment.** If something's not working, you still have time to get the tech people in to work out the bugs. You may be able to delegate this testing, but that depends on the competency level of the staff. I generally arrive between 60 to 90 minutes early so I can test all the audio-visual equipment personally.

If the meeting is off-site, are people available to help you set up? If you've used the venue before, did the staff previously handle the logistics capably?

✔ **Be sure to have the needed charts, graphs, handouts, and any other material critical to your presentation.** Bring extra copies of handouts or other items that attendees may forget.

> ✔ **You may want to check the heating or air-conditioning system.** That way, you can be sure participants won't be leaving the room for their sweaters or opening the door to get a breeze.

Launching the meeting

No matter the meeting's length or formality, the most important rule to launching your meeting off right is to start on time. Even if some of the folks haven't yet arrived. Even if your boss hasn't arrived. If your office environment is one in which start times aren't respected and attendees walk in 10, 15 minutes late, resolve to do your part to reeducate your people.

How you launch the meeting has a lot to do with your success in maintaining control. If the meeting is with a customer, client, or prospect, you may want to allow for a little more small talk, but otherwise dispense with the chitchat before the meeting begins. Suggest that if people want to catch up, they should come early.

Begin by taking five minutes to establish the ground rules:

> ✔ Define the main purpose and objectives quickly.

> ✔ Make sure an agenda is visible to all attendees. When attendees can follow the flow, you have fewer distractions and interruptions.

> ✔ Tell the group what you want to have accomplished by the time you end the meeting at the appointed time.

> ✔ Explain whether attendees should hold questions until a certain point on the agenda.

> ✔ If you have a large number of attendees and are concerned that some members will hold the floor, advise the group of discussion guidelines. For example, you may want to explain that everyone will have an opportunity to speak, but each person can hold the floor for only three minutes at a time before someone else gets to speak.

> ✔ If your meeting is scheduled for longer than an hour, plan for a break and let the attendees know about it. If everyone knows they'll get a bio-break at a given point on the agenda, it'll help reduce walkouts that disrupt the meeting as people leave one by one. Be sure to tell them how long it'll be. (Five minutes? Ten minutes?) Then reconvene when you say you will.

> ✔ Ban cell phones and BlackBerries! Allow me to climb up on my soapbox: I thought it was bad enough when meeting attendees kept their cell phones on ring and then actually carried on hushed conversations as

the meeting was conducted around them. Now it's worse: They're busy checking messages on their smartphones and text-messaging — who knows whether it's business or personal?

As part of your meeting preamble, tell the folks to turn off their cell phones or whatever electronic devices they have with them and put them away. You may even tell them that if a phone rings during the meeting, discussion will halt until the phone is turned off and the interruption is concluded. This usually shames people enough so that they're willing to adhere to the rules.

Keeping the meeting moving

As for smooth-running meetings, the agenda is your best friend. There's a reason you come up with one: to make sure you accomplish what you set out to do when you scheduled the meeting. Sticking to the time parameters also establishes you as a person of your word and sets a positive precedent for future meetings, so follow the plan.

Dealing with habitual latecomers

If attendees typically arrive at meetings late, deal with the problem head-on: Talk with the culprits individually. Visit habitual latecomers before the meeting to make sure they arrive on time, or chat with them after the meeting and ask for their cooperation in arranging their schedule so they can arrive on time in the future. If that doesn't work, you may have to resort to stronger action:

✔ Reward early attendees. Give the on-time people single gifts of company logo wear, coffee cups, movie tickets, or coffee shop gift cards.

✔ Hand out the most desirable projects or assignments in the first five minutes, leaving the tougher or less desirable assignments to the tardy people.

✔ Create a late-meeting fund. Latecomers have to kick in some cash to the kitty. I suggest making the late fee enough to cause a bit of pain but not a financial hardship. Depending on your work environment, this may be $5 or $100. Asking people to pay up can be touchy, but if you have a relatively informal environment, you can establish that late funds go to the company's charity of choice or have the money go toward coffee and doughnuts for the department.

✔ When the appointed time for the meeting arrives, lock the door. This suggestion isn't for the faint at heart — you're sending the message loud and clear, preventing latecomers from slipping in under the radar. Latecomers either have to knock and ask to be let in or must return to their offices and miss the meeting.

Your skill as a facilitator can also influence the movement of a meeting. Here are some tips for staying on track:

✔ **Get input from participants as you go along.** Your ability to ask questions and involve each participant keeps everyone engaged and the momentum going forward. You shouldn't have to backtrack, because attendees contribute to the conversation before you move on to the next major topic.

✔ **Don't adjust the time given to each topic as you work through the agenda.** This virtually guarantees that you'll get behind and either meet longer than scheduled or simply not get through all the items. And you know what that means: another meeting!

If something doesn't look like it'll be resolved in time, you may want to create a smaller group to meet and discuss solutions so you can come back to the larger group at an appointed time. Put that separate meeting on your action list and set it up at the end of the current meeting.

✔ **Remind attendees of the agenda.** The agenda serves as your enforcer when someone gets off-track or goes on a little too long. For instance, you can say something like the following:

- *"Joe, you make some good points, but I promised we'd end the meeting at 2 p.m., and if we're going to get everything done, we have to stick to the agenda. I'll make a note of your concerns to follow up after the meeting."*

- *"That's an important point — can we add it to the end of the agenda and discuss it if we have time left?"*

✔ **Never rehash, backtrack, or review to catch up late arrivals.** Set the standard that they need to bring themselves up to speed after the conclusion of the meeting. It's a monumental waste of everyone's time to rehash the last ten minutes because of someone else's lack of regard.

✔ **Give attendees a ten-minute warning before the end of the meeting.** Just as the last two minutes are critical in a football game, the last ten minutes of a meeting carry that level of importance. If attendees have been out of the game mentally, you can now grab their attention. If they've been with you the whole time, they're alerted that it's time to wrap up and focus on the conclusion.

Assigning action items

As the meeting leader, your job is to make sure that action items are agreed upon and assigned with specific instructions. Failing to assign action items can turn a meeting from a productive collaboration into a colossal waste of time. Especially when the situation is time-sensitive, you can put a project at great risk if no one puts the action items into action.

After you identify an action item, record it and either assign it then and there, or wait until the discussion has concluded and assign all the action items at once. Be sure to clarify the following:

- Who's responsible for seeing that the action is fulfilled
- What, exactly, needs to be done
- When the action item must be started and completed
- Where the choke points of the project are
- The interim timelines for each phase of the project
- Who is to be notified of progress and at what points of the process
- The expected outcome

Don't neglect this critical step in the meeting process. Without it, you may find yourself in yet another meeting revisiting the same issue — and discovering that because of delay, the project is at risk.

If you want career advancement and an increase in income, make sure that as a meeting participant, you're stepping up to volunteer for action items that benefit the company and group. The people who are engaged are the people who earn more income.

Summarizing and concluding the meeting

Work in time at the end of the agenda — at least five minutes — to review the meeting. Your job as the meeting leader is to make sure that all attendees

Making plans without a little fire behind them

When we were first married, Joan and I would talk about upcoming plans or errands we had to accomplish. We might discuss that we needed to buy charcoal for our weekend cookout, for example. Joan and I were always in complete accord in these discussions. But more often than not, when it came time for the cookout — and we were without charcoal — we'd look at each other and say the same thing: "I thought we agreed that you were going to get the charcoal." Well, we had agreed — that we needed charcoal. We just didn't pin down the action item and to whom it belonged.

understand and accept the outcome and follow-up action from the meeting. In your summation, be sure to touch on these points:

- ✔ Key highlights of presentations and discussions
- ✔ All action items and to whom they're assigned
- ✔ Unresolved issues and how they'll be addressed
- ✔ Any follow-up activity, including setting the next meeting

Take this opportunity to ask whether anyone has questions, concerns, or issues he or she feels are unresolved. Your primary objective is to make sure everyone understands what's been decided upon and to ensure that anyone with action items on his or her plate is aware and has taken ownership of that responsibility.

If the questions are very specific and do not pertain to the whole group, or if they're more complex and require more time than is left in the meeting, simply make note of any comments and commit to addressing them after the meeting — this isn't the time for continued or protracted discussion. You don't want to waste the group's time if you need a protracted discussion with one person. A quick judgment at this stage allows you to avoid boring others and wasting their time.

Don't extend the meeting, even if you didn't complete everything you'd hoped. Agree to set another meeting, or if a couple of people can address and resolve the other agenda items, suggest that those folks stay after to tie things up.

Following Up for Maximum Productivity

Most people forget a large chunk of what happened at a meeting. They leave the meeting and walk back into their office with tasks that have piled up in the last hour. Their minds move to those quickly even before you've left the meeting room. That's why you should usually plan to spend at least an hour following up on your meeting to ensure an effective outcome. Follow-ups should be twofold: communicate the results of the meeting and periodically review the status of action items:

1. **Within 24 hours, distribute the meeting notes to all attendees.**

   Send out an email that summarizes the same points you made at the end of the meeting regarding decisions you agreed to and responsibility for action. By putting your understanding in writing — and requesting confirmation from the recipients — you further clarify what happens next.

This way, no one can drop the ball and later on claim that that's not the way he or she understood it. Be sure to give notes to any other employees who weren't invited but may be affected or involved in the action items.

2. **Keep an eye on the list of action items covered in the meeting and check in with each associated individual regularly to see how he or she is progressing.**

Also make sure that you continue to remind that person of the time line of completion that was arranged at the meeting. Then make sure that you hold him or her to the time line.

No, you're not responsible if an employee doesn't follow through. And no, it shouldn't be your job to hover over all the meeting attendees who were assigned action items. But in terms of protecting the time you've invested in the project, it's well worth the few minutes it takes to shoot off a reminder or a quick status request by email.

To help you stay on track with the check-ins, keep the notes visible so you're reminded of them throughout the day. Or add notes to your day-planner to remind you to check on an employee's status. For example, if one attendee was asked to send out an announcement in the company newsletter by Friday, list on your to-do notes to check in with the individual on Wednesday.

Part V
Maintaining Efficiency When Working with Others

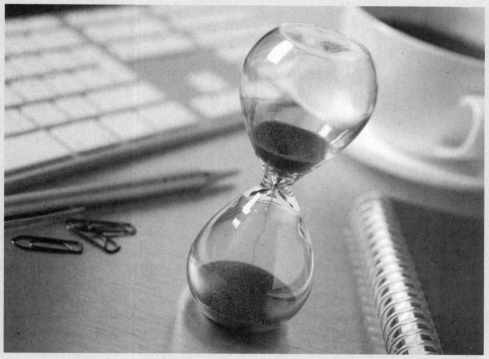

Photo courtesy of Getty Images/iStockphoto

In this part . . .

- ✔ Discover how to manage meetings, appointments, presentations, and other activities spent with colleagues, clients, and business associates.

- ✔ Learn how to conduct informative and productive yet expedient meetings.

- ✔ Find out how to make the most of your time when you're in the sales field.

- ✔ Learn how to be the most time-efficient executive or boss.

- ✔ Discover how to coach others to make the most of their time . . . and yours!

Chapter 19

Time Management for Administrative Staff

The absent-minded boss and the capable secretary (the power behind the office) are all-too-familiar stereotypes in TV and movies. You know, the bumbling department head who oversleeps on the day of the big presentation to the company's biggest client? The administrative assistant comes to the rescue and whips up a presentation with minutes to spare, succeeds in winning over the CEO, and persuades the client to double their business — finally stepping back to give full credit to the ever-clueless boss.

I sure hope that most of international megacorporations aren't operating under these circumstances! But I can say this with certainty: No matter how organized and capable the head of the department or company is, the administrative staff plays a key role in the smooth operations and ultimate success of any business. An organized and efficient assistant helps keep the boss and others in the department on track, often managing multiple appointment schedules, arranging meetings, facilitating communication, anticipating the needs of the organization, and responding to them in a proactive manner. A good assistant supports the department and business objectives and takes on duties that free up others at the management or executive level so the bigwigs can use their expertise to do what they do best: lead, sell, create, produce, or facilitate.

Virtually all the information in this book is of value to administrative staff. In this chapter, however, I zero in on the unique circumstances of the administrative person and how to use time management to further success — for the individual, the department, the boss, and the business.

Recognizing Common Pitfalls

For the administrative person, some responsibilities that come with the territory are prone to begetting *busy-ness* — meetings and phone calls, for example. In and of themselves, they're benign, but an inefficient participant may misuse, confuse, and abuse them. As an administrative assistant, answering the phone and taking notes in meetings may be part of your job description, which can put you at the mercy of others.

Getting a handle on busy-ness generators is important to your productivity, both on a daily and long-term basis. Administrative staff members are especially vulnerable to the following time-zappers:

- **Regular meetings:** In many meetings, a lot is discussed, little is shared, and even less is acted upon. Chapter 18 tells you how to take control of meetings efficiency — even when you're not the one leading the meeting.

- **One-on-one meetings:** You may be trapped with a long-winded supervisor or employee who frequently veers off topic. Chapter 9 helps you deal with talkative co-workers, and Chapter 17 includes tips on dealing with your boss.

- **Phone calls:** Calls may come from customers who have difficulty communicating what help they're looking for. I tell you how to handle phone calls quickly and productively in Chapter 15.

- **Piles of paper:** Papers may seem to get moved from point to point on your desk — but never get filed, acted upon, delegated, or even recycled. Check out Chapter 7 to discover how to handle paper *just once*.

- **Stalled projects:** You may get stuck waiting for direction from a supervisor or co-worker who's either unavailable or unwilling to offer a decision. In Chapter 18, I offer some strategies for having a meeting that will help a stalled project move forward.

See Chapter 9 where I go deep into Evernote, CRM solutions, Skype, and Zoom, and check out Chapter 10 to get tips for controlling email overload.

Keeping Your Eyes on the Goal: Your Boss's Lead

First and foremost, it's critical for you to know your boss's goals — from big-picture vision (where does your boss see the company in five years?) to weekly or even daily to-do priorities. Without that understanding, you may put all your energy into creating an ultra-sophisticated, cross-referenced computerized filing system that puts the Library of Congress to shame — when what's really important to the boss and the company is high-touch customer service and time spent attending to clients. So get a hold of these goals and consider them your Ten Commandments from 9 to 5.

Over the course of my career, I've worked with some outstanding support staff — and others who, well, may have been better suited for another career. I can tell you that the one defining skill that the best assistants shared was this: They understood what made me tick. They made an effort to discover my goals and business priorities. They observed how I operated and liked to communicate. They found out my strengths as well as areas in which I relied on them for help.

Those assistants who caught on to my business approach were then able to complement my strengths with theirs — they were better able to be proactive and work independently. They were more productive and made efficient use of the eight-plus hours each day that we worked together. They became a critical member of the team. In this section, you find out how you can do the same.

Boosting your admin image: Ask and you shall receive

The administrative assistant who builds a communicative relationship with the boss or department, contains busy-work to a minimum, and recognizes and focuses on the critical goals is bound to be perceived as a valuable member of the team. Using your well-honed time-management skills to coax order and more productivity from the staff helps the business and positions you as an indispensable player. I hope your boss recognizes this and rewards you well.

If not, it's perfectly okay to remind the boss of what you contribute to the bottom line. When it's time for performance evaluation, try to quantify your efforts as they pertain to sales: For example, by supporting a sales staff of three, you're freeing up X amount of their time to devote to revenue-generating, which may translate to Y more sales for the company. Then do the math: Your efforts add Z dollars to the company's bottom line. That ought to get the boss's attention!

Getting face time with the boss

Regular meetings with your supervisor are critical to making sure you're in sync with his or her priorities and that you're investing your time and energies into the appropriate tasks. You may run across owners of entrepreneurial startups, corporate department heads, and CEOs of Fortune 100 companies. But as for meetings, there are only two types of bosses in the world: those who love meetings and those who hate them.

Dealing with a meeting-phobe

I admit it: I hate meetings. I'm a driven, get-it-done guy who assumes that because *I* know what needs to be done, everyone else does, too. Besides, I don't have time for meetings — there's too much to do!

I know, I know — shame on me. But in the real world of business, meeting-phobic executives are certainly not the exception. If you find yourself reporting to someone who'd rather have a root canal than sit in a meeting, it's your challenge to wrangle regular face-to-face meetings in as painless a manner as possible.

The key to convincing your boss to meet with you is to show her the benefit of regular meetings. Explain that by meeting regularly, she'll get more done, reduce interruptions, and improve her chances for advancement and raises. Tell her that meeting for 10 minutes a day or 30 minutes a week will save her from having you come in to ask questions to clarify projects.

After you establish the value of these meetings, you'll be more likely to convince your boss that more time or greater frequency would benefit both of you. Start small and work up to that more-frequent or longer meeting. Also, be sure not to overstay your welcome. If the meeting is for 15 minutes, then be ready to leave at that point. Give your boss, not you, the power to extend the meeting. You'll leave the boss wanting more, which is a good strategy.

If you can't convince your boss to hold regular one-on-one meetings, try these other tactics to get more time with your boss:

- ✔ **Make it informal.** Instead of asking for a sit-down meeting, grab the boss for a stand-up conversation at the water cooler. Stop in — when you know things are slow — and ask whether it's okay to interrupt with a few questions.

- ✔ **Make it short.** Whether scheduled or impromptu, keep the encounter brief — perhaps no longer than a half hour. Make sure that the boss understands from the outset that you'll be quick. Perhaps begin with a statement like "I have three quick issues I want to run by you."

- ✔ **Make it productive.** That means you should know exactly what you want to accomplish or find out from this exchange. Ask specifics rather than generalities: "Does the *X* project take priority over the *Y* project?" rather than "What are our priorities this week?"

✔ **Make it online.** If your boss travels or works away from the office, you can meet online. When you meet via Skype, Zoom, GoToMeeting, or join.me, you can meet in shorter, more-frequent intervals. The technology of today enables face-to-face interaction without being physically in the same room . . . or even in the same country. Using technology to increase communication, check results, ask questions, and determine next steps can add to the volume and quality of work. With web-camera technology, you can see facial expressions and interpret passion for a project, and develop priorities more easily. The ability to see other parties can also help your boss more clearly understand your concerns and issues.

Working for a meeting-phile

If you find yourself working for a meeting advocate, you shouldn't have a problem with face-to-face communications. A boss who is partial to formal meetings may schedule a standing weekly meeting or even a daily status review.

On the downside, a meeting-driven manager may be prone to *micromanaging* — getting involved in what you and other employees are doing and perhaps creating friction and inefficiencies. Having too many meetings diverts energy and resources from more-productive activities for you and the boss. And the excess can be a sign that your boss is avoiding decision-making and action.

If you find yourself meeting to death, you may need to step up and guide the meeting through specific questions that lead to action:

✔ "What is our agenda for this meeting?"

✔ "What are we hoping to accomplish by the end of the meeting?"

✔ "What action point do you want me to record?"

✔ "Who do I assign this to?"

✔ "What time frame should we attach to this?"

Asking the right questions

Now for a little reality check: Odds are your boss's goals don't exist in list form. In fact, your boss may not even be able to *articulate* these visions. In reality, many supervisors aren't necessarily good communicators, effective time managers, or very well-organized. (So how did they ever get promoted? You'll have to read another book to find that answer.)

You won't always work for an individual who can communicate, is organized, manages time well, or even has leadership qualities. But that doesn't let you off the hook for pursuing an understanding of your boss's goals and objectives. It's your job to seek out this understanding through observing, interacting, and questioning.

If your boss is unable to communicate well, you can ask questions to draw out the guiding goals and objectives. Try some of these to elicit information regarding big-picture goals:

- ✔ "Does the company have a corporate mission or vision?"
- ✔ "Where do you see this department in three years?"
- ✔ "What do you think is more important in the long run: X or Y?"
- ✔ "How do you measure your own success in your job?"

A supervisor who's ineffective at communicating big goals may also struggle to convey what's important on a day-to-day basis. Your interviewing skills come in handy in this situation, as well. First, start with direct questions about what the boss wants:

- ✔ "What do we have to accomplish?"
- ✔ "What are your priorities for me?"
- ✔ "How can I best support your efforts?"
- ✔ "How should I accomplish this task?"
- ✔ "What's the standard in terms of quality?"
- ✔ "Who else do I need to involve? Who can provide me with more information?"
- ✔ "Can I check back to make sure that I'm heading in the right direction?"
- ✔ "Do we have any immediate problems to address before we can proceed?"

To flesh out further detail, employ what I call an *add-on technique,* attaching a time frame to your question to power up focus, production, and better time management. Here are some examples:

- ✔ "What do we have to accomplish this week/today/before lunch?"
- ✔ "What are your priorities for me for this quarter/this month/this week/in the next hour?"

Another technique I recommend is to follow up any of the boss's responses with this question: Besides that, is there anything else? Here's why: First, it helps identify anything else that needs your attention in the time frame given. Second, it forces your supervisor to pay attention to what he or she is saying. When people are busy, they have a tendency to switch to auto-pilot and not really think deeply about what they're doing. By following up with the anything-else question, you give the boss an opportunity to stop and think through what he or she has just charged you with and determine whether everything has been covered.

Adopting Strategies to Stay On Track

Good news: Just because you leave work every day with a stack of papers on your desk or email still sitting in your inbox doesn't mean you're doing a bad job. On the contrary, if you end each day with everything accomplished on your to-do list and ready to face the next day with a clean slate, you probably *aren't* doing your job (that or your company may be in trouble).

Fact is, when a company finds itself scrambling to keep up with business, it's usually a sign of robust health. And employees who are weighed down with the heaviest workloads are those who management considers indispensable. You've heard the old saw "If you want something done, give it to a busy person."

So when your boss hands you yet *another* top-priority project, consider it a compliment! What determines your success is how you protect your workspace and focus from invasion and how you prioritize your work, tackling the tasks that are most important first.

Starting with a few simple steps

Sometimes you need to slow down in order to speed up, to put a halt to *busyness* so you can get down to business. It's easy to get sucked into a vortex of activity at the office, drowning in a whirlpool of tasks and to-dos so that you can't even stop long enough to ask for help. Have you ever said to someone who offered to help you with a project, "I'm too busy; I don't have time to show you how to help me"?

Too frequently, that frenzy of activity is obscuring the fact that, well, you're not accomplishing very much. When you find yourself swimming in circles, it may be time to stop the frantic flailing and come up for air. By doing so, you may just discover you're not as far from shore as you feared. Here are some steps you can take:

- ✓ **Get to work a bit early so you can review, reload, and get ready for a productive day.** Employees with refined time-management skills arrive regularly from 5 to 15 minutes before their work shift. This is especially true for administrative staff — individuals who support supervisors or a group of people. As soon as the others arrive, they may commandeer your schedule. A quiet time to prepare for the onslaught helps minimize inevitable diversions.

- ✓ **Work routine rest stops into your daily schedule to review and evaluate your progress.** I suggest scheduling at least 15 minutes at the end of the workday to take measure. Keep track of how you spend your time by assessing the tasks according to four main categories: revenue supporting, service supporting, meetings, and project supporting. (Figure 19-1 provides a snippet from a time-tracking sheet you may want to use; I include a full sheet in the appendix.) Did you accomplish what you'd intended? What went well? What went poorly? Who and what interrupted your efforts? What changes would improve the situation? What do you need to accomplish tomorrow? What adjustments to your schedule can you make?

- ✓ **Take a work break in the middle of the day.** You may be tempted to work through lunch, but working an eight-hour-plus day without a break to clear your head and step away will *not* help you accomplish more. If you don't want to take an hour, fine. Get away for a *half* hour. Leave your desk behind and meet a friend for a quick bite or a walk. At least head for the company break room.

Do not — I repeat — do *not* take lunch at your desk! You end up taking business calls, answering co-workers' questions, and jumping up if your boss calls your name. You need at least 30 minutes to clear your mind, exercise your body, or enjoy a change of scenery so you can use your time more effectively the rest of the day.

Protecting peak productivity periods

Most people are at their peak in the morning hours. But whatever time you're most productive, do your best to set aside that period for tasks that require greater attention and focus. If possible, relegate meetings, filing, simple administrative tasks, and other no-brainer activities to other times of day; devote your concentrated energies to challenging projects.

Safeguarding your peak time may be tough. Administrative folks are typically extremely exposed to interruption. Often, their desks are set in an open area, accessible to everyone in the office. And these people are frequently responsible for answering incoming calls for several people.

Time	Activity	RS	SS	M	PS
		RS	*SS*	*M*	*PS*
7:00-7:30		*RS*	*SS*	*M*	*PS*
7:30-8:00		*RS*	*SS*	*M*	*PS*
8:00-8:30		*RS*	*SS*	*M*	*PS*
8:30-9:00		*RS*	*SS*	*M*	*PS*
9:00-9:30		*RS*	*SS*	*M*	*PS*
9:30-10:00		*RS*	*SS*	*M*	*PS*
10:00-10:30		*RS*	*SS*	*M*	*PS*
10:30-11:00		*RS*	*SS*	*M*	*PS*
11:00-11:30		*RS*	*SS*	*M*	*PS*
11:30-12:00		*RS*	*SS*	*M*	*PS*
12:00-12:30		*RS*	*SS*	*M*	*PS*
etc.					

Figure 19-1:
What a time-tracking sheet for an admin assistant might look like.

_____ Total Revenue Supporting Hours (*RS*)
_____ Total Service Supporting Hours (*SS*)
_____ Total Meeting Hours (*M*)
_____ Total Project Supporting Hours (*PS*)

Here are a few tips for protecting your periods of peak productivity:

- ✔ Use the time-block system (see Chapter 5) to schedule your most productive hours.

- ✔ Say no to *multitasking*, which involves juggling several tasks at one time. (See Chapter 2 for more on the perils of multitasking.)

- ✔ Post a sign or implement some sort of signal to alert other employees to hold off interruptions until a given time. You may not be able to completely block disruption, but you can reduce it.

- ✔ Enlist your boss's support in guarding your time blocks. Ask whether you can get phone relief during this time (maybe someone else can man the phones for an hour). If you can't get help on a routine basis, at least ask about getting it as needed.

- ✔ When given a project with a deadline, make sure your supervisor understands the time resources the task requires. (Bosses are notorious for underestimating the amount of effort required to complete a project.) He or she may then be more supportive of your need for distraction-free time blocks.

Getting your priorities in order

The first thing you need to do is make sure your priorities are straight. Whether you get that information from the boss or in a departmental meeting or you're following your gut, you want to be clear on what's most important — what projects command your attention *first.*

Typically, the money-generating activities (or in the case of an administrative assistant, the supporting activities that lead to money-generating activities) are what should come first. Having been in sales for more than half my life, I'm highly attuned to the importance of bottom-line activities. But the fact is that *all* companies are in sales to some degree. And all employees — even those who don't sell or direct sales — are connected to the sales efforts of the firm. There's really nothing more important in any company than increasing sales and therefore increasing profit.

You may be an administrative assistant in the IT department or in finance, but if the sales team fails, everyone in the company is at risk. So if you need to type a sales proposal, book a sales appointment for your boss, or send information that was requested by a new potential customer, these activities take precedence over the day-to-day paper pushing that most administrative staff members engage in. In a very real sense, your job and the future of the company rely on the sales department. Anything you can do to support and enhance sales efforts increases your value.

Seeking clarification about your objectives

Regarding activities whose priorities aren't clear, there's a wrong way and a right way to get clarification. Instead of posing an open-ended question (which is a *good* thing to do when you want to get people to talk), giving your boss a multiple-choice option can help narrow the focus and make it easier to get an answer to one:

> Wrong: "Okay, what exactly is my priority here?"

> Right "I'm currently working on A, B, and C. In order to know how to best schedule my time, which one — A, B, or C — is the most critical?"

Now, let me throw you a trickier situation: Suppose you support several people in the department and two people are insisting that their project is priority. Your first step is to try to talk to the two of them together. By acknowledging the importance of both projects and linking the prioritization to a common goal, you're more likely to get the two of them to mutually agree on the priority:

> "I'll do my best to get both of these projects completed as quickly as possible. But which project do you believe is the most critical to our department's bottom line?"

If they don't agree? Well, you'll have to rely on the boss to be the tie-breaker.

Creating and qualifying a comprehensive task list

As soon as you've established your objectives, it's time to make a list of everything you have to do. Administrative assistants tend to be good list-makers — a skill that everyone should acquire. But there's more to making a good list than meets the eye.

The key to constructing a good task list — whether on computer or with notepad and pencil — is to focus on the *what*. Getting diverted by the *how* and *why* drains the efficiency out of this important step in prioritizing. As you jot down those projects, don't question, judge, or analyze a single item — just get them all down. By taking this productive step, you'll find you have time later to dissect the particulars of each project.

Use the list-making tools that come with your software to keep track of tasks and projects. Microsoft Outlook, for example, has a Tasks feature. You can reorder, add, and eliminate items as much and as often as necessary without wearing out erasers and using up your notepad.

As soon as you have your full list, you're ready to establish the order of attack. Instead of creating a numerical order from 1 to whatever, group the items based on when they must be completed (***Note:*** This task follows the process I outline in Chapter 5, but because administrative assistants often don't have the *delegate* and *eliminate* options, I've reduced the number of categories and broke them out according to the urgency of the task):

1. Critical to complete today

2. Preferable to complete today

3. Important to finish in the next few days

4. Can be completed within a week or longer

A common tendency for those who love lists is to finish the items that can be crossed off quickly. It's so satisfying to see those check marks by the completed tasks — the more, the better. The smarter strategy, however, is to do the most important items first — not the ones that take the least amount of time to finish. That doesn't mean, however, that you put your efforts *only* on that reorganization proposal, deferring everything else until it's completed. It means you have to break down the big job into many smaller but critical steps. Thus, number one on your list for tomorrow is *not* "finish reorganization proposal" but rather "review staff suggestions for reorganization proposal."

Did you cross off all your critical-to-complete-today tasks before you went home? That, in my book, is the measure of a successful day. A productive and efficient administrative person probably finishes the preferable-to-complete-today items, and maybe a few others, before going home, ready to tackle the constantly adjusting list again the next morning.

Chapter 20

Time Management for Salespeople

A salesperson does so much more than simply sell. A salesperson prospects, qualifies, cold calls, warm calls, networks, follows up, generates leads, serves customers, asks for referrals, develops marketing plans, prepares proposals, handles objections, role-plays and rehearses, researches, troubleshoots, files, mails, and asks for the close.

Yet all this boils down to that most fundamental function: making the sale. Boosting the bottom line. Generating revenue. Producing income. The efforts and energies of the salesperson all have to flow in the direction of selling. And the more time the salesperson can devote to making the sale, the more successful the salesperson becomes.

Top performers use their time more effectively to create and convert leads at a higher rate per hour and invest less time convincing people to buy, to buy through them, and to take action now. In the world of sales, time management is a critical skill.

Through decades of experience as a sales leader, sales coach, motivational speaker, and consultant, I discovered that few sales professionals understand exactly how to effectively invest their time when faced with the many tasks required of the job. Early in my career, I developed a system for time management that has served me and thousands of my clients well. By sticking with this program, I achieved and exceeded any sales goal I ever set for myself. And you can, too. In this chapter, I share these not-so-secret secrets with you.

Breaking Your Time-Investment Portfolio into Three Categories

Just as a good financial planner chooses diverse investments to balance a portfolio, a professional of any sort balances the way he or she invests time in the many job-related tasks required on a daily or weekly basis. And just as the well-balanced investment portfolio differs for individuals at various life stages, time investment varies according to profession.

For the salesperson, that time-investment portfolio divides naturally into three categories of activities that make up a salesperson's job:

- ✔ Direct income-producing activities (DIPA)
- ✔ Indirect income-producing activities (IIPA)
- ✔ Production-supporting activities (PSA)

Figure 20-1 shows an ideal breakdown of your time into DIPA, IIPA, and PSA. When I take on a new client in my practice as a sales coach, the first thing I look at is where the salesperson invests his or her time. In the vast majority of cases, I discover the time allocation between DIPA and PSA is completely out of whack, with the person spending as much as seven hours a day on these production-supporting activities and as little as an hour — sometimes less — on tasks that produce income!

In this section, I discuss what each of these categories entails.

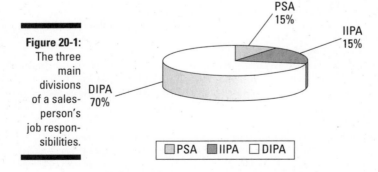

Figure 20-1: The three main divisions of a salesperson's job responsibilities.

PSA
15%

IIPA
15%

DIPA
70%

☐ PSA ◼ IIPA ☐ DIPA

The money-makers: Direct income-producing activities (DIPA)

The job of a salesperson is to create and keep customers — after all, these are the people who produce income. To keep customers, you have to understand their expectations of service and performance and then ultimately deliver on that while communicating at regular intervals, checking the customers' results, and gauging how satisfied they are with the service.

When working with customers, you should also explore other problems and challenges that your customers are experiencing. You can then provide solutions that enable them to reduce or eliminate those problems. Significant time can be saved by cross-selling products and solutions to existing customers. This can save you a large amount of time in working to acquire new customers. In sales, you want and need new customers, but if you can sell more to people with whom you already have business relationships, your income is more stable and consistent.

As a salesperson you might sell payroll services to companies. If your firm also offers accounting services or retirement plan compliance management, cross selling those services as well to your existing customer base can create more income and potentially fewer customer accounts to service.

Customers, whether they represent a high-dollar or low-dollar account, require a certain level of personal interaction with a salesperson. By using your relationship and exploring other additional services you can provide your clientele, you increase sales save yourself (and your client) some time. Remember: Business owners or managers want high quality-service from the fewest number of vendors. This saves time when problems and challenges arise and reduces invoicing and accounting as well.

Any and all activities that lead to producing revenue for the company — and thus income for the salesperson — are considered *direct income-producing activities,* which I refer to as DIPA. What, exactly, can DIPA tasks consist of? Here are some of the biggies:

- Prospecting
- Cold calling
- Warm calling
- Calling on past clients to make more sales
- Seeking leads from your sphere of influence

✔ Networking

✔ Following up on leads

✔ Qualifying prospects

✔ Preparing and making sales presentations

✔ Overcoming objections

✔ Closing orders

The secret to success in sales is maximizing your DIPA time. The activities that comprise DIPA have a higher hourly value than anything else you do during the day. The most successful salespeople make a conscious decision to invest more time in DIPA as soon as they understand the value and power of actions directly linked to dollars.

How much time you can invest in DIPA depends on what you're selling and on your service support system. At a minimum, you want to invest 60 percent of your time in DIPA daily. Certainly, more is better and increases sales more quickly. Also, you want at least half of that time to be in the prospecting and lead follow-up categories of DIPA.

As a sales professional, speaker, and coach, I've discovered three actions that lead directly to leveraging your career and increasing your income: personal development, role-playing, and evaluating personal progress (I discuss all three in the "Planning your day around DIPA" section, later in this chapter). I've yet to meet a salesperson who didn't achieve top level when he or she consistently applied these three DIPA actions over time. The best news of all is that you can dive into these actions from day one of your sales career and never stop.

The prep work: Indirect income-producing activities (IIPA)

As a salesperson, you keep busy with a lot of actions that, although they don't directly bring in income the way prospecting, following up on leads, or making a sales presentation does, are essential because they support these activities. Indirect income-producing activities, which I call IIPA, include the following:

✔ Developing programs to generate leads

✔ Creating marketing strategies

✔ Developing promotional pieces, such as brochures and mailings

✔ Encouraging brand-building and product awareness among the public

✔ Tracking, monitoring, and reviewing sales results

✔ Using social media platforms, such as LinkedIn, Facebook, and Twitter

Although critical, IIPA shouldn't be time-consuming — keep these tasks to an hour or so (or 10 to 15 percent) of your day.

Many salespeople have a pretty easy time finding the right balance of IIPA time. Those who find it more challenging tend to lean toward the marketing side of sales: creating new marketing strategies or perfecting sales processes or sales systems.

It seems as though everyone invests a fair amount of time on social media websites. For salespeople, social media provides a way to create leads and generate sales while sharing everything from personal experience with a product to special pricing events. Sometimes, those who see your postings will be curious about you and your company, and they might check out your profile on LinkedIn. So remember to keep your information current, responsive, and (most of all) professional.

The amount of time you invest on social media needs to be balanced. Far too many salespeople have gotten caught up in reading and posting, much to the detriment of their sales efforts. It's easy to lose track of time and end up spending hours on, say, Facebook, and before you know it, the day is over.

Social media is an IIPA that needs to be done, so to avoid wasting time, take 15 minutes when you come in to post an article or blog post in LinkedIn or share a quote on Facebook. Then move on to other tasks. During your lunch time, catch up and engage with a few people; then create a post for the end of the day. Your business-related social media efforts should total around 30 minutes a day.

In coaching thousands of salespeople, I've observed that the overload of IIPA usually comes in bunches. It's not a day-to-day problem but rather a weekly or monthly challenge. A salesperson devotes a few days straight to tracking, analysis, or marketing strategies, for example. Based on a 40-hour work week, if you invest, say, even 80 percent of your time for four workdays in a month, that equates to 26 hours of time invested in IIPA, for a total of 16 percent of your time.

Although important to your overall results, marketing efforts can consume more of a bite in your schedule than is warranted. Overinvesting time in IIPA can throw off your DIPA attention and, as a result, lower your sales. If you see evidence of this, here's the solution: Pick up the phone now.

Administrative stuff: Production-supporting activities (PSA)

Numerous tasks support the direct and indirect income-producing activities — you know, all the administrative details (processing orders, crafting emails, servicing customers, monitoring delivery and implementation of what was sold, and filing paperwork) that are unavoidable parts of the job. These tasks don't generate revenue or even indirectly lead to income, but someone has to do them as part of the DIPA and IIPA process.

As a salesperson, keeping in touch with your clients, confirming specific service details, and ensuring customer satisfaction are important tasks that lead to long-term business relationships. And the only way to have long-term clients is to meet with potential customers.

Calling on a prospect is clearly a DIPA action; then developing a sales proposal for the prospect is an IIPA project. But the actual process of compiling, organizing, and sending of the proposal — and all this process entails — is a production-supporting activity (PSA). The administrative staff often manages these tasks, but even among the most fully staffed sales departments, the sales folks themselves have to handle some of the PSA tasks.

Your goal is to reduce the time you invest in PSA to the smallest amount possible. Are you controlling your time so well that you're investing 10 to 15 percent — or less — in this area? The PSA work's value is set by what an administrative assistant in your company earns per hour. If more than 10 to 15 percent of workday hours are spent on administration tasks each day, you run the risk of not achieving your financial goals.

Although DIPA can be worth thousands of dollars an hour, PSA time is probably valued at $10 to $20 per hour, depending on the market rate for good administrative help. The time you devote to the big-money activities is diminished, and you earn much less than you could.

Letting the numbers scare you straight

After asking hundreds of thousands of salespeople the normal amount of time they invest daily in DIPA and PSA actions, I've come to the universal numbers of two hours per day in DIPA and six hours per day in PSA. Does that sound like you? Here's a scenario that'll scare you straight. Say you earn $100,000 a year and work about 2,000 hours over that time. That means your value or worth is $50 per hour, or $400 a day based on 250 days of work.

Sounds pretty good, doesn't it? Even if you invest the majority of your time in constructing, filing, copying, attaching, researching, organizing, compiling, and emailing a proposal, you're making decent pay for secretarial work. But consider this: Administrative skills have a market value of $15 per hour. So if you're spending six hours of your day on PSA, your earnings for that time are a total of $90 — which means in the two hours you spend on DIPA, you're earning $310, or $155 an hour. That's more than ten times the value of your PSA time!

Here's the time investment of a typical salesperson:

✔ **DIPA compensation:** 2 hours × $155 = $310

✔ **PSA compensation:** 6 hours × $15 = $90

See where this is going? Yep, if you invert those activities — working six hours on DIPA and two hours on PSA, your earnings would be $960 a day, or $240,000 a year. I know you may feel sick at this point, realizing how much money you may be leaving on the table. That's the normal reaction I get from salespeople when we look at the real numbers and costs of PSA. The good news is that now you're aware that you have a choice in where you channel your efforts, you can make a change.

Everyone knows about lawyers and their billable hours, the time they bill out to clients. I was recently having lunch with a friend, a long-time attorney, and asked him what his goal was for daily billable hours. "Seven hours," he replied without pause. He knew his number.

Think of your DIPA time as billable hours and your PSA time as nonbillable hours. A $100,000-per-year salesperson who reduces PSA time by one hour per day and invests that hour in DIPA can see at least a $38,750 increase in income. In practice, the increase is typically more than that because the salesperson creates more momentum, increases his or her sales skills, and increases confidence.

Tracking Your Time to See Where You Stand

It's hard to know exactly how much time you spend on DIPA, IIPA, and PSA functions unless you've tracked your activities over a period of time to determine an average. Taking stock is important, and it supports an undeniable truth in sales: When performance is measured, performance improves.

Recording your activities

By tracking your time usage, you're guaranteed to increase your time effectiveness. Figure 20-2 shows a form I use at Sales Champions to help our clients record and report how they use their time in half-hour increments — in the appendix I've provided a full blank form for you to use. Most people have between 16 and 20 half-hour increments to invest at work daily. Here's how to use this form to help you make the most of those increments:

✔ Keep the form with you and fill it out as you go. Don't wait until the end of the day to complete it — you're bound to forget something.

✔ Track yourself for at least a week — longer is better. This allows for daily anomalies and helps create more of an average workflow.

Repeat the time-tracking process at least every six months. Over time, habits and behaviors may creep into your routine to diminish your effectiveness. A routine check-up keeps you on track.

Time	Activity	*DIPA*	*IIPA*	*PSA*
7:00-7:30		DIPA	IIPA	PSA
7:30-8:00		DIPA	IIPA	PSA
8:00-8:30		DIPA	IIPA	PSA
8:30-9:00		DIPA	IIPA	PSA
9:00-9:30		DIPA	IIPA	PSA
9:30-10:00		DIPA	IIPA	PSA
10:00-10:30		DIPA	IIPA	PSA
10:30-11:00		DIPA	IIPA	PSA
11:00-11:30		DIPA	IIPA	PSA
11:30-12:00		DIPA	IIPA	PSA
etc.				

Figure 20-2:
Tracking
activity by   DIPA Payoff Hours   _____
the half   IIPA Payoff Hours   _____
hour.   PSA Payoff Hours   _____
Total Hours   _____

The indirect income-producing activities are more subtle, and the definition of IIPA is more fluid than the definitions of DIPA and PSA. For your sales products or the services that you sell, what you consider to be IIPA may be different from what I do. There's no question that prospecting or lead follow-up is a DIPA action; and there's no question that crafting documents, collecting data, and other administrative activities are PSA actions. However, the middle ground is more open to interpretation. The ambiguity can lead to a misrepresentation of your time.

My best coaching advice is to free yourself to decide which sales-creating actions fit in each category. Really define your DIPA, IIPA, and PSA actions and create a list for each category so there's no guesswork and faking yourself out when your time allocation is off.

Evaluating your time-tracking sheets

The most successful salespeople are brutally honest with themselves and confront their strengths and weaknesses. They're able to look at their performance in an objective, real, honest, and constructive fashion. To get the most out of your personal evaluation, you should assess where you currently are with your time management before you plan how to allocate your time, noting where you're doing well and where you have room for improvement. Use your time-tracking sheets to identify how much time you spend in each category and when you perform tasks of a certain type. You can then use the review questions in this section during your self-evaluation sessions.

Looking back at your day

How often do you exclaim at the end of the day, "Where did the day go?" When you feel as though you've gotten nothing of significance done in the last eight hours on the job, go back and review the mix of PSA, IIPA, and DIPA. Then pinpoint the problems, plan for the next day, and nail down a schedule that ensures maximum productivity and keeps you on the path toward success. Ask yourself the following questions to identify what to change for tomorrow:

- ✔ When did you invest in DIPA in your day? Did you put off tackling your DIPA tasks until your day was derailed by interruptions?
- ✔ Were you so engrossed in IIPA tracking that you spent more time than you intended in analyzing the results?

- ✔ How did you break down DIPA time in terms of prospecting, lead follow-up, and sales presentations?
- ✔ Did you lose momentum by jumping back and forth between prospecting and lead follow-up?

Keep a level head as you evaluate your productivity by accepting that although today is gone, tomorrow is a new opportunity to get it right.

Reflecting on your week, month, quarter, and year

At the end of each week, wrap up with an evaluation of how you did, asking yourself the following questions. This needn't take any longer than 90 minutes.

- ✔ How much time did you spend in each category? Is your time investment a little off-balance?
- ✔ How many contacts, leads, appointments, and sales did you complete? Were those numbers better or less than your goals for the week?

When you're comfortable that you have a good handle on what happened this week, then evaluate what needs to happen *next* week:

- ✔ What needs to change next week to close any gaps?
- ✔ Which areas of DIPA do you need to focus on?
- ✔ How much DIPA time do you need to hit or exceed your sales goals?
- ✔ How can you increase the hours you invest in DIPA, and who or what can help you do so? What are the barriers to increasing DIPA time?

Repeat this process at the end of the month, quarter, and year, asking yourself how far behind you are for the month, quarter, or year to date. Your monthly reviews may take a couple of hours; a quarterly evaluation, perhaps a half-day. And at the end of the year, you may want to set aside a day or two to replay the whole year. Your yearly reviews differ in scope from your weekly and monthly recaps because you're looking for big-picture trends rather than daily or even hourly work routines.

Several years ago, my annual self-evaluation uncovered that if I don't take an extended break from work at about the ninth week, my effectiveness drops dramatically. I need at least a five-day break to recharge my batteries. If I don't put that break in my schedule, my intensity, focus, concentration, and results drop dramatically with each subsequent week. Most people limit their work patterns and intensity. Understanding your rhythm can dramatically increase productivity and results.

A DIPA success story

Kim, a one-on-one coaching client of mine, is an outstanding salesperson based in Eugene, Oregon. Every week, Kim gives me a report of her sales activity and time-investment breakdown into DIPA, IIPA, and PSA. I've worked with her for a handful of years and watched her income skyrocket from just over six figures to approaching seven figures this year. Her secret? She makes certain that her DIPA accounts for 75 percent or more of her time invested each week. She works an average of about 42 hours per week, with as much as 85 percent of those hours invested in DIPA. In addition, better than 50 percent of the DIPA hours invested are in the prospecting and lead follow-up segments of DIPA. She spends very little time in PSA. It's not a surprise that her income is higher than that of most heart surgeons in her town!

Planning Your Day around DIPA

Your first step in improving your time management is to decide to make DIPA a priority, to commit to it, to just do it! Stuff happens, and this is no greater a truth than in the world of sales. If you don't place your direct income-producing activities in your schedule, chances are that stuff will come along to commandeer your time — and the DIPA won't get done. If you fail to plan out the *where, when,* and *how* of your DIPA for the week or day, you can plan to fail.

Picking time for DIPA and using that slot wisely

Because DIPA tasks are the most important, you want to put those actions in the part of your day when you have the most energy, intensity, and focus. When are you better, sharper, or thinking most clearly during your day? When do you have the most energy and greatest focus? For most people, this period of high productivity is typically in the morning, but doesn't have to be.

Aligning your most productive time periods with your most important DIPA tasks is critical to your success on a daily basis. Whether you're an up-at-daybreak person like me or more like my wife, Joan — whose engine is misfiring until her second latte kicks in sometime between 9:00 and 10:00 a.m. — you want to determine your personal prime time sooner rather than later.

The best way to arrive at your alignment is through personal observation. Monitor yourself for a few weeks. You may even journal through your day, finding the sweet spot where you're most productive. You can also seek out the opinion of those who know you well. Ask your spouse or significant other, your co-workers, or your sales manager. You can even ask a parent, someone who's followed your biorhythms from your birth.

If you discover that your best time of day is the afternoon or evening, be especially diligent in protecting that high-powered period. As your day progresses, you encounter more opportunities for stuff to happen and derail your plans for an afternoon of DIPA. I'm not saying you can't do it, but just be aware that if you book your direct income-producing activities later in the day, you have to be extra wary of distractions, glitches, interruptions, and other trip-ups. (For advice on handling interruptions, see Chapter 15.)

Getting off to a good start

I'm at my best first thing in the morning. I have a greater storehouse of energy to invest, better intensity, and laser-like focus at that time. One of my critical DIPA actions is writing (as in this book). So when I'm in the middle of a book, I devote my early-morning hours to writing. In fact, I often wake up extra early to squeeze more morning into my day. With a 13-year-old and a 9-year-old, most mornings at my house are like a fire drill (and about that noisy), so it's not unheard of for me to be at my desk writing as early as 3:00 a.m.

When selling was my primary job — as it was for decades — I blocked my prospecting and lead follow-up time first thing in the morning as well (although I assure you I wasn't calling prospects at 3:00 in the morning!). I wanted to be sure that I aligned the high-production time with high-production action.

Giving priority to prospecting

Too many salespeople and even some sales trainers lump in lead follow-up with prospecting. Big mistake! These two actions are very different. *Prospecting* is the act of generating leads. *Lead follow-up* is keeping in contact with the leads in order to convert the leads into appointments or customers. During lead follow-up, you can dump some leads because their desire, need, ability, or authority isn't high enough or definable enough for you to serve them.

Combining prospecting and lead follow-up in one category is a mistake because most salespeople then take action only on the lead follow-up portion. When you're not creating or working new leads, your production and sales are only as good as the leads you have already. What happens if the leads are really low quality? What happens to your sales and earnings? Everything in terms of production, sales, and personal income is negatively affected.

I recommend investing at least 25 percent of your day — or at least two hours — to prospecting. You should also work to make that time consistent each day, meaning no bingeing on prospecting. Schedule the two hours each day and sew them in the schedule. Don't get to the end of the week, find out you're behind, and try to do marathon sessions to catch up.

Part of your prospecting investment is in *qualifying* prospects — determining their motivation, time frame, expectations, and experience; and which other companies may be competing for their business. You also want to know how they're going to make the decision. The questions you ask, whether on the phone or in person, help you use your time in the most efficient manner by eliminating prospects who don't exhibit the characteristics of a customer. The process also helps you craft the most on-target proposals to the prospects who do qualify as customers. Here are the three core elements to qualifying a prospect:

- **How much?** What's the size of the potential order? What can you expect in orders for the future? Can this prospect buy other products and services from you? In the scope of your current clients, where does this prospect fit?

- **How soon?** What's the time frame to buy? If the prospect is six months away from the final decision, a lot can happen to derail the sale. You also have to invest six months of calls, email, question answering, meetings, and presentations. However, if the prospect views you as a last-minute entry to the game, the prospect may perceive you as too risky because you haven't been part of the deliberations long enough. Some of selling is being there at the right time.

- **At what cost?** What's the cost in terms of your time, effort, energy, and emotion to create a sale? Some customers take large volumes of time for little return. You need to determine the costs and ask whether the sale is really worth it.

Leaving time for following up on leads

Lead follow-up is the process of converting your leads into customers — or at least into appointments. During lead follow-up, you can dump some leads when you determine they don't really meet the customer profile or it's clear that they're not in a position to buy at this time.

You should be spending less time on lead follow-up than on prospecting. Shoot for a 2:1 ratio at a minimum, or an estimated one hour per day. If you invert this ratio, you may run out of leads sooner than you anticipate — and find yourself playing prospecting catch-up.

If you have an overabundance of leads, then swing the percentages to lead follow-up for a few days, a week at the most. Just don't remain there too long, or you'll find your new leads dwindling.

Blocking out time for sales presentations

Many sales are completed in the sales presentation, where you're meeting face to face. But the online presentation world — such as meeting via Skype, GoToMeeting, or JoinMe — has exploded and creates options and efficiency in sales. These programs create a personal connection and offer a more experiential presentation than can be done over the phone, especially if you send supporting documentation beforehand. These type of sales presentations can save time. They require preplanning and scheduling, thus I rarely recommend doing an online presentation on the fly even those online presentations offer that level of flexibility.

Preschedule sales presentations in your time-blocked schedule. (Turn to Chapter 5 for more on time blocking.) As a salesperson, I knew how long a sales presentation took to conduct, so I typically had preplanned slots to do them. When I was prospecting, I'd use alternate-choice closes to garner appointments, such as "Would Wednesday at 1:15 p.m. or Thursday at 3:15 p.m. work better for you?" It kept me focused on booking appointments, and it increased my effective use of time through better organization of my schedule. It also helped me avoid the poor technique that most salespeople employ, which is asking, "When do you want to get together?"

Planning for personal development

The books you read, seminars you attend, CDs you listen to, and videos you watch can all have a dramatic and positive influence your level of sales success. When you invest your time into these learning activities, you can count on a healthy return. Although formal classes and classroom study are good ways to continue your quest for knowledge, you can squeeze in lots of learning opportunities without giving up vast amounts of time. Here's how:

- ✔ **Sign up for seminars.** Sales and motivational experts make speaking tours to many cities throughout the country, and they frequently offer workshops or programs that may be no more than a day or a half-day in length.

- ✔ **Turn your car into an audio university.** Make the most of your commute. Turn off your favorite top 40 station or talk radio show and stick in a book-on-CD or recorded podcast instead. The number of books offered today in a downloadable audio format via Audible.com or Amazon.com is staggering. Use the time to expand your knowledge about your industry, your career, or human psychology. With the amount of time you spend in your car over the course of a year, you can theoretically put in enough hours to earn a college degree.

✔ **Learn while you fly.** Turn business travel into an opportunity to bone up on a new topic. After you reach that comfortable flying altitude, you're free to turn on the laptop or pop on your earphones for CD study.

✔ **Attend webinars.** The training webinar is ubiquitous today. There are literally thousands from which to choose each day. Many experts offer free or low-cost webinar subscription services, which give you the opportunity to follow and learn from someone you respect.

Continuing education: A lifelong journey

I remember attending my first professional sales seminar like it was yesterday. I was fascinated with the speaker's understanding of how to become more successful, how he broke success down to a simple series of actions. One of those actions was personal development. He asked the attendees how many books they'd read in the last year. I was relieved we didn't have to share our responses with the group. Reviewing the last few years out of college, I could count the number of books I'd read on the fingers of one hand. And it occurred to me at that moment that there was a direct connection between the low numbers in my bank account and the number of books read, seminars attended, and self-improvement CDs listened to.

That was 25 years ago. The amount of time and energy I've invested in continued learning and personal development is immeasurable. I couldn't count all the books I've read or experts I've listened to, but I can tell you they far exceed the number of fingers and toes I have — and probably the total fingers and toes of my family, employees, and professional colleagues combined. And undeniably, my bank account reflects the riches and wisdom I've collected.

Wherever you are in your journey of lifelong learning — whether you have a high school diploma or a doctorate degree; whether you're fresh out of school or many miles into your career — you can reap great rewards from continuing the process of learning. Don't feel limited to the confines of formal education; the knowledge you pick up from printed and audio books, downloads, CDs, seminars, continuing education courses, white papers, podcasts, webinars, and computer studies goes a long way in boosting your sales success.

Role-playing: Getting ready for prime time

I put a great deal of emphasis on role-playing in preparing for appointments and sales presentations. These dress rehearsals are much more than a fun and frivolous exercise; they're a critical step in increasing a positive outcome from a direct income-producing experience. If you invest your time in role-playing, and perfect your scripts and delivery skills, you're bound to grow your sales results.

The time to practice isn't when your commission check is on the line! Here are some tips for working in some practice through role-playing:

- **Set a time and place to role-play and put it in your schedule.** Don't book appointments in your role-playing time — protect role-playing as if it were an appointment itself. Role-playing is usually the first thing sales-people cut when they get busy.

- **Start with your appointment-setting techniques.** These are the most important because if you can't get in front of the prospect to make a pre-sentation, it doesn't matter how good your presentation is.

- **Enlist a partner.** To really role-play well, you need a partner. Why not practice on someone other than a prospect? You can find another sales-person in the office or you can ask someone who has a vested interest in your career.

   Early in my sales career, my wife, Joan, listened to literally thousands of my sales presentations, objection-handling scripts and dialogues, and trial and final closes. In fact, to this day she could probably outsell most of the sales-people in the field because she knows the scripts and can deliver them!

- **Have your partner offer various responses (without setting out to antagonize you).** The objective of role-playing is to develop good skills and gain confidence. You want to practice making the sale. You want stalls, objections, and problems brought forth from your role-playing partner. The other person just doesn't have permission to be a jerk.

To improve the quality of your message, you can rely on the two following theories:

- **The *X* Theory of Success:** Becoming proficient at anything always takes a certain amount of time, which I call *X*. *X* is different for each person because it's based on innate talents and previous experiences and skills. The more talents and previous experience you have, the less practice you need.

   For example, to deliver your presentation with power and conviction, handle objections, and persuade the prospect to sign the contract, you may need 100 practice sessions. I may have a tougher time and may need to practice 200 times before I get it down pat. However, the issue isn't that I take twice as long as you to achieve success but that I have an idea of where X is and that I'm working toward it regularly.

- **The Y Theory of Choice:** After you know how many times you have to practice your presentation, you can choose how long you'll take, which is the *Y Theory of Choice* in action. You can take ten years, five years, two years, one year, or perhaps even just six months. For example, if I conduct my presentation live only in front of prospects and don't practice, it'll take me a long time to reach my 200. If I'm in front of prospects three or four times a month, I may need more than five years to complete my 200 presentations.

Your success in improving the quality of your message is determined by crossing the finish line (X) and using the shortest amount of time (Y) to get there. A top salesperson uses a combination of presentations to prospects and a larger number of practice or role-playing sessions to advance further faster when striving to improver message quality.

Evaluating your sales presentation performance

The time you invest in evaluating your personal performance absolutely earns a DIPA rating. What you do with your time, how you invest it, how you make decisions, how you use your skills, how you work to improve — all these actions influence your personal productivity, and all warrant your most honest attention. (Although some people may feel that self-evaluation is IIPA, I really believe most salespeople don't invest enough time in evaluation, limiting their improvement.)

If you have aspirations to improve and increase your income, you have to be willing to critique your performance. Ask yourself the following questions:

- How is your opening statement? Does it create a high level of connection and interest?
- Do you harvest viable leads?
- How effective is your lead follow-up sequence?
- How well do you deliver your sales presentation?
- Do you give yourself high marks in confidence, conviction, enthusiasm, and assertiveness?
- Do you listen or speak more than your prospect?
- How well do you present benefits aligned with the needs of prospects?

✔ What's the conversion rate of leads to sales presentations? What's the conversion rate from leads to sales? What's the choke point to improvement in this area?

Also do sublevel evaluations for a sales presentation in the area of objections-handling and closing. These two areas really separate the top-level salespeople from the middle of the pack:

✔ How well do you know the objection scripts furnished by your company? Do you practice them weekly?

✔ Can you deliver them under pressure in a sales presentation with eloquence?

✔ At the end of an objection that a prospect raises, can you shift to closing?

✔ In closing, do you ask for the order in closing more than four times?

Honest personal evaluation takes guts. Focusing on your problems, mistakes, and faults isn't fun. Although many salespeople may rank prospecting as their least-favorite activity, I suspect that personal evaluation is really the most difficult task. But if you never look in the mirror, you may never glimpse those ugly truths and correct them so you can achieve the success you deserve.

Scheduling your DIPA time

To make sure you focus on the most essential direct income-producing activities, be sure to separate out the most important and devote a specific amount of time to each. Of the many DIPA functions that you regularly undertake, a handful are critical to perform regularly, if not on a daily basis. To stay focused, set aside time specifically for each function. Don't lump everything together in a single DIPA time slot.

As you schedule time for your direct income-producing activities, consider these tips (and see Chapter 5 for more-detailed guidance on scheduling your time):

✔ **Batch like activities together.** Don't make two prospecting calls, do a couple of lead follow-up calls, and then go back to more prospecting. This disintegrates into multitasking, which is inefficient.

✔ **Set aside at least one hour at a time.** Give yourself enough time to build momentum for greatest productivity.

✔ **Schedule a break between activities.** Giving yourself 15 minutes to stretch your legs, return some calls, or even get a cup of coffee enables you to clear your mind and transfer your thinking to a new prospect, lead follow-up call, or other action.

Incorporating IIPA into Your Day

After you've worked your schedule around your direct income-producing time, it's time to fit indirect income-producing activities (IIPA) into your day. Because they aren't linked as closely to bottom-line measures, IIPA tasks shouldn't take up as much of your energy, but in no way should you overlook them, either. Your goal is to budget time for them but keep them from eating into the most lucrative activities.

Using IIPA time to review sales results

By figuring out what works — and what doesn't — you can channel your efforts into activities that multiply your income. Examining how many leads a particular marketing piece generates, tracking the conversion rate of leads to sales, and plotting average order and average commission all fall under IIPA.

The time you spend gathering and analyzing data doesn't earn you money directly, but it does show you what works and which DIPA efforts you may need to tweak. For example, say your tracking reveals that from 20 leads, you convert only one of those to a sale. The barrier is likely between the leads and the sales presentation. I'm simplifying (you may have problems at the presentation level or at other stages, too), but the point is that by analyzing each step of the sales process, you can zero in on your strengths and areas of further work. Here's what you may discover from results tracking:

- **You're pursuing low-quality leads.** This may be true, but most of the time, it's not the case. Check with the other salespeople — if they're achieving low results from these leads, the problem probably *is* with the quality of the leads. However, if other salespeople are booking five appointments to your one appointment, look elsewhere for the problem.

- **Your lead follow-up strategy is off.** Take a look at your lead-qualifying tactics. You may not be doing an effective job of determining the time frame, motivation, and urgency of your prospects. You may not be assessing the level of competition or the level of commitment. The result is that you end up spending a lot of time pursuing individuals who should've been eliminated during your lead investigation.

- **You failed to grab the prospect's interest.** From the first moment of contact, you have seven seconds to hook a prospect. You need to hit that prospect between the eyes with your value proposition. What benefits you are offering with what you're selling?

Keeping IIPA in check

To keep IIPA in check while staying on top of everything, I suggest these four tactics:

- ✓ **Relegate IIPA to the afternoon.** Unless you don't fully engage in the day until noon, you want to set aside the morning for your most important income-producing activities. IIPA functions typically don't require the same level of energy as DIPA. And because they aren't as critical as DIPA, holding off on IIPA ensures that you wrestle the most important activities first, before something comes along to derail your day.

- ✓ **Work on social media IIPA in bursts.** Schedule two or three 15-minute segments of social media interaction a day. Keep that in balance!

- ✓ **Keep IIPA to 90 minutes or less a day.** Marketing, social media, evaluating others' sales performance, analyzing your lead follow-up, scheduling the next day's setup, and reviewing call sheets are all effective uses of IIPA time, provided you don't spend hours daily doing them.

- ✓ **Use the end of the day to prepare for tomorrow.** One of the best uses of IIPA time is preparing your sales calls, sales strategy, opening statements, and call objectives for the next day. Investing a mere 15 to 30 minutes today means you're able to instantly click into DIPA tomorrow. You'll be less likely to stall, evade, and avoid the calls if your call sheets or call logs are on your desk.

Even if you do most of your prospecting and lead follow-up out of your computer customer relationship management (CRM) program (see Chapter 8), I still encourage some salespeople to at least print out a hard copy of their calls on paper during their IIPA time today before they leave. Some salespeople get overwhelmed with the call numbers in their CRM. Engaging in creative avoidance is harder when you see all these names on a page rather than on a computer screen. Some salespeople are better with a list and can see the check marks on their page. If that works better for you, do it. Technology for the sake of technology doesn't necessarily make things better.

Decreasing Your PSA Time

The goal of any salesperson is to get those administrative production-support activities (PSA) down to well under two hours a day, freeing up more time for prospecting, calling, lead follow-up, and other direct income-producing activities (DIPA). Awareness is the first step toward the proper alignment of DIPA to PSA. For a good gauge of where your time is going, track your daily activities for a period of several weeks using the form in Figure 20-2, earlier in this chapter.

Armed with the understanding that spending time on PSA saps your DIPA energies, you may be tempted to set a zero-tolerance policy for PSA. The truth is you'll never be able to avoid PSA actions completely, even if you employ an army of administrative help. Here's the conundrum: The more you invest in DIPA, the more PSA actions you generate. The two are interconnected. You make prospecting calls (DIPA), and a prospect wants a brochure, marketing material about a product, a quote, or even a sales proposal (PSA). Or you make a sale to a prospect (DIPA), and you now have to write the order, turn it in, follow up on the order and administrative team, coordinate delivery, check back to make sure the customer is delighted and using your product, and possibly train the customer on the use (PSA). So frustrating though it may be, generating more PSA work because you're increasing your sales is a good thing. Your goal is simply to keep the PSA in check, making sure that you keep your DIPA-to-PSA ratio at a healthy 6:1.

PSA functions surrounding sales tend to be recurring, requiring weekly or even daily attention. Here are several ways to keep these supporting tasks on a firm leash:

- ✓ **Streamline the process.** Determine whether you can create a system to make a PSA process faster, possibly eliminating some unnecessary steps. It takes almost as much time to assemble one marketing material package and brochure as it does ten; invest the time to create the ten and have nine ready to go out the door.

- ✓ **Create templates.** Don't craft a sales or lead follow-up letter from scratch each time. The same goes for proposals. You can take a basic format and customize it for individual use.

- ✓ **Batch your work.** Make your PSA calls one after another. Bunch together the PSA actions as much as possible so you can move quickly from one similar call or action to another.

- ✓ **Eliminate the step.** Sometimes examining the process reveals that you don't need to do a particular task at all.

- ✓ **Delegate.** Is administrative help somewhere in your sales department? Can you find someone to lend a hand? Can internship programs provide some eager business students who want to learn the business from the ground up? A talk with your sales manager may help.

- ✓ **Hire help.** If you can't get support within your department, are you willing to pay a few bucks for it? Maybe you can hire a college or high school student, a stay-at-home parent, or a part-timer who just wants a low-pressure opportunity to earn a little money. For many of the PSA tasks that aren't proprietary, the work can be done off-site.

Remember: If you don't have an assistant, you *are* one. What I mean is this: If you don't have someone you can delegate the mailing, faxing, research, typing, low-level customer service, and a host of other actions to, you become the administrative assistant — and you earn your income commensurately.

✔ **Turn PSA work into DIPA work by asking for a referral.** When you have to do PSA work, you can often take the opportunity to get in a little DIPA action at the same time. For instance, customer service follow-up calls are part of your PSA. Checking to confirm that the prospect or client has received expected materials or information is a routine task that doesn't relate directly to generating income. But don't stop there — get some extra mileage from this PSA effort by turning your customer service call into a prospecting call: Ask for a referral.

It's never too early in a sales relationship to begin building a referral base. A truly qualified referral request, however, takes a little time and attention. Be ready to invest at least five minutes in conversation to avoid appearing like a hit-and-run referral driver. You may use a great segue statement like this: "I have a very important question to ask you." This statement forces a pause, builds anticipation, and sets the tone for a meaningful conversation. And it requests permission to explore client or prospect contacts. You may even use a script like this to help you:

"I'm delighted that I've been able to serve you. I was wondering about others you might know who would also benefit from my service. Could we explore for a few minutes other individuals you believe I might be able to serve?"

Questioning the way it's done

My late friend Zig Ziglar told a story about a 5-year-old boy watching his mother prepare a holiday meal. The boy asks her why she cuts off the end of the ham. "I don't know," she says. "My mother always did it this way." Now the boy says, "Let's call Grandma and find out why." So they call Grandma and ask her why she always cut the end of the ham off. Her reply? "The pan was too small."

People often continue to do their jobs a certain way because that's the way they've always done it. Sometimes the original reason for doing it is no longer relevant. Critically questioning your production-support activities can help identify and eliminate needless tasks, freeing up your energy for more-important activities.

Chapter 21

Time Management for Business Owners and Executives

Corporate executives and business owners are two of the most stressed-out and time-shorted categories of workers in the business world. A number of circumstances heighten the time pressures on these folks: Company leaders are charged with creating strategic plans and carrying them out. Entrepreneurs in the start-up stages are taxed with nurturing a fledgling business until it can fly on its own. And both feel the burden of bottom-line pressures: Is the company hitting the revenue goals? Are you making a profit? Are you growing the way you should? Are you in the black? What new products and services can I bring to the marketplace that will create a profit?

Here's another observation about these business leaders: Even after they've succeeded in launching and maintaining a viable and thriving enterprise, they can't seem to get off that fast track, gotta-do-everything-myself, 24/7 treadmill. Even when the business stabilizes and matures, these executives and owners struggle against pulling back, balancing their lives, and transitioning away from their insane work schedules. They seemingly become addicted to time deprivation.

If you suspect you're addicted to work stress, read on. In this chapter, I walk you through a successful withdrawal process to help you grow your business, empower your employees, and take a look at the big picture. It's painless, I promise. And I'm with you every step of the way.

Stepping Back and Observing Your Time Investment

Owners and executives may believe that a million things a day eat away their time. But in his book *The E-Myth* (HarperCollins), entrepreneur Michael E. Gerber claims that all the time spent falls into one of three big categories — and your business success depends on your ability to align these three realms in your schedule so you achieve the right balance:

- **Growth activities:** Expansion, increasing the customer base, adding to the product or service line, and other growth-oriented energies are what drive the long-term success of the business.

- **Work *in* the business:** This includes the administration, management, and internal operations of the company — in essence, what occurs within the company.

- **Work *on* the business:** These activities often involve stepping back and evaluating what's happening, assessing challenges, and looking for new opportunities.

To get your time under control, you have to be able to identify how you're spending it. The process is just like following a household budget: Before you can successfully manage your paycheck, you log your expenditures to determine where it's going.

Time-tracking is important for everyone, but executives and business owners can especially benefit from this self-knowledge. I use the chart in Figure 21-1 to help my clients monitor their time usage daily in each of the three time categories: growth, *in*, and *on* work.

What I've discovered over the years is that after tracking their time for a few weeks, most executives discover that they spend more than 80 percent of their time on working *in* the business. They typically spend less than 15 percent in growth activities and less than 5 percent working *on* the business. I've also found out that this is not the best time-mix formula for a successful business.

Owners and executives should invest 40 percent minimum in growth, no more than 25 percent in working *in* their business, and at least 15 percent of their time working *on* the business. I'm not a dilettante about the percentages — they vary upon your circumstances. You have some wiggle room to increase growth and *on* activities and even reduce the *in,* but this formula offers an excellent guideline. (And the best way to stick to the guideline is through the application of a time-blocked schedule. Turn to Chapter 5 for more on that.)

Time	Activity	Growth	In	On
7:00-7:30		Growth	In	On
7:30-8:00		Growth	In	On
8:00-8:30		Growth	In	On
8:30-9:00		Growth	In	On
9:00-9:30		Growth	In	On
9:30-10:00		Growth	In	On
10:00-10:30		Growth	In	On
10:30-11:00		Growth	In	On
11:00-11:30		Growth	In	On
11:30-12:00		Growth	In	On
etc.				

Figure 21-1:
Activity-
tracking
by the half
hour.

Growth   Hours_____

"In"   Hours_____

"On"   Hours_____

Total   Hours_____

After tracking your time daily, use the T-chart in Figure 21-2 for an entire week, compartmentalizing your week in the three areas of *growth, in,* and *on.* It'll give you a road map so you can determine what to delegate and to whom you should delegate the lower-value *in* activities. You need only write an action or activity down once. At the end of the week, walk through the

Activity Analysis T-chart

Growth	In

On

Figure 21-2:
A weekly
T-chart
helps iden-
tify tasks to
delegate.

Total Growth Hours _____

Total "In" Hours _____

Total "On" Hours _____

actions and determine how to delegate the low-value ones to another person or remove those activities. If you have to keep those activities, try to figure out where you may put these actions in the schedule so you can do them more efficiently or at a time when your energy is lower.

Increasing Time on Growth Activities

When identifying growth activities, look for things that offer long-term returns on investment. In the world of sales, for instance, direct income-producing activities (DIPA) are always considered growth activities (turn to Chapter 20 for more on DIPA). Here are some examples of growth areas:

- ✔ Prospecting for new customers
- ✔ Following up on sales leads
- ✔ Developing customer service strategies to maintain and up-sell existing clients
- ✔ Coaching and training staff
- ✔ Developing yourself professionally
- ✔ Developing strategic alliances
- ✔ Launching new products or services

Such growth activities demand a higher focus and energy level than the *in* and *on* work categories. That's why it's wise to schedule these efforts first rather than last. Use a time-blocking system (see Chapter 5) to schedule your growth activities, and tackle them when your energy level is at its peak — before the day's troubles and surprises start sabotaging your schedule.

The amount of time you devote to growth depends on your work. If your business is sales, I recommend dedicating no less than 50 percent of your day to growth, whether you're actively selling or leading a sales team. If you're leading a team in an area other than sales, I recommend spending at least 40 percent of your time in growth. Whether you should set aside time on a daily or weekly basis depends on your job, but it's likely to be a daily activity.

Track the percentage of your overall time spent on growth: Do a back-end analysis to verify that you're putting in the necessary amount of effort. You may have a day spent putting out fires, but evaluating your growth activity regularly allows you to allot the needed catch-up time before the week is out.

Your success in allocating the proper amount of time to growth activities requires a commitment. Start by setting a goal to spend a specific number of hours on a daily or weekly basis. Write it down and post it where you can see it each day. Put a sticky note on your computer monitor or put an index card on your bulletin board or even on your mirror at home. This visual reminder reinforces your good intentions and helps you discipline yourself to stay focused on growth.

Sticking with activities that don't bring an immediate return takes discipline, and growth activities are definitely a long-term investment. If necessary, share your growth commitment goals with others: a colleague, your administrative assistant, or another executive.

Responsive Tasks: Decreasing Your "In" Time

Here's an astute observation from British scholar C. Northcote Parkinson that has become universally embraced as Parkinson's Law: "Work expands to fill the time available for its completion." It's no more apt than when describing the activities of the *in*-the-business category — you know, all the administration and management stuff.

Awareness is the first step toward reducing the *in* time investment in your business. Identify the *in* activities and how much time you're spending on them, and you're soon on your way to whittling them down. I have one simple measure for recognizing *in* activities: In most cases, they're *responsive* tasks: efforts generated by some external trigger. This trigger can be a staff person who has asked for direction or a customer who has a question about your product. These activities aren't necessarily one-time incidents; the same external triggers can create fixed routines that end up on your desk. Consumer inquiries, for example, lead to a standard response process that involves sending out an information packet. Or the need for your employees to keep you in the loop results in a weekly staff meeting. These triggers — all part of doing business — often turn into processes and procedures that demand your attention and keep you working *in* the business.

The reports, the ordering, the return phone calls, the administration and filling orders, and keeping order and all the routine details that must be done — it's easy to let them consume all your time because they all *need* to be done. And frequently, they're activities that take little thought or effort — or even time. Problem is, in total they derail all the effort and energy you ought to be putting into growth and working-*on*-the-business activities. This section tells you how to cut *in* activities down to size.

Solidifying your organizational chart

The hierarchical structure you follow can have an impact on the effective time management for you and all the employees within that structure. Unfortunately, especially with a young company, when a business grows too fast or changes too drastically, it's easy to end up with an organizational chart that's stunted or entangled with limbs that just get in the way. When this happens, you can count on more of the workload shifting to the executive and leadership branches of the company.

Businesses that rely on a build-as-you-go organization chart typically end up with the same structure. And it looks something like Figure 21-3.

Figure 21-3:
An orga-
nizational
(org)
chart with
everyone
answering
directly
to the
executive.

The owner or key executive is the hub of the wheel, and all the areas, departments, or segments of the business connect to the hub. All decisions, employees, customers, and problems end up on the center desk. Under this structure, the employees are rarely empowered to make decisions at a level that makes operations efficient. In fact, this type of structure results in constant involvement from the hub, which means regular interruptions, low productivity, high frustration levels, and more work hours. Hub leaders find themselves staying late and working weekends, not because business is booming but because they're too busy juggling all the hats to get three, four, or more jobs done by the end of the workday.

Business leaders, be warned! Without a clearly established hierarchy that distributes decision-making and empowers employees, you — the executive or owner — get stuck as the hub, impaled by a circle of spokes.

What's most important for an effective organizational structure is a hierarchy with a solid foundation. And the traditional *pyramid* organizational chart, shown in Figure 21-4, is most widely used for good reason. It allows for the logical distribution of responsibility and decision-making — and level-appropriate weights — to a larger base. It relies on a chain of command in which the responsibility levels are clearly defined. This structure fosters a sense of ownership and responsibility at all levels. The upshot? Employees who have a clearly defined organizational chart to follow with a strong set of job tasks or job descriptions feel the highest sense of ownership, and what gets owned gets done!

Figure 21-4:
A pyramid structure empowers workers and reduces your burden.

Crafting clear job descriptions

Hiring capable people allows you to spend fewer hours *in* your business, and the first step to getting the right folks in the right seats is to have a clear set of job descriptions. You need to know precisely what you want the candidate to do.

Let my people delegate!

The challenges of building sound organizational structures are not just a 21st-century problem. In fact, this organizational overload has been around since Biblical times. Even Moses had his struggles with spreading the work. After leading the Israelites out of Egypt and into the wilderness, he found himself settling all the disputes for the whole nation of Israel. (Perhaps those run-ins with the Pharaoh made him particularly sensitive about "pyramid structure"?)

A typical day started first thing in the morning when Moses took his "seat of judgment" and ended at dark. It took his father-in-law, Jethro, the original productivity coach, essentially to say, "Wait a minute. Why are you the only one charged with this job?" Some translations indicate he said, "This is not good. You're going to wear yourself out and the people, too." Jethro then coached Moses through developing the first organizational chart and delegating some of the decision-making to others.

However, good job descriptions are just as essential for your current employees. After all, the best way to keep yourself from hovering over the desks of your employees is to give everyone a clear idea of what's expected of them and then let them do their jobs. If all your employees are armed with a clear understanding of their responsibilities, you're bound to spend more time making progress and waste less time stepping on or over each other — and your pyramid organizational structure (see the preceding section) is much more likely to stand the test of time.

Be sure a detailed, clear job description exists for each person on your staff or in your company — including you. You should be as familiar with a job description as the employee in that position is. A good job description should

- So clearly describe the particular role in the company that it could be used as a want ad that would bring in the ideal candidate for the job

- Be so detailed that your employee can use it as a pretty good guide to follow — even in your absence

Think specifics: Sure, your sales reps are supposed to sell your product, but that's not enough for a job description. What, exactly, do they sell? How do they sell? What must they do in order to sell — make phone calls? Set face-to-face appointments. Go door-to-door? How often? Monthly? Weekly? Daily? Hourly? And there's more. Does their job require certain skills? What's their top priority? Second priority? Third? Do they have to know how to use a computer? Certain software programs? What decisions do they have authority to make? Who, within the company, must they interface with?

Putting together a solid job description is more science than art, and it often requires someone with a human resources sensibility. In an existing company, check with the HR department first — you may discover that job descriptions exist for the positions you need to define. Or maybe you can start with an existing description as a template to develop new descriptions.

Creating room for growth with supplemental task lists

A supplemental task list — to complement a job description — provides employees room for growth and advancement. It also strengthens the base of your organizational pyramid, allowing you to delegate more tasks and lighten your own load. The supplemental list includes the tasks you want to transfer to employees from either yourself or someone else in your department. For instance, a task list for an administrative assistant may look something like this:

- Answer all incoming calls, screen calls, and take care of any calls that you can handle, if not take complete messages.
- Return phone calls (within three hours or at least same day).
- Open and distribute all incoming mail, except anything marked *personal.*
- Schedule all appointments and make sure that they're reflected in the scheduling program or day planner.
- Review the daily appointments; send thank-you notes as necessary.
- Complete all correspondence in a timely manner.
- Order supplies. Keep enough on hand so you won't run out at any time.
- Handle all mailing functions — sending mailings, buying postage, and so on.
- Update and maintain current mailing lists.

And here's a sample task list for a salesperson:

- Make 105 outbound calls daily.
- Make contact with at least 25 people per day.
- Complete 125 contacts weekly.
- Schedule 15 sales presentations weekly.
- Conduct ten sales presentations weekly.

✔ Sell five water filtration systems weekly.

✔ Practice scripts, dialogues, and objection handling for 30 minutes every day.

✔ Complete daily tracking report.

Devising a management plan

One step toward managing the *in* work is to develop and use an effective management plan. You don't need a manual the size of the New York City phone book; a *management plan* is simply a set of key guidelines and procedures that you and your staff can follow for greater productivity and focus on the goals. Here are some tips:

✔ **Base it on the core values.** A key component of your management plan is the core values and goals — the mission of your company (see "Planning Ahead: Your 'On' Time," later in this chapter). The mission serves as the umbrella under which everything else is sheltered.

✔ **Plug in the organization chart.** Establishing the who's-responsible-for-what flow helps keep everyone — including you — on the right track (see the earlier "Solidifying your organizational chart" section).

✔ **Add the job descriptions.** Include the detailed job descriptions of each person on your staff — and don't forget your own (check out the two preceding sections).

✔ **Gather activity-tracking charts on everyone in your company/department.** Have your staff fill out the activity-tracking chart in Figure 21-1 so you have a better idea of where everyone spends time currently.

As these components come together to form the management plan, you're bound to discover you still have some gaps in data. To gather that information, answer questions such as the following:

✔ How many people do you interact with regularly? How many people *should* you interact with?

✔ What are the top five time-wasters for you? Why?

✔ What are the top five time-wasters for the department/company?

✔ What are the daily or weekly time commitments that you can't change?

✔ What are the functions and work that only you can do?

✔ Are there any tasks or activities that only one or a few individuals can do?

With the answers to these questions, you're well-equipped to draw up a manifesto of the overall functioning of your area — establishing how much of the *in* work is to be performed and by whom. The goal of this process is to pinpoint the *in* work that can be removed from your plate and placed in the most appropriate spot.

Empowering your staff

When all decisions, both major and minor, need to be run through the executive, you end up with a tremendous waste of time. That setup does not motivate the employee and bogs down the executive. The solution is to *empower employees* to identify problems and come up with solutions — in other words, let them do their jobs.

In empowering others to make decisions, you have to accept that mistakes will happen. Give employees the freedom to make decisions and mistakes without fear of recrimination. If there are some areas so critical that you can't risk an error, then identify yourself as the final *okay* for those issues. (And hope that you aren't the one who makes the mistake!)

Some people claim they can do an activity faster than it'd take them to train someone, so it's not worth it. Sure, you may save time on this occasion if you just do the job yourself, but this outlook is only for the short term. I call this the *incandescent blind spot:* Compact fluorescent (CFL) light bulbs may cost twice as much as traditional incandescent bulbs today, but adding up the energy savings and a lifetime at least twice as long, there's no doubt that the CFL bulbs are the big cost-saver. Likewise, when you train your staff to take on some of the *in* activities that hijack your time, you save in the long run. Now that's a bright idea!

Encouragement can go a long way. Almost 20 years ago, I introduced a policy in my company that has dramatically reduced my *in* work. I call it the *No Problems, Only Solutions Policy,* and it works like this: Employees aren't permitted to come to me with a problem — unless they have at least two solutions. Everyone from the frontline administrative assistant to the senior executive is held to this rule. Prior to this, I realized that I employed smart people but didn't encourage them to use their problem-solving abilities. After I established the No Problems policy, I discovered it gave me more freedom, more time, and numerous teaching and coaching moments. I gained insight into how my employees thought. It also gave me a moment to encourage and further empower them.

Developing workers' talents: The secret of great leaders

Who's a great leader is always apparent when you look back to see how many of that leader's people advanced through the ranks to hold higher positions. You can find one of the best examples of this phenomenon in the field of athletics. Look at great football coaches, for example, and note that they often see their trusted assistant coaches get head coaching positions. It's almost as if there were a family tree that sprouts one head coach after another because of the immersion in values, excellence,

high expectation, training, and coaching. Head coaches such as Bill Walsh, Bill Parcells, and Tony Dungy have all developed numerous lieutenants who became head coaches themselves. That should be the goal of any executive or business owner: to develop the talent within and empower that talent to take on a greater role, increasing the overall success of the organization while reducing the exec's *in*-the-business time.

Organizing Daily Priorities

In any entity (but more so in small businesses), daily productivity can make or break a company. Your ability to set priorities and execute them impacts your customers, employees, and bottom line.

The most effective executives have a system by which they organize and prioritize their day. This section looks at a simple but effective prioritization system that identifies what's most important, what to delegate, and what to eliminate.

Establishing your daily priorities can help you make each day a 10. The system that I created a few years ago, known as the Daily Priority tool, enables you to get maximum value from your time. Turn to Chapter 5 to learn how to have a more organized day.

Planning Ahead: Balancing Your "On" Time

On time is planning time — and it's the most often overlooked process in business. That planning should have its roots in your company's vision and values, which are at the core of your business success. Make sure you establish those visions and values with careful thought, communicate them to everyone on the staff, and continue to convey and instill them through ongoing coaching and accountability among all employees. Here are the major ideas you need to outline:

✔ **Core purpose:** Why does your company exist? And don't say "to turn a profit." Profit is the result of a well-run company that has a clearly defined mission. This core purpose should be easily summarized in one or two sentences.

In my company, Sales Champions, our core purpose is "To teach and inspire people to use their God-given gifts to create excellence in life." One of my all-time favorite core purposes is from Mary Kay Cosmetics: "To provide unlimited opportunity to women." It has nothing to do with cosmetics — it's about people. I believe that if Mary Kay Ash had found another vehicle that would provide more opportunity to women, she would've changed businesses.

✔ **Core values:** These are the enduring tenets that guide your mission. Core values should be so simple and straightforward that you could explain them to your children. What are the values you'd hold onto even if they became a competitive disadvantage? For example, at Sale Champions, some of our core values are "hard work and continuous self improvement" and "exceptional execution of the fundamentals." Sony Corporation mentions "being a pioneer — not following others" and "doing the impossible," and Nordstrom values "service to the customer above all else." You save time by clearly knowing and living your core values — and having your staff know and live them as well.

Your core purpose and values serve as the foundation of your *on* responsibilities: your strategy, tactics, timing, people resources, and finances. They sit at the heart of every action, thought, hiring, firing, strategy, tactic, and expenditure. Aligning your big-picture view with your mission and values is a process that successful companies engage in regularly, investing at least 15 percent of their efforts in *on* activities.

Because planning time is so important to your success, you want to be sure that *on* time gets attention. The best way to identify your *on* duties and ensure they get the necessary attention is through weekly tracking (see Figure 21-1 for the activity tracking chart).

Take a look at your *on* tasks — study them to determine their frequency, asking yourself questions such as the following:

✔ Do these tasks happen or need to happen every day? Every week?

✔ Is this a periodic or even one-time activity?

✔ Have you neglected some planning activities that should be on the weekly or daily list?

✔ Are there easy opportunities to invest more time in *on* activities?

All staff members should be investing some time during their day in *on* time. Teaching the importance of *on* time is the first step. If you're leading other managers who get the standard of daily and weekly *on* time that's prescheduled, hold them accountable for it in your meetings. It'll be as hard for you to adhere to *on* time as it is for them, so ask them to hold you accountable to your *on* time as well.

Setting aside daily and monthly "on" time

On time has a tendency to be squeezed out more than the other two segments for a busy owner or executive. It gets the leftovers rather than the first fruits of your labor. But you need *on* time to evaluate your previous course so you can plot the adjustments you need to stay on track. Use this reflection time to set priorities, establish goals, and revise existing processes to further your efforts.

At a bare minimum, I recommend at least 30 minutes at the end of the day to review the day — you want to get insight from your day so you can improve tomorrow. Ask questions like the following:

✔ What went well today?

✔ What didn't go well today?

✔ What did you learn today?

✔ What would you have done differently?

✔ What are your priorities for tomorrow?

These questions and others like them will finish off today and set the table for tomorrow. I also advise that you schedule review time at the end of every week and month. An hour or two may be enough for an end-of-week wrap-up; for a month, you may need a half day.

Most people have fewer than 1,000 months in their whole lives, and you likely have more than a quarter of them gone as you're reading this book. So at the end of a month, you need to look at how the past month stacked up. Are you progressing toward your goals and objectives? What are the goals and objectives for the next months? What do you need your staff to focus on for the next 30 days? Take about a half day of *on* time to do a thorough evaluation of your month so you can invest it in the next month.

Performing a quarterly and yearly review of "on" time

You need to schedule quarterly and yearly reviews — wonderful predetermined *on* time breaks — with adequate amounts of time that correspond to their length. Owners and executives frequently omit the quarterly pause of *on* time — it really demands a day of uninterrupted focus — but that time is well worth it. Here's what to review:

✔ Where are your goals versus actual year-to-date results?

✔ What were the biggest challenges during the quarter?

✔ Has the competition changed in the quarter? Have the economic conditions changed?

✔ Do you need to make any adjustments in your strategy, tactics, lead sources, customers, products, presentation, marketing, or staffing?

This is the time to review the business plan, staff, goals, and results. You have enough time and data to be able to make course corrections in your business or department, being confident that you're not being reactionary.

An off-site *on* day is the best strategy because it reduces distractions.

The end of the year is a time for the most thorough analysis and evaluation. Over the years, I've personally found the last week of the year to be my favorite. I take the whole week to replay the year and invest the whole week in the *on* business activities. The *on* time of this week can ensure that the new year is your most productive and fruitful ever.

Chapter 22

Coaching Others to Manage Time Effectively

*I*f you have employees who report to you, being a good time manager isn't enough. For maximum benefit, your staff members also need to improve their time-management skills. Coaching your employees is part of your job, and improved time management makes everyone's job, including yours, much easier.

Walking each of your staff members through this book may be the best solution, but most managers (even you, with your new and improved time-management skills) probably can't devote a block of time to a mini-seminar for each of your employees on the whole book. However, you may want to walk your people through Chapters 4 and 5 and through the appropriate chapters in Part V — or simply provide this book as a reference. May I say I'd be pleased and proud to see a copy of *Successful Time Management For Dummies* on the desk of each person in your department?

But you can do more. This chapter offers a helping hand in getting your staff on board as to the value of time management and in helping them embrace strategies and techniques for lassoing that most important of resources: their time. In this chapter, I show you how to take a hard look at your employees' current time-management practices and how to develop a growth plan that you all buy into. I walk you through ways to ensure that the plan sticks and help you support your staff's efforts. Then I offer some strategies for handling situations in which an employee fails to improve.

Finding Out Who'd Benefit from Training

What you accomplish is a direct result of how you use your time. Pretty simple, right? So how *are* your employees using their time? Your first step in getting your employees on board with time management is to find out how efficient they are currently and to assess their strengths and weaknesses in terms of time management.

You may begin by reviewing their past performance evaluations and spending time observing your staff and their work habits. Then, most importantly, talk to each employee, getting input about the challenges and goals in time management.

Using the four probabilities of success as a gauge

As you gather information about an employee's time-management strengths and weakness, you may find it helpful to consider the four probabilities of success:

- ✔ Knowledge
- ✔ Skill
- ✔ Attitude
- ✔ Activities

When you improve employee performance in any one of these areas, your staff becomes more productive — and the individuals on your team become more successful.

Knowledge of time-management principles

A strong knowledge of proven time-management principles can increase the volume of work your staff can complete in an eight-hour day. Additionally, employees need to have a solid knowledge of their job and the responsibilities expected of them. When evaluating an individual's time-management potential based on knowledge, answer the following questions — based on your observations:

- ✔ Does the employee have the knowledge necessary to do his or her job in an efficient manner?
- ✔ How well-defined are this employee's life and business goals?

✔ Is the individual aware that time management is an important priority?

✔ Are the business goals yours or the employee's?

✔ Does the employee know how to work effectively to meet time goals?

✔ Do you talk about goals frequently and specifically enough?

✔ Does the employee understand the 80/20 rule: that 20 percent of effort brings about 80 percent of results? (See Chapter 5 for more on the 80/20 rule.)

Skill in time-management techniques

Skilled time managers usually acquire their expertise through practice, trial-and-error, and daily use of techniques (as well as a few failures). Your staff has to develop time-management expertise in the same way.

Employees who have time-related skills — such as the ability to organize themselves and their work area and use tools such as Evernote, Google Calendar, a CRM (customer relationship management) solution, time blocking, and organizers — are likely more efficient. Look at your staff and ask the following questions:

✔ Is the employee able to use organizational techniques and tools, including technology?

✔ Does the individual's work area seem organized and tidy?

✔ Do you notice that the person has difficulty diverting interruptions?

✔ Does the employee prioritize each day for the next before leaving for home?

✔ Have you noticed whether the employee regularly uses a planning system to track upcoming commitments or even the next day's work? Does he or she do this every evening or only once in a while?

✔ Is the staffer able to use a scheduling system to organize his or her day?

✔ Is the employee able to consistently keep commitments — including arriving at work and making it to meetings on time?

Attitude toward improving time management

Attitude is one of the most important factors in success. Maintaining a positive attitude is a choice, however, and it's one you have a right to expect your employees to make. A poor attitude leads to negative results and — you guessed it — more wasted time. Even if skills and knowledge are on the weaker side, a good attitude makes for faster and greater improvement in time management skills. As you study your employees, ask these questions to determine their attitude toward time management:

- ✓ Is the employee open to learning new techniques and skills to increase productivity?

- ✓ Has the individual proactively sought out advice or made efforts to improve time-management practices?

- ✓ Has the staffer exhibited a positive attitude in other situations in which improvement was needed?

- ✓ Does the employee convey confidence that he or she is able to develop more time-efficient habits?

Activities

In the business world, action is king. The biggest increase in productivity comes from selecting the right activities on which to spend your time. In Chapters 19, 20, and 21, I outline areas in which administrative employees, salespeople, and executives have to spend their time to produce better results more efficiently. As you evaluate your employees' activities, you may include these questions:

- ✓ In which activities does the person spend his or her time?

- ✓ How does the employee's eight-hour day break down? What percentage of his or her time is spent on each of these activities?

- ✓ Does the staffer avoid or postpone activities he or she doesn't like?

- ✓ What activities is the individual most comfortable doing? Are those activities best for the department and the company?

- ✓ Does the employee accept direction in terms of prioritization of activities?

Tapping into an employee's motivation

One critical key to success in helping an employee manage time is to involve the individual, so be sure one of the first steps you take is to confirm employee buy-in. You want to put together a plan in which the employee has as much ownership as you do, and that means involving him or her at the outset.

You can't afford *not* to pass along time-management tips to your employees. I liken true coaching to exercise: It may seem inconvenient and time-consuming, and sometimes it is, but the benefits so far outweigh the effort that it's impossible to justify skipping it.

If you're like most managers, you may find that training your employees in time management helps you improve your own time-management skills further. Teaching others is the best way to reinforce your knowledge and discover even more about a topic.

Don't neglect the costs of employees who work excessively. Some people feel that how many hours they work in a week is a badge of honor. This warped thought process leads to excessive time at the job, which can lead to burn-out, lower production, and lower levels of job satisfaction. If the employee isn't salaried, then overtime costs are significant to companies as well.

Discerning whether your employee is ready to change

My experience coaching thousands of people worldwide has taught me that most people don't change their time-management (or any other) strategy unless they're experiencing some type of pain: They've had enough, heard enough, or hurt enough:

- ✔ **Had enough:** They're frustrated and feel like they're always at work. They've missed enough dinners with family, T-ball games, swimming lessons, kindergarten graduations, and nights out to say, "I'm going to make a change." This one is the best of the three options because it's created internally, so it has greater odds of sticking. The employee may come to you for guidance.

- ✔ **Heard enough:** When a staffer reaches the "had enough" level but still presses on, ignoring repeated warnings in various forms, it may be time for the manager (that's you) to step in and have some serious discussions with him or her. Using this book, as well as stories of your victories and failures in time management, can bring the situation to light.

  I'm not suggesting nagging as a strategy to improve an employee's time management; I *am* suggesting that repetition and consistency of message have their place.

- ✔ **Hurt enough:** As a manager, friend, and colleague, "hurt enough" is the learning experience you want employees to avoid. An employee comes home one day and the kids and spouse are gone because he or she was *never* home. Or employee health issues border on catastrophic because he or she never "had time" to attend to his or her physical well-being.

Spend some time talking to the employee and you're bound to discover whether he or she has reached — or is close to — one of these crossroads. Then you want to try to connect with the person on an emotional level.

Helping your employee want to change

Most human beings make decisions — even big decisions — largely based on emotions. Then they justify those decisions with logic, data, or facts.

Achieving buy-in from employees isn't solely about goals, benefits, and time management skills. It's also about employees' emotions.

Tapping into your employees' feelings can help you persuade them to try your new time-management strategies. Try these questions to explore their emotions regarding time management:

- ✔ *"How do you feel when you miss your quota for the month?"*
- ✔ *"How do you feel when you're interrupted regularly by others?"*
- ✔ *"What are your feelings when I delegate a few projects in a row?"*

Next, use follow-up questions to move from emotions to action:

- ✔ *"How can I help you reduce those feelings? How can you reduce them?"*
- ✔ *"What can I do to help you feel more positive and energized rather than drained and frustrated? What can you do?"*

The answers — or *emotions* — your questions elicit help prompt your employee to buy into a plan for improved time management. Tell your employees that based on their responses, you'd like to work with them to develop a time-management plan with concrete steps they can take to improve their skills.

Establishing Goals

As soon as you understand a staff member's problem areas, the next step is to develop a plan to overcome these challenges and turn the employee into a productive, efficient dynamo. One of the first items on your agenda when you want to overhaul employees' time-management skills is to establish goals. As you craft the goals, you may want to turn back to Chapter 3 for more advice.

When establishing an employee's time-management goals, keep these pointers in mind:

- ✔ **Cast the goals in a positive light.** Instead of "stop coming in late," try "work to consistently come in on time or earlier."

- ✔ **Make goals realistic.** Goals should be challenging but not so difficult that the employee may become discouraged. If an employee is always late for work, insisting on 100-percent on-time arrival starting on day one may be setting the bar too high.

- ✔ **Break goals into manageable steps when possible.** What steps does your employee need to take to accomplish the goals? For instance, you may have your employee identify his most important tasks before trying to put them in order.

✔ **Make goals measurable.** First, determine how you can measure the progress:

- By projects completed?
- By an increase in responsibility?
- By adherence to new time-management strategies and systems?
- By a rating system you develop?

Then make sure you can measure the goals using numbers, whether percentages, totals, number of first-time responsibilities, or specific figures. With a measureable component, a goal such as "finish projects on time" becomes "strive to increase on-time completion of projects from 1 in 5 to 4 in 5" or "commit to completing all projects within 24 hours of the original deadline."

✔ **Give a target date for goals.** Without establishing a "by" date, your employees are less likely to be as motivated to do the hard work of change. To make sure the time line you attach to the goal is realistic, ask these questions:

- When do you want to see improvement? Next week? Next month? Next quarter?
- When is the employee's next performance review? Is it reasonable to expect X amount of improvement by that time?
- Are there company deadlines that have an impact on how quickly improvements need to be made?

With a target date, "reduce the number of interruptions to four times per morning" becomes "reduce the number of interruptions to four times per morning by month's end."

Have your employees develop *skills time lines,* which determine which skills, tools, or systems they must learn and implement and by what dates. Help your employees create their time lines, but let them do the bulk of the work themselves: It builds employees' ownership of the goals, and it teaches them the skill so they can do it themselves the next time.

Incorporating Tools and Strategies

Chances are your employees could use some tools, technology, and resources to assist with the process of adopting new time-management skills. As you put together your plan, select the tools you believe are most pertinent and work them into your overall strategy. Of course, all the content in this book is of great value, but here are some helpful tools and strategies your employees can use to address common time-management challenges:

- **Find where the time goes with time-tracking charts.** Plenty of people have difficulty identifying where their time goes. Your employees who struggle with productivity probably believe they're getting a lot done, when in all likelihood their days are peppered with disruption, drained from wasteful meetings, and dissolved by unimportant but time-consuming tasks.

  A time-tracking chart (see the appendix) commands users to look closely at their day, half-hour by half-hour. This tool is sure to unearth the worst time-stealing culprits, and the discovery of "where the time goes" is likely to liberate the employee into a more productive state of being.

- **Identify what comes first with the prioritization tool.** Some employees struggle with determining what's really important — which projects are most critical to address or which job to tackle first every day. What these folks need is a way to help them order their priorities. The prioritization tool spelled out in Chapter 5 helps individuals gather all their projects or tasks and go through a careful and deliberative process to put them in order. This is a process that you and the employee may want to work through together because work priorities are a combination of personal and business interests.

- **Get a grip on the day/week/month with time-blocking.** Who doesn't get so overwhelmed by a busy schedule that he or she misses an important meeting, forgets about a family event, or double-books appointments? The person who uses the time-blocking tool! By introducing your employees to time-blocking (see Chapter 5), you help them open the door to achieving so much more. Because time-blocking brings in all aspects of your life, from work to personal, those who use it often discover that they don't have to sacrifice family for work — or vice versa.

- **Head off drag time with the 11 a.m. rule.** As you direct your employees to block their time, arm them with the *11 a.m. rule,* scheduling the most important tasks of the day before 11 a.m. For most people, the hours before 11 a.m. are most productive. Workers tend to have more energy at the beginning of the day and, typically, there are fewer interruptions, problems, and "fires" to serve as distractions. When your employees tackle the most important tasks during their peak performance period, they're investing their best hours in the most critical activities before the day wears them down.

- **Combat interruptions with do-not-disturb policies.** All employees struggle with interruptions, but administrative staff are especially vulnerable. You may want to institute a time during the day when administrative employees are relieved of phone duties and other potential distractions (if you have more than one administrative assistant, rotate schedules so they're not all using their quiet time at once).

If a staff member has his or her own office, suggest that he or she shut the door, essentially hanging up a do-not-disturb sign. You can also have employees hang actual do-not-disturb signs if they work in a bullpen environment or cubicle. Help communicate their off-limits time to other staff members so they can be more productive.

Encourage employees to make the most of these time periods — somewhere between 60 to 90 minutes at a time — saving that time for the projects and tasks that require concentrated effort or intense focus, such as writing a report or doing research.

As you and your employee develop the plan for more effective time management, start small and then build on that. By starting small, you encounter less resistance. Employees won't roll their eyes when they see you coming, knowing you're on this "new time-management kick." And they won't secretly hope it all blows over so they can return to status quo in a few weeks. Instead of pressing the employee to commit to doubling productivity, begin by getting the individual to incorporate time-blocking or reducing daily interruptions into his or her daily routine. Focus on one small tool, strategy, or routine for a few weeks.

Fostering Partnership and Encouraging Success

I'm a big productivity and efficiency nut. I want the best possible value out of every second in life. When I was younger and attended conferences or read books, I came away with 101 new ideas on how my companies could operate with higher returns. I wanted to implement them all by *yesterday*.

My staff members started wincing when I brought my new ideas to the office, and they especially dreaded my return from conferences because I could point to XYZ Company, which was doing business this way and was hugely successful. I had validated results! But I can tell you, I didn't generate buy-in when I came back.

Time management is an evolving process. Acquiring new skills, making noticeable improvements, and completing complex projects are big steps. That means they take time, which means greater potential for an employee to veer off-course. You can't meet with the employee, set up the plan, and walk away, expecting everything to work. The employee is accountable for achieving these benchmarks, but you, as manager, have accountability, too. You have to nurture the process along the way. In this section, I explain how to approach the time-management plan as a partnership between you and the employee.

Setting up benchmarks and check-ins to instill accountability

As for accountability and performance change, two universal truths stand out:

- ✔ When performance is measured, performance improves.
- ✔ When performance is measured and reported, performance improves *faster*.

So as you put together the improvement plan, define *benchmarks* — progress stops along the way to the time-management goals (see the earlier "Establishing Goals" section) — and set check-in appointments in which you and the staffer meet to assess progress.

Check-ins with your employee may be frequent at first and become less frequent as time passes. You may schedule daily check-ins in the beginning, moving to weekly, biweekly, and monthly progress reports as the employee builds his or her time-management skills and achieves greater confidence. As you schedule the progress report points, determine the following:

- ✔ Whether employees need to hand in their measurement and tracking tools daily, weekly, or monthly; I have my employees hand in daily reports that track their activities by the half hour and show how they prioritize their tasks and projects
- ✔ Whether you'll meet face-to-face daily, weekly, or monthly to discuss employees' progress

If you can, schedule weekly or at least regular sessions with an employee, each session lasting at least a half hour. In addition to checking the benchmark status and getting an update from the staffer, you can introduce a new time-management technique. These sessions can help you keep tabs on the individual's progress and inspire the employee to stick with the effort.

Employees want to see improvement fast, or they may begin to think this time-management stuff is a bunch of bunk. So come up with some measurable and reasonable benchmarks that are certain to motivate the staffer to progress.

Taking a team-based approach to time management

If you feel uncomfortable engaging so personally in the lives of your team members, consider a group goal-setting session limited to business topics. Take your team off-site for an afternoon or, even better, a full day. Discuss departmental objectives, quotas, and benchmarks. Ask for input on goals, strategies to attain them, and bottlenecks where time is wasted or service doesn't meet the standard.

Set goals as a group and make sure everyone commits to them as a team. Then determine a team reward that energizes employees. Make it clear the reward is available to everyone who works toward it. The reward needs to be their idea: their reward and their commitment to deliver with excellence.

You may establish weekly time-management classes to raise awareness as well as skill levels, but make sure employees green-light the idea before you begin, or your results may be less than stellar.

Being consistent

If you delve into successful time-management strategies, you find that consistency is the secret sauce of success. As a manager looking to groom your staff into better time managers, consistency is important both in terms of what you should expect from your employees and what they should expect from you.

Model the behaviors you'd like employees to exhibit. Establish routines and then help employees develop their own routines. As you keep tabs on an employee's progress toward better time management, be consistent with the following:

- ✔ Employees' schedules
- ✔ Strategies for minimizing interruptions
- ✔ Meetings and appointments
- ✔ Memos
- ✔ Time-block schedules
- ✔ Priorities
- ✔ Expectations

When your staff members are confident that the priorities you set for them yesterday won't turn on end today, and when they can look to you as a manager who consistently makes appointments and meetings on time and responds promptly, they're more likely to embrace their time-management goals and improve their performance.

Fulfilling your role as a mirror

As your employees' manager and coach, you're in the mirror business. Ask employees to articulate their goals and then serve as a mirror to show them how what they do daily reflects what they claim they want. When you mirror an employee's vision — rather than your own expectations — you're more likely to motivate positively. Consider these two statements:

> *"You're not going to do a good job on this project if you're getting distracted by other things."*

> *"You shared with me that this project was extremely important to you. How do you see yourself completing it while directing most of your energy to these other tasks?"*

The first casts the goal as yours — not the employee's — and your feedback comes off as a reprimand. But when mirroring the employee's interests, as the second statement does, you come across as an ally in your employee's success.

Here are some effective mirroring phrases:

- *"You said you wanted to invest x hours a week in this activity. How are you doing so far? What do you need to do to improve that? What can I do to help you?"*

- *"What changes are in order to allow you to achieve those goals you told me about?"*

- *"Can I hold you accountable for meeting your goal?"*

The more clearly you see employees' goals, the more effectively you can remind them of their goals and reinforce that how they manage their time helps them achieve their goals.

Waiting for the "Aha!"

I once had a salesperson who struggled with a number of key issues but especially with investing too much time in unqualified prospects. He wanted to save these people, but he couldn't help them because his prospects hadn't arrived at a point where they wanted to change — and *not* changing didn't hurt them enough.

The salesperson called me and asked what to do with a prospect he hadn't closed. After listening to his story, I knew the prospect wouldn't be converted to a customer because he didn't meet the criteria for Sales Champions' pros-

pects. I asked the salesperson a few questions, and suddenly, the conversation changed. My salesperson took the lead, telling me why he should abandon this prospect and move on, even though he'd invested hours in moving the prospect toward a sale.

I asked myself, "Has he finally gotten it? Did he just put the puzzle together?" Before he hung up, he said, "Dirk, I get it!" That was the moment I'd been waiting for: the got-it moment. All the sweat, worry, and frustration had been worth it.

Dealing with a Lack of Progress: Can This Employee Be Saved?

When you make a commitment to help an employee improve, you invest time of your own and you understandably don't want to give up, even if things don't appear to be progressing. Unfortunately, not everybody can be saved. Sometimes, even though you follow all the steps I outline to help your staff members attain time-management enlightenment, you can't get through. In these circumstances, you may have to take a good, hard look at the situation and make some tough decisions.

If you're committed to healing your problem employee no matter what, be careful. Early in my sales management career, I was determined to make a particular salesperson better. I vowed that I'd make him into a good salesperson, even if it killed me. It almost did! I worried more about this salesperson and lost more sleep over him than any other I've had in my career. It was a big waste of time and energy because I was really more determined to make him a success than he was.

Before you invest the time in trying to save an employee, determine whether this is a problem that *can't* be fixed. Look for these signs:

✔ The employee has consistently failed to meet time-management benchmarks and goals established in your plan.

- ✔ The employee has failed to use the time-management tools you identified in the plan.

- ✔ The employee is neglecting opportunities to acquire knowledge or skills that could help him or her attain time-management goals.

- ✔ The employee has displayed a negative attitude despite your efforts to connect time-management improvement to his or her goals.

- ✔ The employee's time-management failures are having a measurable impact on your department or company goals. (Consider measurements such as revenue shortfall or missed deadlines.)

- ✔ The employee's limitations are having a detrimental effect on other staff.

If your employee meets even one of these criteria, you, as a manager, need to take action. Here are your options.

Accepting them, warts and all

If you're like most managers, you probably have at least one employee whose use of time makes you bite your lip (and your tongue). Despite your efforts and encouragement, you haven't seen any improvement. But because of other merits or strengths that the employee brings to the company, you may choose to let it go. Say, for example, the staffer is a prolific producer of business and meets all responsibilities, but simply can't manage her own time and often spends evenings and weekends in the office. Because her challenges don't affect her performance or disrupt anyone else in your department, you may be comfortable resigning yourself to this failing.

When evaluating this employee, address and document this shortcoming during the annual review. Your staff members need to be held accountable for their ability — or inability — to meet the goals you've set for them.

Giving it one more try

The original time-management improvement plan you mapped out with the employee should have had some give built into it. For example, the benchmarks you set may have allowed for extra time if the employee struggled a bit achieving that point. But if you want to give the employee one more chance, have at it: Be prepared to go through the discussion, review, and perhaps revision of the improvement plan, identifying tools and setting up a time line.

Maybe your problem employee only needs fine tuning. Answer these questions:

- ✔ What adjustment in the employee's time-management process would improve his or her performance?

- ✔ What skill, if he or she mastered it, would make this employee more productive?

- ✔ How can you help this employee increase his or her earnings?

- ✔ What would have to happen to allow this employee to leave work at 5 p.m. rather than 6:30 p.m. each night?

I suggest, at this juncture, that you tighten up the time frame for improvement. Suppose you originally had an overall time line of six months, with interim benchmarks every two weeks. This go-round, establish the expectation that the goals must be met within two or three months. After all, with all the time you've already invested in this employee, it's reasonable to expect results a lot earlier. In addition, be sure to clarify the consequences should the employee fail to improve at the end of this time.

Saying sayonara

One of my mentors, Dave Doeleman, taught me, "If you can't *change* people, you have to change *people.*" Time-management skills are critical to the success of an individual and to the team. If you have an employee whose failure to meet time-management goals is affecting the success of your area, and if you've done everything you can (as outlined in this chapter) to help the employee attain time-management skills, then you may find yourself obliged to let the individual go and replace him or her with someone who has his or her time under control — or who shows promise of developing the skills.

Part VI
The Part of Tens

In this part . . .

✔ Examine time-wasting habits and discover how to go from a time-waster to a time-saver.

✔ Learn how to develop positive habits that will save time for you and possibly those around you.

Chapter 23

Ten Time-Wasting Behaviors

With all the things you have to accomplish in a given day, wouldn't it be nice if the day were just a bit longer? Before you start thinking of ways to slow the rotation of the Earth, try to cut out some serious time-wasters — or at least reduce the amount of time you devote to them; it'll seem like you're gaining one, two, three, or even more hours to your day to invest in activities and pursuits that are important to you. Here are some of the most voracious devourers of your precious time.

Failing to Stop and Think

When you spend too little time in preparation, you're forced to spend too much time in execution. The time you invest in collecting, compiling, and organizing your thoughts before you begin a project pays off in time savings and in the quality of the outcome.

Not only does planning ahead eliminate problems before you start, but it also helps you imagine how you'll perform the task. When you address the situation in advance, you feed your subconscious with the tools and information it needs to work on the problems, often without your awareness. That's kind of like sticking bread dough in a warm space and letting it rise overnight — just consider your planning efforts to be the leavening that brings your projects to rise to their full potential.

Preparation is valuable in efforts big and small. Even 10 minutes at the end of a day to review your schedule and set out the materials you'll need is sure to increase your productivity and effectiveness the next day.

Multitasking

The scientific evidence overwhelmingly suggests that *multitasking* — switching back and forth between two or more tasks — is an extremely ineffective way to get things done. Researchers say that when you multitask, you're making your brain take time to switch to a different skill set and a different memory experience.

One study shows that when people who speak two languages are asked to switch between languages when counting objects, they have to slow down for each switch — even the language they're most familiar with. Another study indicates that when people start-stop on several tasks in a given time period, they increase the time needed for completion by as much as 500 percent.

Sometimes multitasking can't be helped: You're cooking dinner, helping one child with her homework, and telling another where he can find his soccer shoes. And sometimes multitasking doesn't affect productivity: You're reading a book while listening to jazz and stopping occasionally to respond to your spouse who's reading next to you.

For those projects and tasks that require your best effort, you're better off to focus on one at a time. Here's how to keep yourself focused on the task at hand:

- ✔ **Turn off or mute the ringer on your cell phone, or forward your phone to go directly to voice mail.** Even if you intend not to answer the call, the sound halts your attention and slows your progress.

- ✔ **Turn off the text chime on your phone.** You can create instant communication with your circle of friends and colleagues through text, but the challenge is the constant state of interruption that it causes. Create an electronic-free segment of your day. You accomplish more in that timeframe than any other during your day.

- ✔ **If working on the computer, set your email program so you're not notified every time you receive a new message.** You may check your email at certain time intervals or even arrange to check and respond to email in your time-block schedule. Turn to Chapter 5 for more about time-blocking.

- ✔ **If you're working on a report, article, or some project that demands a lot of concentration, set aside at least one hour of uninterrupted time.** You may not be able to finish it in that hour, but you'll get a good jump on it. An hour of focus is about all most people can do on an intense project without some type of break to get a cup of coffee or visit the restroom or just do a stretch.

See Chapter 15 for tips on handling interruptions.

Working without Breaks

There's a point of diminishing return where your focus and concentration start to fall dramatically. Too many people grind through, skip breaks, and cross that threshold. They sit and read the same paragraph over and over again because they're tired and out of focus. They review the same report again without realizing it until they're halfway through it.

Everyone needs breaks from routine and the tasks at hand. You should take frequent breaks but for very short durations. If you're given two 15-minute breaks a day plus your lunch hour, I suggest trying to take three 10-minute breaks or two 5-minute breaks and two 10-minute breaks for the day. I'm not suggesting taking more time than you're allowed by your boss, but to use it in short spurts to regain your focus and energy.

To achieve a true break, take a walk around the block. Leave your office and move your body. The act of physical movement connects with cleansing your brain, relaxing your mental muscle, and relieving stress. Don't take a break at your desk; detach from the project you're working on for at least 10 minutes.

Demanding Perfection

If you're expecting perfection from yourself or others, you're wasting your time. Letting imperfection keep you from pursuing recreational interests or your career goals can end up limiting your fulfillment in life.

The amount of time, effort, energy, and emotion required to achieve perfection dramatically reduce production. You may invest as much time and energy to move from a 95 percent performance score to the 100 percent mark as you do to go from 0 to 95 percent. You're much better off investing your energy in starting something new than focusing on perfection. Production beats perfection.

And if you refuse to give it a go until you're perfect, how will you ever get to be perfect? One of history's most prolific inventors, Thomas Edison, made hundreds of failed prototypes before he perfected inventions such as the light bulb.

Worrying and Waiting

Hand-in-hand, *worry* and *waiting* are two time-wasters that can undermine your success and happiness in life. Worry usually comes from dwelling on factors that you can't control. It's scary to think about overpowering forces that can have a devastating impact: a downturn in the economy, a hurricane, global warming. But if you spend time worrying, you're not spending time on ways you can prepare for or avoid such forces. Renowned self-help guru Dale Carnegie viewed it this way: "If you can't sleep, then get up and do something instead of lying there worrying. It's the worry that gets you, not the lack of sleep."

Another exercise to help you overcome worry is to ask yourself these four questions:

- ✔ What am I really worrying about?
- ✔ What can I do about it?
- ✔ What will I do about it?
- ✔ When will I take action?

A first cousin to *worry* is *waiting* — not the waiting for your spouse to meet you for dinner. Or the waiting to hear back from a client about your proposal. Or the waiting for the price on HDTV to go down. I'm talking about the waiting that often accompanies worry, the waiting that keeps you from taking a productive course of action.

Why not know now rather than later? If that client hasn't called you back, call her. You're going to find out the answer, anyway. If she gives you the bad news that you lost the competition for the business, find out now so you can do something about it or replace the business by prospecting. If you're waiting for the price of a TV to go down, how much do you really expect it to fall? Is enjoying it for a few months in your home worth a couple hundred dollars?

Hooking Up to the Tube

According to the Nielsen Company, the average person in the United States watches more than 28 hours of TV a week. Think about it: If you could eliminate that much viewing time, it'd be like having an eight-day week. Just think of all you could do with 28 extra hours: read a good book, spend time with your family, take a class, start working out — and even get a good night's sleep!

If you're a committed TV watcher, kicking the habit cold turkey probably isn't realistic. The withdrawal pains would be too severe. And truth is, television isn't all bad. Just like coffee, a little bit can do you some good. But to me, 28 hours of TV a week is the equivalent of a four-cup-a-day espresso habit.

Here are some ways to wean yourself off evenings and weekends glued to the couch:

- ✔ **Leave the TV off if you're not watching it.** Some folks like to have the tube on for company, but it's too tempting to wander over and plop yourself down if Oprah is hosting a controversial guest or the tribe is about to cast another member off the island.

- ✔ **Preplan your TV schedule.** Decide what's really important for you to watch. On Tuesday evening, if it's the 9 p.m. crime investigation series, so be it. But don't turn on the TV until it starts, and turn it off immediately upon seeing the closing credits.

- ✔ **Schedule no-watch zones throughout your week.** Maybe set aside a specific weeknight or weekend day when all household TVs remain off.

- ✔ **Reduce the number of TVs in your home.** Keep the TV out of the kitchen and bedroom, especially. Just as diet experts advise weight watchers to eat only in certain places in their houses, limiting the number of TVs helps keep the habit under control.

- ✔ **Prerecord what you want to watch and view it on your own schedule.** The added bonus? You get to skip over all the commercials, which reduces your viewing time by about one-third!

Surfing the Web

Nothing is wrong with hanging ten on the Internet — as long as the *ten* isn't ten hours. I'm not exaggerating when I report that although studies indicate the average per-day time online is one or two hours, a measurable percentage spend seven or more hours a day glued to their monitors! Studies also show that Internet time is increasing — and usurping other activities, including watching TV and reading.

The Internet is incredibly valuable as a time-saving tool. Just think how much faster pulling data and tracking down information is than in the past. But the Web is a storehouse of *useless* information as well. You can spend hours sifting through waves of data in search of what you really want to know, and before you know it, more than half the day has passed. Your original intentions suffer a wipeout as you get pulled off-course by information undertow.

When using the Internet for research or information-gathering, it pays to stay focused on your mission: What are you in search of? The annual report from a company you're pursuing as a client? The best bed-and-breakfasts available in St. Thomas in May? Don't get sidetracked by related information that steers you off-course. Put specific phrases in quotation marks to get exact matches or use the advanced search features to avoid certain words or limit your search to .org, .com, .gov, or .edu sites as needed. Bookmark sites you find especially useful, or copy and paste important info into a separate document, along with the URL where you found it, for later reference.

The biggest time-waster on the Internet is social media. There. I said it! The hours that most people spend on Facebook, Instagram, Twitter, and other sites is staggering. According to Ipsos Open Thinking Exchange, the average person ages 18 to 64 spends 3.2 hours a day on social media.

The best way to avoid the time-creep of wasted time in social media is to set limits. Set a limit of 30 minutes so you don't review every post and video that arrives in your newsfeed. Additionally, remove or block posters who are not real friends or post views you don't want to read. This can save time as well as emotional energy drain.

A big use of the Internet is for recreational pursuits: music, shopping, computer games, blogs, virtual worlds, porn. My advice: In some cases, you're best to cut off this activity completely. Many of these online behaviors can lead to serious problems, addictions, financial risk, and even personal safety issues. In other more benign situations, it's still a good idea to keep the online activity to a minimum and find your kicks in the real world instead.

Getting Caught in Junk Mail Undertow

As if it weren't enough to be inundated with credit card offers, catalogs, and direct marketing materials in your mailboxes, now your email inboxes are slammed with unsolicited tidings, commonly known as *spam*. At least email offerings don't waste the thousands and thousands of tons of paper that get tossed in the recycling bin. But everyone wastes too much time sifting through both paper and electronic mail to make sure they don't miss critical correspondence.

Recently at our house, I collected a month's worth of junk mail, which included 30 catalogs addressed to Joan. Interesting thing: She had only ever ordered from two of the catalogs. Apparently, these catalog companies sold her name to the other merchants.

Selling or exchanging mailing lists is a common practice among catalog companies. I bet if you check in the stack of offers you receive, you'll find a few different companies that misspell your name in exactly the same way. Coincidence? I don't think so.

Getting off all these lists is more of a challenge than it ought to be. Calling the company and asking to be taken off its list doesn't always work. And after you do get off a list, the same company may purchase a new list with your name on it, and the mail starts up again. Although many companies commit to purging your name from future purchased lists, this just doesn't always happen.

Being removed from some email lists can also be difficult. When you unsubscribe, it might trigger more activity because the sender has now confirmed yours is a live email address. Too, those companies may take you off their list, but they might give your address to another company. If you want to reduce your email and not receive further information from a legitimate company, simply unsubscribe. When you respond to spam, all you do is confirm your email address. The spammers know that the address is good and that a person opened their email. Now the spammers have three options: continue to send spam email to you, trade your address to another spammer, or sell your email to others . . . none of these options are good for you.

You can take some steps to reduce the deluge of paper and electronic mail that comes your way. However, it does take a little bit of a time investment to stop this time-waster:

- ✔ Register with www.dmachoice.org to be removed from direct-mail lists for up to three years.

- ✔ Go to www.optoutprescreen.com to get off mailing lists for prescreened credit and insurance offers.

- ✔ To reduce your catalog load, sign up with www.catalogchoice.org. You can manage your mail by selecting which catalogs you'd like to continue to receive and which you don't.

- ✔ Online, install a good spam manager program. Most capture the spam mail and offer you the opportunity to view it if you choose.

Be prepared: It can take as long as 10 weeks to see a reduction in your junk snail mail. Also, be sure to enter the names of all the people in your household — as well as variations of your name and address. Joan was actually receiving two catalogs from one fashion company: one to Joan Zeller and one to Joan Seller.

Killing Time in Transit

I used to envy those folks living in major metropolitan areas who could take advantage of efficient mass transportation. With the idea of hopping on a train and spending the commute reading, catching up on reports, and scheduling business commitments while leaving the driving to others, I wouldn't care if the commute were an hour!

That was an unrealistic fantasy, of course — my job required lots of driving to places not well-served by public transportation. That meant long, unproductive hours behind the wheel. Unproductive, that is, until I discovered that my automobile provided me with one of the most valuable opportunities I could've imagined. My vehicle became my very own *auto-university*.

At the time I turned to the cassette player — then to a CD player, and now an iPod or MP3 player. I turned my vehicle into a classroom for skills development and self-improvement. Instead of listening to commercial radio, switching stations as I drove out of signal, I put my ears to work listening to motivational speakers and how-to books on everything from personal finance to personal relationships.

I recommend some of my favorite audio programs from over the years: Jim Rohn's *The Art of Exceptional Living,* Earl Nightingale's *Lead the Field,* Brian Tracy's *The Psychology of Achievement,* and *Goals,* by my good friend, the late Zig Ziglar. I also recommend some of my own CD programs, which you can find at www.dirkzeller.com.

Although there's nothing wrong with listening to music or radio talk shows (one of my very best friends owns a number of radio stations), when you spend a lot of time in your car, you're better served by putting some of that time to good use.

Spending Time with Negative People

One way to bring down your energy level, reduce your enthusiasm, darken your outlook, slow your productivity, and drain your glass from half-full to almost-empty is to invest your time in negative people. The more you reduce the influence they have on your life, the happier and more productive you can be.

Easier said than done, I know. Chances are you have at least one foul-weather friend in your close circle. And you're likely related to someone who likes to remind you that you're not living up to your potential or that everyone is out to trip you up. Your negative associates don't necessarily focus their malcontent mojo toward *you*. They may, in fact, look at you as a shining success while they cast themselves as a poor victim of the world's injustices. But their pessimism is bound to rub off on you.

I don't suggest that you abandon friends and relatives who are suffering through hard times, whether due to illness, financial problems, or personal troubles. I'm talking about avoiding those people who are prone to see the negative side of life, no matter how much good fortune they have.

Do your best to minimize the time you spend in the company of curmudgeons and contrarians. Not only do you take back valuable time to direct toward positive endeavors, but their absence also breaks the dark spell over your optimistic outlook.

Chapter 24

Ten Time-Efficient Habits

Time management isn't a talent you're born with. You may need an amazing set of DNA to sing opera, win a triathlon, or get signed by the New York Giants, but with time management, you can work your way up to champion level without having the efficiency gene. Successful time management is a matter of habit. And in this chapter, I present you with the ten best habits to adopt for winning at time efficiency.

Start Your Day Early

Most people are more productive in the morning. That's logical: After sleep, you have more energy, you're more alert, and you've had less "day," when everything that could go wrong does. No doubt, a half-hour first thing in the morning is easily worth two hours at the end of the day.

When I have deadlines to hit and projects to complete, I set my alarm clock for a couple of hours earlier than normal. That's much more effective for me than trying to squeeze in the time in the evening. I'm generally too tired to focus well. I may go to bed as early as 8:00 p.m. in order to get up at 3:00 a.m. to put in some dedicated time. The house is quiet. I'm refreshed. My mind is alert. And my productivity is at its peak.

You don't have to set your alarm for the crack of dawn. An extra hour can buy you plenty of bonus time to take a big bite off your to-do list. Even just a half-hour earlier a day adds 182.5 hours to your year — 23 additional workdays:

365 days × ½ hour ÷ 8-hour workday ≈ 22.8 workdays

It really is the closest thing to buying more time.

Plan for the Next Day

Set aside time every day, at the end of the workday or before you wind down in the evening, to set up for the next day. Investing a half-hour, even as little as 10 or 15 minutes, can guarantee a higher return on productivity in as little as 24 hours.

As you confirm tomorrow's schedule and add to your to-do list, take your entire day into account — not just your work hours but your personal obligations, too. Think through all that you hope to accomplish, from the time the alarm clock goes off (need to take the cat to the vet or pick up dry cleaning?) through your workday (what meetings and presentations are scheduled?) and through the hours you have before your day concludes (time to return some phone calls to family and friends?). Then adjust your schedule accordingly.

As you set aside some uninterrupted planning time, do the following:

- ✓ Review tomorrow's work commitments and be sure your schedule is up-to-date.
- ✓ Integrate any personal appointments into your schedule, too.
- ✓ Make sure you have no scheduling conflicts. (Does your morning meeting allow you to get to your noon dentist appointment on time?)
- ✓ Add any items you didn't get to today.
- ✓ Anticipate and work in any plans or arrangements necessary for accomplishing tomorrow's to-dos.
- ✓ Identify your top priorities — if everything that could go wrong does, what do you absolutely have to accomplish?

See Chapter 5 for advice on planning your days using time-blocking.

Take Care of Your Health

Taking steps to stay well is one of the best time investments you can make. After all, if you lose work time because of frequent illness or you just don't have the stamina to put in a full day of activity, you lose productivity and get behind at work and at home.

Eating for optimal performance

You don't have to fuel up like a mountain climber or marathon runner, but eating healthy is as important for desk jockeys as it is for anyone who requires his or her body to be in top shape. A proper diet ensures the physical and mental energy required for a productive day. Here are some eating tips:

- **Schedule your meals.** If you have a tendency to skip meals, work them into your daily schedule, along with your business meetings and personal appointments.

    - **Breakfast:** Don't skip breakfast. Starting the day on an empty tank means you'll run out of steam before you get everything done.

    - **Lunch:** The break in the middle of the day works to rejuvenate you as much as the food you consume.

- **Pass on the empty calories.** A bag of chips and a soda may stop your stomach from growling, but it doesn't provide the slow-burning fuel you need to make it through the day. Choose a high-protein snack bar instead.

- **Choose small frequent meals throughout the course of the day.** Eating just one big meal or two big meals may leave you full and lethargic.

- **Eat a balanced diet.** Learn the basics of nutrition and let science, not the latest diet fads, guide your food choices. (For more on basic nutrition, visit www.mypyramid.gov or check out *Nutrition For Dummies,* by Carol Ann Rinzler [Wiley].)

Exercising for energy and stamina

I can't count how often I hear people say that physical activity helps their mental outlook as much as their physical well-being. Scientific evidence supports that exercise stimulates chemicals that send positive thoughts and increased energy to the brain, all sensations important for peak productivity.

So if you often talk yourself out of going to the gym because you don't have time, consider that you don't have time *not* to.

Carrying extra pounds is hard on your body, and it definitely slows you down — not the best condition for maximum time efficiency. But even folks who don't have a weight problem benefit from regular physical activity. To up your productivity, follow this advice:

- ✔ Work some physical exercise — as little as 20 minutes — into your schedule every day.

  If scheduling exercise time is difficult, work it into your day in small increments: Park farther from your office to get in a brisk walk; take the stairs instead of the elevator; use your lunch hour to get in some walking, stretching, or even a half-hour in the gym. Lift hand weights, do squats, and/or do crunches in your living room. Don't refuse to work out simply because you can't do a full hour — you're missing out on valuable opportunities to work your body. A little bit does go a long way.

- ✔ Find an activity that gets your heart rate up — walking or running, bicycling, swimming, or an aerobics class — and participate two or three hours a week.

- ✔ Find an activity you enjoy instead of forcing yourself to follow some unappealing regimen.

Sleeping for rejuvenation

Getting enough rest to recharge is paramount. Going to bed early enough so you're well rested can improve your time management and energy level the next day. Know your amount of needed rest that your body craves. Establish your schedule to coincide with that amount.

One of the best techniques for helping yourself recharge with sleep is napping. I'm especially fond of afternoon naps on weekends. They help me to catch up on my rest and wake up really refreshed.

Set Aside Downtime

An issue that's gotten a lot of press in the world of parenting is overscheduling children. Child development experts point out that kids' schedules are so packed with school, music lessons, sports activities, play dates, and other commitments that they have virtually no downtime in which to develop their creativity and imagination.

Whether you call it prayer, meditation, clearing your mind, quiet time, or goofing off, adults need these unstructured blocks of time, too. Extremely busy people may find it hard to justify doing nothing when so much work awaits them, but these periods of reflection stretch your thinking muscles, release built-up stress, and lead you to new insights and greater understanding. And that's hardly "nothing."

I notice a significant improvement in my effectiveness, energy, and outlook when I adhere to a morning routine that starts with prayer and reading the Bible each day at 5 a.m. Here are some ways to find a quiet time that works best for you:

- ✔ Sit outside, in your backyard or a public garden, and let your mind wander.

- ✔ Take a walk with no destination in mind.

- ✔ Listen to wordless music.

- ✔ Meditate.

- ✔ Read spiritual, inspirational, or thought-provoking material.

- ✔ Pray — most religions have some tradition of daily prayer.

Plan Meals for the Week

My mother, one of the most efficient people I've ever known, demonstrated her organizational proficiency by deliberately planning our meals. She sat down each week with paper and pencil and mapped out our meals for the next seven days, considering our schedules, special occasions (birthdays, for example), and what items were on special at the grocery that week. She reviewed the cupboards and pantry to make sure she had all the ingredients she needed, and then she made her grocery list. When she hit the supermarket, she shopped with a plan: Not a superfluous minute was wasted on impulse. She was a mom on a mission — she knew what she wanted and where to find it. And she only had to do it once a week — no quick stops for a forgotten ingredient. My mom's extreme efficiency in meal planning paid off in time freed up to enjoy dinner and conversation with her husband and sons.

Make a habit of making a once-a-week meal plan so you don't have to waste time contemplating what to eat — no more frantic sweeps through a fast-food drive-through because you don't have anything in the house.

You can apply a weekly-plan habit to aspects of your life other than meals as well. For instance, plan what you're going to wear each day so you can be sure everything is washed, returned from the dry cleaner, shined, and repaired.

Delegate Almost Everything

Figure out what's most important to you, and delegate everything else. In Chapter 5, I walk you through the process of identifying your priorities. As soon as you have that list (and I suggest you write them down and keep them in front of you), you can better determine which activities support those priorities and which, though necessary to complete, can be handled by someone else.

Sometimes, what seems like an activity to be delegated is, in reality, one that's close to the heart of your most cherished values. I can't say that I'm big on playing tea party. But the joy I see in my daughter Annabelle's face when I join her on the floor with her dolls brings me joy and deep fulfillment. I wouldn't delegate doll-playing to anyone. On the other hand, I detest yard work. Of course, it's important to me — and my neighbors — to keep up with cutting the grass. But in my grand list of top priorities, spending time in my yard doesn't even make the top 100. So I delegate it, along with other manly responsibilities such as changing the oil in my car, repairing a leak in the sink, and other choice tasks. Faced with one of these activities, I join my daughter on the floor for a doll tea party and say, "Pass me the imaginary cream, please."

Say No More Often

You've heard it said that if you want something done, then ask a busy person to do it. It's true that the most productive people seem to be able to juggle more responsibilities and activities. But what a too-busy person achieves in quantity often comes at the cost of quality. To get the most satisfaction out of the work you do and the pastimes you engage in, you need to protect them from getting swallowed up by other commitments.

The demands on your time are limitless. Time is a finite resource. Figure out how to recognize when the hourglass is almost out of sand, and protect your time by saying *no*. Return to your list of priorities and evaluate whether your plate is filled with unrelated commitments. If so, scrape them off as possible to make room for the things that really matter to you. And when the next wave of people serves up more requests for your time, politely put your hand over the plate and say, "No, thank you. I'm full."

Always Use a Time-Management System

To best retain your time-management skills, adopt a system for managing your time. And stick to it. With regular use, such a system gets easier to use and brings a greater return with time. In Chapter 5, I show you how to use time-blocking, a system I stand by because I've seen how it yields success time and again.

Simplify Your Life

Just as material possessions take up space in your home and office, they also clutter up your time. I have a client who lived in Manhattan for several years and decided he needed to buy a car. He kept it for less than a year before he realized it was costing him money and time: filling it up, maintaining it, parking it, insuring it. He initially bought the car because he thought it'd simplify his life, but he quickly realized it added complexity that he hadn't imagined. Life was much simpler when he relied on taxis and subways.

Most people have too much stuff. There are 2.3 billion square feet of self-storage, translating to 7 square feet for every man, woman, and child in the United States. Storing stuff has moved from transitional storage to permanent storage, and more than one in ten households rent a storage unit. Imagine the amount of time and money spent to store things no one is using.

Having and caring for possessions takes a lot of time. The fewer you have, the simpler life becomes. I'm not suggesting you return to Walden Pond or join a commune. Nothing's wrong with having things that bring you happiness and pleasure. If you love getting in your daily laps and spending time sunning yourself by your in-ground swimming pool, savor the joy it brings you whenever you can. But the more you can divest yourself of your other leisure toys, the more you're able to focus on your time enjoying the pool.

Return to your priorities list and take stock of how your material wealth aligns with your goals. Identify what relates, and get rid of as much of the rest as you can. Having fewer material burdens is one of the most liberating feelings you can experience.

Begin Every Day at Zero

Leave all your baggage from the day before where it belongs: in the past. Whatever mistakes, disappointments, losses, embarrassments, and failures you suffered yesterday don't have to affect the outcome of today.

As the saying goes, the past is history. The future is a mystery. Today is a gift; that's why they call it the *present*. Unwrap each day with the anticipation and expectation of unfolding a wonderful day of production, success, fulfillment, service to others, results, and relationship-building. Use your time to create the largest, best, most significant return on your time as possible.

Index

Goals (Ziglar), 328
gold customer category, 111
GoToMeeting online meeting platform
  alternative meeting options, 242
  engaging through online platforms,
    124–125
GoToWebinar online meeting platform,
  125
Groups feature (Facebook), 148
growth activities, 290–291
guest list, meetings, 236–237

• *H* •

half hour activity tracking, 289
handouts, meeting, 244
hashtags (#), 149
headsets, 172–173
health
  exercise, 333–334
  nutrition, 333
  poor procrastination costs, 208–209
  sleep habits, 334
  taking care of, 333–334
heating and air-conditioning system, 245
Hill, Napoleon
  Think and Grow Rich!, 36
hiring help, 285–286
hobbies, 60–61
home office
  advantages, 73–76
  chairs, 78
  computers, 79–80
  creating productive environment in,
    73–74
  desk, 78
  desktop, 79
  disadvantages, 76–77
  discipline and accountability
    assessment, 74–75
  equipment, 78–80
  ergonomics, 78

establishing boundaries, 80–81
  feelings of isolation, 82–83
  interruptions, 77, 81–82
  laptops, 79
  lighting, 80
  location, 77
  music in, 80
  noise-canceling options, 80
  scanners, 79
  working with kids at home, 82
  workspace in, 77–78
hourly income
  boosting, 45–46
  calculation, 43–45
household tasks, 60–61
human resources
  decreasing *in* time, 292–293
  resource needs, 39
Hussain, Anum
  Twitter For Dummies, 153

• *I* •

IIPA (indirect income-producing
    activities), 268–269, 283–284
impromptu meetings, 237
in time, decreasing
  awareness as first step toward, 291
  daily priorities, organization, 297
  empowering employees, 297–298
  job descriptions, crafting, 293–295
  management plan, 296
  No Problems, Only Solutions Policy, 297
  organizational chart, 292–293
  task lists, 295–296
inbox, 87
incandescent blind spot, 297
income, hourly
  boosting, 45–46
  calculation, 43–45
indirect income-producing activities
    (IIPA), 268–269, 283–284

Notes

Notes

About the Author

Dirk Zeller started his entrepreneurial business career more than 40 years ago through lemonade stands. He has been recognized as an efficient time manager and top sales performer in every field he's entered, from professional racquetball to business sales of advertising, marketing, and event sponsorship to consumer-direct sales fields such as real estate. His time management skills were legendary in the real estate field, where he sold over 150 homes a year while working Monday through Thursday, taking Friday, Saturday, and Sunday off.

Dirk has been teaching, coaching, and training success, sales, and time management strategies to executives, managers, and salespeople since 1998, when he founded Sales Champions and Real Estate Champions. He is one of the most sought-after speakers in time management, peak performance, and sales. He has spoken on five different continents to hundreds of thousands of people.

Dirk is one of the world's most published authors on success, time management, productivity, sales, and life balance. He is the author of ten top-selling books, including *Telephone Sales For Dummies* and *Success as a Real Estate Agent For Dummies*. He has more than 500 published articles to his credit, and over 250,000 people read his weekly newsletter.

The time that's most valuable to Dirk is the time enjoyed with his wife of 25 years, Joan, his 13-year-old son, Wesley, and his 9-year-old daughter, Annabelle. He and his family reside in Bend, Oregon. You can reach Dirk at

Sales Champions
5 NW Hawthorne Ave., Suite 100
Bend, OR 97701
Phone 541-383-0505
Email info@saleschampions.com
Email info@dirkzeller.com
Website www.saleschampions.com

Dedication

Nothing reflects the passing of time more than growth and changes in our children. It seems like just yesterday that Joan and I received the call that changed our lives as we exited my 96-year-old grandmother's funeral. The call was from our pastor's wife, Linda Johnson. She said a baby boy had been born that morning in Hood River, Oregon, and asked if we wanted him. The next day, Joan and I walked out of the Hood River Memorial Hospital with our son, Wesley.

In the last 13 years since that moment, the time has passed like a blink of an eye. We have added another blessing in Annabelle, who also has a divine and miraculous story. In those years, which seem like mere moments in time, it feels like seconds ago we got our first smile, giggle, crawl, and walk out of each of them.

I dedicate this book to my two precious time clocks of life, Annabelle and Wesley. The time with you two moves too quickly. I, as all parents, fight to stay in the moment, enjoy every moment, and relive those moments before they are gone. You two have taught me more about time's value, joy, and its ever-marching-on characteristics than anyone else in my years on Earth. I love you both deeply and praise God for the honor he bestowed on me to be your dad.

Author's Acknowledgments

I always have to thank my team at Sales Champions and Real Estate Champions. It is truly an honor to be surrounded by so many talented people. I must especially thank my senior management team: Wende Fletcher, my office manager, and Julie Porfirio, senior vice president of operations. You both have worked hard to insulate me so I could take on another *For Dummies* book.

To Julie Porfirio, who labored over my handwritten words to type, organize, revise, and edit the whole manuscript — thanks. This book would not have existed without your fine work.

To Stacy Kennedy, my acquisitions editor at Wiley; and Susan Hobbs, project editor.

To my wife, Joan, my son, Wesley, and my daughter, Annabelle. Thank you for your patience and grace. There is a sacrifice of time that we all make when I am writing a book!

Publisher's Acknowledgments

Acquisitions Editor: Stacy Kennedy

Project Editor: Susan Hobbs

Copy Editor: Susan Hobbs

Technical Editors: Angela Jorden

Art Coordinator: Alicia B. South

Production Editor: Vinitha Vikraman

Project Manager: Jennifer Ehrlich

Cover Image: ©iStock.com/Greyfebruary

e & Mac

For Dummies,
dition
-118-72306-7

e For Dummies,
dition
-118-69083-3

All-in-One
ummies, 4th Edition
-118-82210-4

Mavericks
ummies
-118-69188-5

ging & Social Media

ook For Dummies,
dition
-118-63312-0

Media Engagement
ummies
-118-53019-1

Press For Dummies,
dition
-118-79161-5

less

Investing
ummies, 4th Edition
-118-37678-2

ting For Dummies,
dition
-470-90545-6

Personal Finance
For Dummies, 7th Edition
978-1-118-11785-9

QuickBooks 2014
For Dummies
978-1-118-72005-9

Small Business Marketing
Kit For Dummies,
3rd Edition
978-1-118-31183-7

Careers

Job Interviews
For Dummies, 4th Edition
978-1-118-11290-8

Job Searching with Social
Media For Dummies,
2nd Edition
978-1-118-67856-5

Personal Branding
For Dummies
978-1-118-11792-7

Resumes For Dummies,
6th Edition
978-0-470-87361-8

Starting an Etsy Business
For Dummies, 2nd Edition
978-1-118-59024-9

Diet & Nutrition

Belly Fat Diet For Dummies
978-1-118-34585-6

Mediterranean Diet
For Dummies
978-1-118-71525-3

Nutrition For Dummies,
5th Edition
978-0-470-93231-5

Digital Photography

Digital SLR Photography
All-in-One For Dummies,
2nd Edition
978-1-118-59082-9

Digital SLR Video &
Filmmaking For Dummies
978-1-118-36598-4

Photoshop Elements 12
For Dummies
978-1-118-72714-0

Gardening

Herb Gardening
For Dummies, 2nd Edition
978-0-470-61778-6

Gardening with Free-Range
Chickens For Dummies
978-1-118-54754-0

Health

Boosting Your Immunity
For Dummies
978-1-118-40200-9

Diabetes For Dummies,
4th Edition
978-1-118-29447-5

Living Paleo For Dummies
978-1-118-29405-5

Big Data

Big Data For Dummies
978-1-118-50422-2

Data Visualization
For Dummies
978-1-118-50289-1

Hadoop For Dummies
978-1-118-60755-8

Language &
Foreign Language

500 Spanish Verbs
For Dummies
978-1-118-02382-2

English Grammar
For Dummies, 2nd Edition
978-0-470-54664-2

French All-in-One
For Dummies
978-1-118-22815-9

German Essentials
For Dummies
978-1-118-18422-6

Italian For Dummies,
2nd Edition
978-1-118-00465-4

 Available in print and e-book formats.

Available wherever books are sold. **For more information or to order direct visit www.dummies.com**

Math & Science

Algebra I For Dummies,
2nd Edition
978-0-470-55964-2

Anatomy and Physiology
For Dummies, 2nd Edition
978-0-470-92326-9

Astronomy For Dummies,
3rd Edition
978-1-118-37697-3

Biology For Dummies,
2nd Edition
978-0-470-59875-7

Chemistry For Dummies,
2nd Edition
978-1-118-00730-3

1001 Algebra II Practice
Problems For Dummies
978-1-118-44662-1

Microsoft Office

Excel 2013 For Dummies
978-1-118-51012-4

Office 2013 All-in-One
For Dummies
978-1-118-51636-2

PowerPoint 2013
For Dummies
978-1-118-50253-2

Word 2013 For Dummies
978-1-118-49123-2

Music

Blues Harmonica
For Dummies
978-1-118-25269-7

Guitar For Dummies,
3rd Edition
978-1-118-11554-1

iPod & iTunes
For Dummies, 10th Edition
978-1-118-50864-0

Programming

Beginning Programming
with C For Dummies
978-1-118-73763-7

Excel VBA Programming
For Dummies, 3rd Edition
978-1-118-49037-2

Java For Dummies,
6th Edition
978-1-118-40780-6

Religion & Inspiration

The Bible For Dummies
978-0-7645-5296-0

Buddhism For Dummies,
2nd Edition
978-1-118-02379-2

Catholicism For Dummies,
2nd Edition
978-1-118-07778-8

Self-Help & Relationships

Beating Sugar Addiction
For Dummies
978-1-118-54645-1

Meditation For Dummies,
3rd Edition
978-1-118-29144-3

Seniors

Laptops For Seniors
For Dummies, 3rd Edition
978-1-118-71105-7

Computers For Seniors
For Dummies, 3rd Edition
978-1-118-11553-4

iPad For Seniors
For Dummies, 6th Edition
978-1-118-72826-0

Social Security
For Dummies
978-1-118-20573-0

Smartphones & Tablets

Android Phones
For Dummies, 2nd Edition
978-1-118-72030-1

Nexus Tablets
For Dummies
978-1-118-77243-0

Samsung Galaxy S 4
For Dummies
978-1-118-64222-1

Samsung Galaxy Tab
For Dummies
978-1-118-77294-2

Test Prep

ACT For Dummies,
5th Edition
978-1-118-01259-8

ASVAB For Dummies,
3rd Edition
978-0-470-63760-9

GRE For Dummies,
7th Edition
978-0-470-88921-3

Officer Candidate Tes
For Dummies
978-0-470-59876-4

Physician's Assistant E
For Dummies
978-1-118-11556-5

Series 7 Exam For Dur
978-0-470-09932-2

Windows 8

Windows 8.1 All-in-On
For Dummies
978-1-118-82087-2

Windows 8.1 For Dum
978-1-118-82121-3

Windows 8.1 For Dum
Book + DVD Bundle
978-1-118-82107-7

Available in print and e-book formats.

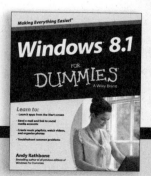

Available wherever books are sold. **For more information or to order direct visit www.dummies.com**

Take Dummies with you everywhere you go!

Whether you are excited about e-books, want more from the web, must have your mobile apps, or are swept up in social media, Dummies makes everything easier.

For Dummies is the global leader in the reference category and one of the most trusted and highly regarded brands in the world. No longer just focused on books, customers now have access to the For Dummies content they need in the format they want. Let us help you develop a solution that will fit your brand and help you connect with your customers.

Advertising & Sponsorships

Connect with an engaged audience on a powerful multimedia site, and position your message alongside expert how-to content.

Targeted ads • Video • Email marketing • Microsites • Sweepstakes sponsorship

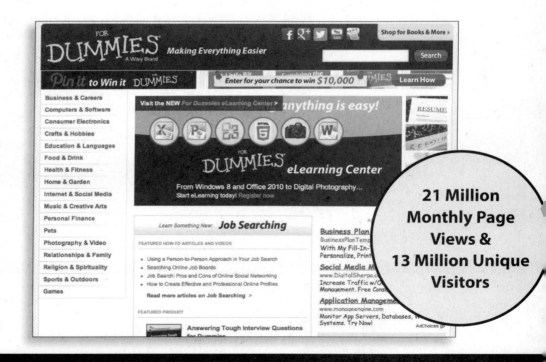

Custom Publishing

Reach a global audience in any language by creating a solution that will differentiate you from competitors, amplify your message, and encourage customers to make a buying decision.

Apps • Books • eBooks • Video • Audio • Webinars

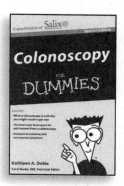

Brand Licensing & Content

Leverage the strength of the world's most popular reference brand to reach new audiences and channels of distribution.

For more information, visit www.Dummies.com/biz

FOR
DUMMIES
A Wiley Brand

Dummies products make life easier!

- DIY
- Consumer Electronics
- Crafts
- Software
- Cookware
- Hobbies
- Videos
- Music
- Games
- and More!

For more information, go to **Dummies.com** and search the store by category.